PRIVILEGING INDUSTRY

PRIVILEGING INDUSTRY

THE COMPARATIVE POLITICS OF TRADE
AND INDUSTRIAL POLICY

Fiona McGillivray

PRINCETON UNIVERSITY PRESS PRINCETON AND OXFORD

Library of Congress Cataloging-in-Publication Data
McGillivray, Fiona, 1967–
Privileging industry : the comparative politics of trade and industrial policy /
Fiona McGillivray.
p. cm.
Includes bibliographical references and index.
ISBN 0-691-02769-2 (alk. paper)—ISBN 0-691-02770-6 (pbk. : alk. paper)
1. Commercial policy. 2. Industrial policy. I. Title.
HF1411.M37573 2004
338—dc21   2003051742

British Library Cataloging-in-Publication Data is available.

This book has been composed in Times Roman

Printed on acid-free paper. ∞

www.pupress.princeton.edu

Printed in the United States of America

1 3 5 7 9 10 8 6 4 2

To Angus, Duncan, and Molly

Contents

List of Figures

List of Tables

Acknowledgments

I AM EXTREMELY grateful for the comments and advice from many people while working on this book. Thanks to Marc Busch, Bruce Bueno de Mesquita, Bill Clark, John Conybeare, John Freeman, Geoffrey Garrett, Mike Gilligan, Joanne Gowa, Ellen Lust-Okar, Mark Kayser, Tasos Kalandrakis, Edward Mansfield, Tim McKeown, Iain McLean, Jim Morrow, Chuck Myers, Bob Pahre, Bing Powell, Larry Rothenberg, Ronald Rogowski, Bruce Russett, Anne Sartori, Alastair Smith, Norman Schofield, Wendy Schiller, and several anonymous referees. I was lucky to have the help of terrific research assistants, both at Yale and at New York University: Sona Golder, Alexandra Guisinger, Nate Jensen, Tanaz Moghadam, and Jason Sorens. Thanks to my mum for her unwavering support. Finally, thanks to Alastair Smith for comments, advice, criticism, tech support, and constant scolding to get the bloody book done.

Portions of chapters 3 and 5 have previously appeared in McGillivray 1997 and McGillivray 2003, respectively.

PRIVILEGING INDUSTRY

CHAPTER 1

Redistributive Politics

DEMOCRATIC PROCESSES are intended to ensure equal representation. Yet the "one man, one vote" ideal does not mean that everyone benefits equally from political processes. Redistribution is the essence of politics, and electorally motivated politicians have incentives to redistribute resources among voters, privileging some at the expense of others. Who wins and who loses from such redistribution is at the heart of democratic politics and is the subject of this book.

Desiring to keep their jobs, politicians are ever willing to give to those who can keep them in power: winners are not chosen randomly. I focus on the winners and losers from trade and industrial policy. Some might argue that trade policy is a fundamentally international issue. Yet despite its consequences for the international flows of goods and services, trade policy is, like industrial policy, highly redistributive. Those people associated with the production of a protected good are privileged, while the population as a whole suffers from higher prices or higher taxes. There is remarkable variance in which industries win and how they are privileged; for instance, imported leather handbags face high tariff barriers in the United States, the Germans heavily subsidize the marine propeller industry, carpet firms are favored with government loans in Belgium, while the Spanish strongly support EU (European Union) quotas for the toy industry.[1]

Democratic institutions are ostensibly designed to serve the majority. Why then should democratic politicians want to enrich some chosen few and forsake others? The answer is political survival. Leaders assist those who can help them keep their jobs; yet who can most effectively help them keep their jobs depends upon the institutional context in which the politicians serve. As such, who the winners and losers are is shaped by domestic political arrangements. Institutional rules affect which industries legislators wish to protect as well as whether they can achieve protection for these groups.

The field of comparative politics seeks to identify the dimensions in which political systems differ and the impact of these differences. Although the myriad of combinations across all of these different dimensions produces a virtually limitless number of possible institutional arrangements, I focus on the impact of two prominent features of democratic institutions: the electoral rule and the strength of political parties. These two features have deservedly received much critical attention as they shape many aspects of political behavior;

for instance, the number of parties, parties' policy positions, the level of political violence, the duration of government, and public policy outcomes.[2] My goal, however, is to explain which industrial groups receive preferential treatment through the redistributive effect of trade and industrial policy.

The institutional features of the electoral rule and the strength of political parties play a key role in sorting the winners from the losers through two processes. First, the combination of the electoral rule and industry geography affects which industries legislators *want* to protect. That is to say, they induce preferences over which groups to protect. Second, the electoral rule and the strength of parties affect which industries legislators are *able* to protect. The legislative incentives created by these features determine how legislators' induced preferences are aggregated into actual policy. Rogowski (1987, 1998; Rogowski and Kayser 2002) is one of many scholars who consider the mapping from electoral rule to trade policy as a single step.[3] As I shall argue, considering only one of these two processes is misguided. While Rogowski's and Kayser's work is extremely insightful, particularly in terms of explaining aggregate levels of protection, I believe it fails to account for the pattern of winners and losers under different electoral systems. Desperately wanting to help an industrial group is not the same as being able to help an industrial group. Similarly, simply because politicians are in a position to privilege an industrial group does not mean they will. It has to be in their political interest to do so. The provision of assistance requires both a will and a means.

The theory in this book is about redistribution. The logic of the theory tells us which groups of voters politicians will favor with redistributive policies. Trade and industrial policy are one means for targeting benefits to voters (Godeck 1985). Other policies, like public spending programs or welfare transfers, also have a redistributive component. So why would politicians use trade and industrial policy rather than other more "efficient" means to redistribute? Rodrik (1995) has been vocal in his criticisms of the trade literature for precisely this reason. While alternative tax-and-spend redistributive policies might have greater economic efficiencies, the question is, are they politically as effective? Throughout the book I argue that trade and industrial policy can be a politically efficient way to target key voters. Whether or not an industry is a good vehicle through which to redistribute income depends on the industry's geography and how it maps into electoral jurisdictions. Politicians do not want to protect any industry per se. They want to assist groups with precisely the right size, spread and location, to target benefits to politically important groups of voters.

While those wedded to the efficiency of alternative redistribution might remain unconvinced of the superior political efficacy of protection, trade policy has another great advantage over direct redistribution: it is opaque (Magee, Brock, and Young 1989). It is hard to know how much has been redistributed and to whom. If the government raises taxes to hand out additional benefits, such as increased welfare transfers, these acts are readily transparent. Tracing the beneficiaries of the U.S. sugar quota is not. Of couse the beneficiaries know who they are, but it is difficult for most voters to figure this out, far less to determine how much extra they themselves are paying for a pound of sugar. It is extremely difficult for voters to judge whether or not the sugar quota is based on sound economic reasoning (to help the beleaguered industry compete with subsidized EU sugar) or political vote-buying (pork for Florida's voters). Trade and industrial policies are also an indirect method of redistributing between geographic regions. For example, the U.S. sugar quota redistributes resources to Florida, Louisiana, and Hawai from the other forty-seven states. Many countries institute rules preventing direct transfers to regional groups; for example, in the United Kingdom, government spending to different regions is strictly controlled by a set of rules that assess need, based on criteria such as demographics and unemployment. However, the allocation of research-and-development funds cannot so easily be monitored or legislated against.

More broadly, there are many different ways that governments can give and take between industries: subsidies, tax exemptions, low-interest loans, debt reduction, tariffs, and quotas. Unfortunately, what makes trade and industrial policy attractive to politicians—its opaqueness—makes it difficult to study analytically. Conceptually straightforward, as a practical matter it is extremely hard to directly assess the level of assistance any particular industry receives. I believe this is why so many of the empirical results in the literature disagree.[4] Looking at different measures of protection can lead to very different conclusions about its causes. As a result, comparative trade research has stalled. Rather than contribute another voice arguing for one measure over another, this research focuses on deriving additional consequences of trade and industrial policy. By deriving alternative dependent variables and testing hypotheses that relate to aspects of trade that are not dependent on direct measures of trade assistance, I hope to forward the study of comparative trade and industrial policy.

The arguments in this book also contribute to the literature on U.S. government redistribution. Scholars of U.S. politics disagree about which groups of voters are "purchased" with government transfers. For instance, Dixit and Londregan (1986, 1998; see also Lindbeck and Weibull 1987) argue that parties target policy transfers to swing voters. In contrast, Cox and McCubbins (1986) argue that parties are more likely to use transfers to reward loyal voters. Both of these arguments focus on only one step of the two-step mapping I propose. Using a comparative framework to consider both steps, I argue that the Dixit and Londregan (1986, 1998) hypothesis applies to one subset of countries— for example, the United Kingdom, Austalia, and Canada—while the Cox and McCubbins predictions apply to a different subset of countries—for example, Sweden, Germany, and Belgium. The predictions in this book are not unique; however, they are sensitive to comparative political institutions and are testable against other theories of redistribution.

Next, and throughout this chapter, I focus on how governments redistribute policy between industries. I use the case of the cutlery industry in the United Kingdom, Germany, and the United States to illustrate how the geographic and structural features of industry and the institutional characteristics of political systems affect how governments distribute trade and industrial assistance.

KNIVES AND FORKS AND TARIFFS

The focus of this book is to explain cross-country differences in which industries governments choose to assist. Take, for example, the cutlery industry: highly protected in some countries, it had been left to the vagaries of market forces in others. In Germany, Britain, and the United States, the cutlery industry had long been in decline,[5] but the recessions of the 1970s threw the industry into crisis.[6] Although the cutlery industry lobbied loudly for protection in all three countries, there was considerable variation in each government's willingness to assist. Successive governments in Britain heavily protected the cutlery industry; its effective tariff rate was as high as 30 percent, far greater than the average level of protection in Britain. By comparison, the German government did much less to support its cutlery industry, giving less than a half of the assistance that the British did, and in the United States, the cutlery industry received only token tariff protection from its government.[7] Based on national security legislation, the U.S. Department of Defense was restricted from purchasing foreign stainless-steel flatware. Apparently using German forks undermined national preparedness.[8]

Why did the British lack the political will to kick out cutlery's crutch of protection? Industry pressure alone was not responsible; if that had been the case in the United States, Britain, and Germany, we would have seen the highest level of protection in the United States, where the industry was largest, or in Germany, where the industry was well organized. In fact, what we observe is protection directly inverse to the size of the industry and uncorrelated with the level of organization. What is missing is a grasp of the political incentives to supply protection. Later in this chapter, I will argue that British cutlery's political leverage was, in large part, due to its regional concentration in the type of electoral districts that make or break governments. In Britain, the cutlery industry was small in size, but its firms were regionally clustered in politically important districts. Cutlery's geography made it an ideal vehicle for the government to redistribute income toward key groups of voters; hence cutlery's high levels of protection. Under the German and the U.S. electoral systems, however, cutlery's geography made protecting the industry much less politically profitable. In the latter case, regional concentration became the cutlery industry's Achilles' heel, the reason it failed to win protection. Throughout the book, I argue that it is the joint effects of an industry's geography and the electoral system that determine the political opportunities for industries, such as cutlery, to gain industrial assistance. This approach differs from extant explanations in which the industry's structure and ability to lobby matters most. Rather than focus on the incentives facing industry to organize and demand protection, I focus on the incentives facing governments to reward particular groups of voters. There are many different ways that government can redistribute resources among voters. Trade and industrial policy can be a politically efficient way to target key voters. Whether or not an industry is a good vehicle through which to redistribute income depends on the industry's geography. The purpose of this book is to show *when* governments use trade and industrial policy for political goals and to show why aiding an industry can be a politically efficient way for government to redistribute from one group to another.

Who the winners are and who the losers are from trade and industrial policy depends on the interaction of industry geography and the electoral system, a two-stage process. In the first stage of the argument, legislators have preferences induced over which industries they want to assist as a function of each industry's geographic distribution and the electoral rule. An industry's geography relative to political jurisdictions induces these preferences, determining whether or not legislators want to privilege an industry. In the second stage, the electoral rule and the strength of parties determine how legislators' induced preferences are aggregated into actual policy. It is one thing for a legislator to want to protect an industry and another for her to be able to do so.

In the case of cutlery, the initial link between industry geography and induced preferences is similar in the United States and Britain (the electoral rule is the same); however, in the second stage, differences in how legislative preferences are aggregated into policy strongly disadvantage a small, regionally concentrated industry such as cutlery in one case but strongly advantage it in the other. Thus the second stage is as important as the first. As I hope to demonstrate, most extant explanations of how governments' choose to redistribute fail because they examine only one of these two stages.

Obviously, the type of electoral system and the strength of parties are not the only political factors that come to bear on the setting of tariffs or on legislative policy making; for example, the role of international negotiations is a common topic of trade research (Grossman and Helpman 1995; Levy 1997; Marvel and Ray 1983; Pahre 2001, 2002). Yet focusing on these features of the political system as a starting point provides leverage in understanding how industry geography and political structure influence other aspects of the political process of trade. For instance, while it is true that international agreements might prohibit policies that governments would otherwise pursue, governments are unlikely to negotiate treaty exemptions for industries that they do not want to protect anyway. On the other hand, they are likely to fight long and hard at the negotiating table for those industries that they deem essential for their political future.

In this chapter, I start by assessing our current understanding of how industry structure and geography influence industrial and trade policies. This issue is far from resolved on empirical grounds. Findings conflict because there is no general, unambiguous relationship between industry geography and political influence. Rather, the relationship between industry protection and industry geography is contingent upon institutional features of the political system. Following this review, I outline my approach in this book and consider some of the data and measurement issues that make testing so difficult in this field. A large part of the problem is that trade and industrial policy lack transparency. In Germany, cutlery gets three times the subsidies that steel gets; however, steel is heavily protected by tariffs. The question is, what size of subsidies to cutlery is equivalent to the dollar amount of tariffs won by steel? Compounding this problem, different governments tend to prefer different policy instruments to favor industries: the Swedes often opt for debt guarantees; the British generally favor regional grants and development subsidies; the Germans make liberal use of tax exemptions; and "Buy America" legislation and tariffs tend to be the United States's policy instruments of choice.

To overcome these problems I use a combination of case studies and statistical tests. Most empirical tests focus on assessing the value of protection, or assistance, an industry receives and relating this to economic and political factors.[9] Unfortunately, even in the case of direct tariffs (which are becoming increasingly rare), industrial assistance and protection rarely leave a smoking gun. As such, many direct tests are inconclusive. Although I do use industry tariff data to test the argument, I supplement this tariff-based test by using my theoretical explanation to derive auxiliary hypotheses. These hypotheses suggest new dependent variables, such as the dispersion of stock prices within capital markets and government influence in the targeting of plant closures within declining industries.

As fans of courtroom dramas know, a case without a smoking gun often needs to be built on circumstantial evidence, and the more extensive and the more varied the evidence, the better the prospects for conviction. Testing new dependent variables does more than simply provide confirmatory evidence of direct tests. Many theoretical perspectives may produce parallel predictions on a particular dimension. When theories make such parallel predictions, it is impossible to distinguish between them without observing how they fare against the evidence on a different dimension upon which they do not agree. Generating additional hypotheses and testing new dependent variables not only supplement the direct evidence supporting one set of theories; it also allows us to differentiate between the arguments within this set.

CONCEPTUAL ISSUES

So why did the cutlery industry receive higher levels of trade and industrial assistance in Britain than in Germany or the United States and in fact higher levels than most other British industries? Protection and industrial assistance are both highly redistributive. By using tariffs, subsidies, voluntary export restrictions, or other nontrade barriers (hereafter NTBs) to protect one industry from international competition, governments either increase the price at which the industry can sell its wares or lower the industry's cost for producing its wares. This assistance provides economic rents for the industry.[10] Those associated with the industry, its employees and owners, benefit from protection. In the short term it is costly for investors to shift capital between industries and costly for workers to find new jobs.[11] Both labor and management have incentives to demand protection for their industry. That said the ease with which labor and capital can shift between industries varies across countries and over time; this will affect the extent that political divisions are based on industry rather than class (Hiscox 2001). For example, in Germany better unemployment benefits make it less costly for labor to shift between industries. Nonetheless, in an industry like cutlery, where it is difficult for workers to carry over traditional skills to other high-paying jobs, the political division in Germany remains firmly along industry lines.

If the industry wins trade assistance, there are often additional kick-on effects for the immediate community associated with the industry. For example, if without trade protection a firm would close, then protection helps the entire local workforce, since the rise in unemployment associated with plant closure would hurt all workers' ability to demand higher wages. The effects of plant closure are often very severe, particularly in small "company towns." When the main employer in a town fails, so do many of the subsidiary and service businesses. Additionally, the local tax base and property values often collapse, hurting the town as a whole.

Protection and industrial assistance target benefits at those people and areas associated with the particular industry. Yet these benefits are not without costs. While protection allows an industry to extract rents through charging higher prices, this harms the welfare of consumers who must pay these, higher prices and, in the case of some NTBs, pay higher taxes. These costs are dispersed, however; everyone suffers slightly through higher prices. The benefits are concentrated among producers.[12] This concentration of benefits and diffusion of costs means producers are more motivated to organize and lobby than consumers.[13]

There can be cases where the costs of protection are concentrated. For instance, if the product of a protected industry is an input for another domestic industry, then that second industry suffers. Cutlery firms, as well as companies that make products such as oil equipment and plastic moldings, are hurt when tariffs are imposed on imported steel.[14] Indeed, President Bush's imposition of steel tariffs in 2002 had severe adverse affects on U.S. auto makers.[15] More generally, rival foreign industries are harmed by protection, since it reduces demand for their products. Foreign governments might impose retaliatory tariffs, which will hurt domestic export industries. However, the likelihood of any particular exporter being hurt by these retaliatory tariffs is small; hence, it is unlikely that export industries will coordinate to oppose protectionist legislation.[16] Of course, as the size of the protectionist demands becomes large, so does the probability that any single exporter will be hit with retaliatory tariffs; this increases the probability that an antiprotectionist coalition will form (Destler and Odell 1987).[17]

While it is always important to bear these exceptions in mind, in most cases, protection and industrial assistance provide concentrated benefit to those associated with the industry and to those in the immediate geographic vicinity. In contrast, the costs of protection and industrial assistance are evenly spread over the entire population. From a purely microeconomic viewpoint, the costs of trade assistance are widely believed to outweigh the benefits.[18]

Redistribution is the heart of my theory. Protection or industrial assistance privilege some groups at the expense of others. Who the winners are and who the losers are is the stuff of politics, not economics. Therefore, with respect to the underlying economic model, I work with the simple stylized fact that protection and industrial assistance provide concentrated benefits to areas associated with the protected industry, with the costs being dispersed over everyone. In the short term, it is costly to relocate capital or retrain workers for a new job. I assume labor and capital within the industry and individuals in the regional community associated with the industry have similar trade preferences. The political division is both between industries and between geographic regions.

Maintaining protection for the cutlery industry meant that at the height of its protection, British consumers paid about 30 percent (this is the approximate effective tariff) more for cutlery than they otherwise would. This protection also harms the interests of foreign cutlery workers. Why would the British government choose to privilege British workers in the cutlery industry at the expense of the general public and workers overseas? The latter is perhaps easy to explain: foreigners do not vote on the government's future. But why help cutlery workers at the expense of the general voting public? Most of the literature focuses on an industry's motivation to organize and its ability to lobby as the reason for its political clout.[19] Such theories would argue that cross-national differences in the level of protection result from cross-national differences in the structure of an industry.[20] These arguments implicitly assume that across all countries, the biggest and loudest demanders for protection are the ones who receive the most assistance. However, politicians do not automatically respond to the loudest demands. They listen to the industries that affect their chances of reelection. Hence, which industries receive assistance depends upon how industry geography and political institutions interact to create an incentive for the government to help an industry. Sure, an ability to shout the loudest might help, but politicians have to be willing to listen.

As a vehicle to motivate my arguments, I concentrate on the case of British cutlery. Using this as an illustrative example, I show that many extant arguments are deficient. In the process of evaluating these arguments, I introduce the components necessary for my theoretical approach.

CUTLERY'S POLITICAL CLOUT

The town of Sheffield, in South Yorkshire, is home to the United Kingdom's table cutlery, handknives, and handtools industry. The manufacture of Sheffield knives can be traced from the fourteenth century. The English poet Geoffrey Chaucer (ca. 1340–1400), said in *Canterbury Tales* of the miller of Trumpington, "A Sheffeld thwitel baar he in his hose."[21] For such a small and industrially fragmented industry, it has received a remarkable level of assistance (Cable 1983). Successive governments in Britain have heavily protected the cutlery industry. As mentioned earlier, in the 1970s, the effective tariff rate for cutlery was around 30 percent (Cable 1983).[22] In the late 1970s and 1980s, the cutlery industry received additional assistance via government grants and quantitative trade restrictions. The British cutlery industry also obtained voluntary export restrictions on a variety of products from Japan and South Korea (Tweedale 1995). Cutlery received higher protection than the average industry in the United Kingdom and higher protection than the cutlery industry in Germany and the United States. In the 1970s and 1980s the effective tariff rate on cutlery in Germany was around 6 percent. The German government supplemented this with a variety of domestic subsidies, mainly in the form of regional grants, which were worth about 1.3 percent of the value added in 1972 (Glismann and Weiss 1980; Weiss 1983). The United States has largely ignored the plight of its cutlery industry. Although it received an effective tariff rate of about 5 percent in the 1980s (Lavergne 1981), it received few domestic subsidies. Since the 1950s there have been a series of on-and-off quotas; however, these have been largely ineffective (USITC 1978, 1985). In no case did state aid prevent cutlery's decline, but in the United Kingdom and Germany, it significantly slowed the process. The decline of the cutlery industry in the United States has been drastic, with cutlery almost completely eliminated from Connecticut, a state that together with New York once formed the basis of the U.S. cutlery industry.

The structural features of the cutlery industry are similar in all three countries. Cutlery is a small industry in decline. It consists of a heterogeneous set of firms, meaning in this case that many of the firms within the industry have

TABLE 1.1

The Industrial Characteristics of the Cutlery Industry Compared to
Other Manufacturing Industries in the United Kingdom, 1980s

Industry Characteristics	All Manufacturers	Cutlery Industry
Employees, 1980	6,264,000	9,200
Gross-output per person (index, 1977)	100	63
Value-added per person (index, 1977)	100	86
Capital employed per person (index, 1977)	100	53
Wage and salary per quarter (index, 1977)	100	57
% share of output from 5 largest firms, 1978	—	43
% employment in firms below 200 employees	23	53
Import penetration. All imports, % by value, 1980	25	38

Source: Cable 1983, p. 13, table 2.

different preferences over trade policy. It is industrially decentralized, meaning that production is spread over a number of firms. Yet cutlery is highly geographically concentrated, since most of its firms are located in close proximity to each other. In the next section, U.K. cutlery serves as a platform from which to assess how industry competitiveness, size, industrial concentration, and geographic spread affect an industry's political leverage.

Declining Industries

The U.K. cutlery industry has been in decline since the U.S. Tariff Act of 1890.[23] However, the British recession of the late 1970s and early 1980s created a major crisis in the industry.[24] In 1980, the industry had a gross output per employee, wage per quarter, value-added per employee, and fixed capital per employee below the manufacturing average (see table 1.1). In the industrialized world, labor-intensive, low-wage, low-value-added industries tend to receive higher than average levels of protection.[25] These industries have a comparative disadvantage in a world market where they face steep competition from foreign imports.[26] This was true for the U.K. cutlery industry. In the 1980s, foreign imports had a 38 percent share of the U.K. cutlery market (see table 1.1). The long-term prospects for the U.K. cutlery industry are bleak.[27] Part of the reason declining industries demand, and win, protection is that it is costly for workers and owners to shift out of the industry.

In labor-intensive industries, large numbers of voters must find new jobs. Politicians often argue that state aid is not intended to prop up declining industries such as cutlery; rather, it is to ease the adjustment process for workers and owners (Baldwin 1989).[28]

There is little doubt that the plight of the cutlery industry—company bankruptcy, heavy job loses, and surging import competition—spurred the government to assist the industry in the 1970s with exemptions from tariff reductions, grants, and quotas (Tweedale 1995). Across countries, there is strong, robust evidence that industries facing a surge in import competition receive more favorable levels of trade assistance (Trefler 1993; Riezman and Wilson 1992; Rodrik 1995). However, not all of the United Kingdom's struggling industries received as favorable levels of assistance in this period as the cutlery industry did; for example the shipbuilding industry was left to sink or swim with minimal political support.[29] This suggests that cutlery's declining competitiveness was only part of the explanation for its privileged levels of government assistance.

Industry Size

The cutlery trade is a small industry and this typically works against an industry's ability to demand protection (see table 1.1). In 1980, cutlery had about nine thousand workers; today that number is about two thousand (HMSO 1983; ONS 2001). That is not a lot of votes. Larger industries have more workers—hence they have more voters, plus they have greater access to funds for lobbying (Becker 1983; Busch and Reinhardt 1999; Caves 1976; Pincus 1975). The plight of large industries is also more likely to be covered in the media and to arouse public sympathy. On the other hand, being ignored by the media can have benefits; smaller-sized-industries are less likely to arouse antiprotectionist opposition than are larger industries (Mayer 1984). Smaller industries are easier to organize and can also be "cheaper" to protect (Olson 1965). Cross-nationally, however, studies have found that industries with larger numbers of employees (large size) tend to receive more favorable levels of assistance (Anderson and Baldwin 1987). Cutlery's small size probably put it at a political disadvantage vis-à-vis other industries seeking protection.

Industrial Concentration

Industrial concentration is defined as the degree to which a small number of firms in an industry dominate the market.[30] In 1980, 55 percent of cutlery workers were employed in firms with fewer than two hundred employees—a far higher proportion than the average for all manufacturing industries (see table 1.1). Small firms, such as Schofields or C. W. Fletcher, characterized the industry. There were a few large firms, such as Viners; in fact, the output of the five largest firms accounted for 43 percent of the industry's output (Cable 1983). Nonetheless, compared to other industries, cutlery was relatively industrially decentralized.

Industrially concentrated industries, where the benefits of protection are shared among a few large firms rather than many smaller firms, have stronger incentives to organize and lobby.[31] For an industrially decentralized industry, the costs of lobbying probably exceed the benefits of protection. Individual firms have incentives to free ride on the efforts of others (Cornes and Sandler 1996; Olson 1965). If these firms want to organize and be effective, they need to coordinate lobbying activities. This can be difficult to achieve. On average, industrially concentrated industries win higher levels of trade protection than industrially decentralized industries (Anderson and Baldwin 1987; Riezman and Wilson 1992). Cutlery's industrial decentralization should have undermined its ability to organize as an industry and demand assistance. Yet as I describe in the next section, cutlery had a prolific lobbying history.

Firm Heterogeneity

The structure of firms is important in determining trade preferences (Milner 1988). In a heterogeneous industry, many of the firms within the industry make different products, play different roles in the production process, or rely in different ways on export and domestic markets. In the case of cutlery, firms had different trade preferences because some firms—typically the larger ones—used semifinished cutlery imports in the production process. Viners, for example, cared less than smaller firms about the artificially high cost of U.K. steel because a large part of its business was importing semifinished products, finishing them, and then stamping "made in Sheffield" on the final product. Using the Sheffield trademark on semifinished imports created much fury among the smaller firms.[32] If firms have different preferences about how the government should help, this can undermine the industry's lobbying efforts (Milner 1988). Cutlery certainly has a rich and complex history of lobbying in the United Kingdom. However, it does not have an effective lobbying history, in part because the industry was divided over goals (Cable 1983).

Cutlery is a highly fractured industry on both management and labor sides, with numerous business and union associations. Cutlery has four manufacturing associations: the Cutlery and Silverware Association (CSA), the Federation of Cutlery Manufacturers (FBCM), the Sheffield Spoon and Fork Makers Association, and the Manufacturing Silversmiths Association (Cable 1983; Tweedale 1995). Among the things they disagree about is the type of trade assistance the industry should receive: tighter protection or more restrictive quotas on semifinished products. Unionized cutlery workers are split between three rival unions: the National Union of Goldsmiths, Silversmiths, and Allied Trades (NUGSAT), the Transport and General Workers (TGWU), and the General and Municipal Workers (GMWU). The unions have typically lobbied for the industry (Cable 1983) but, like the manufacturing organization, are at odds over goals. The industry is split between four manufacturing associations and three unions. These divisions partly reflect the industrial heterogeneity of the industry and partly reflect the structure of unions in the United Kingdom. Cutlery was organized, but industry heterogeneity undermined cutlery's ability to coordinate effectively to demand protection. Thus it remains to be explained why cutlery won such high levels of government assistance.

Geographic Concentration

Numerous scholars have contended that geographic distribution affects an industry's ability to lobby and secure assistance.[33] Geographical concentration relates to the spatial concentration of firms within an industry. The cutlery industry is about as geographically concentrated as it is possible to get—over 50 percent of the industry is located in the town of Sheffield in South Yorkshire.[34] Most scholars argue that geographic concentration has a positive effect on an industry's level of protection. Nevertheless, there is disagreement whether it is spatial proximity or asset specificity that positively affects a geographically concentrated industry's ability to organize.

Industries that are spatially proximate are thought to benefit from lower transactions costs in organizing industry-wide lobbying activities and mobilizing industry workers to vote (Busch and Reinhardt 1999; Chwe 2001; Pincus 1975; Schonhardt-Bailey 1991). Spatial proximity makes it easier for firms to coordinate lobbying activities (Chwe 2001). The spatial proximity of workers and firms in Sheffield lowers communication costs within the industry. These workers share social networks (down at the pub—the British version of the water-cooler effect). If communication costs are low, firms are able to sanction free riders; this makes it less costly for firms and workers to organize as an industrial lobby.

Others argue that geographically concentrated industries are more politically active because their assets are highly specific (Alt et al. 1996). As it is difficult for labor and capital to shift out of such industries, they have incentives to organize politically to defend their jobs and investments. Cutlery workers are highly skilled, but only in the cutlery trade; these skills do not transfer easily to other industries. In Sheffield, it is difficult for unskilled laborers to find new employment (Hayter 1985). Nowadays, the local council is the largest single employer in the city. Labor has incentives to organize, raise funds, and get the vote out in an effort to save immobile jobs.

In a different line of argument, economic geographers make the point that a geographic concentration of firms in an industry—geographic agglomeration—improves the competitiveness of individual firms (Krugman 1991; Sabel 1989; Scott 1988).[35] We might therefore expect geographically concentrated industries to be less in need of protection. In the case of U.K. cutlery, however, innovation in the industry stalled in the 1800s despite the benefits of geographic agglomeration (White 1997).[36]

The empirical findings on the effect of geographic concentration on the level of protection are ambiguous. In some studies, geographic concentration is positively related to levels of protection. In others the effect is negative, and in still others, no significant effect is found (Anderson and Baldwin 1987; Hansen 1990; Lavergne 1983; Nelson 1988; Pincus 1975; Rogowski 1997, 1998; Schonhardt-Bailey 1991). Part of the problem is that in many studies, industrial concentration is used as a proxy for geographical concentration (for example, Cable and Rebelo 1980). However, an industry that is industrially concentrated is not necessarily spatially concentrated. For example, the car industry in Australia is industrially concentrated in a handful of firms, but car plants are spread throughout the country. In an important step forward, Busch and Reinhardt (1999, 2003) construct a measure of geographic concentration that captures the spatial relationship between geographically proximate firms. They categorize geographic concentration as a decreasing function of the physical distance from plants of workers to the national midpoint of an industry. Using NTBs in the United States and Europe, they find strong evidence that geographically concentrated industries receive more favorable trade assistance. Although Busch and Reinhardt's measure of geographic concentration captures spatial concentration, this does not necessarily measure an industry's regional concentration. For example, the footwear industry in the United States is heavily located in the states of Maine and Missouri. According to Busch and Reinhardt's measure of spatial dispersion, the footwear industry is geographically dispersed; however, footwear is regionally concentrated in only two of fifty states. Later in the book I argue that when the theoretical focus is the government's decision to supply protecion, rather than the ability of industry to demand protection, regional concentration is a more relevant concept than spatial concentration.

Cutlery is an industry that is both spatially and regionally concentrated. How does this geographic concentration affect cultery's political clout? Cutlery has a strong history of lobbying for import-relief. For such a small, industrially decentralized industry, it has made noisy demands for aid. Unfortunately, it is hard to determine the impact of geographic concentration in this case. Spatial concentration in one town probably explains why cutlery is highly organized; however, firm industrial heterogeneity has prevented the coordination of lobbying activities. One might expect that geographic concentration—most cutlery firms working together in the same city—would generate coordination over time. The spatial proximity argument assumes that workers from different plants and firms rub shoulders together because they work closely together. Yet cutlery firms are described as aggressively independent.[37] In Sheffield, spatial proximity seems to breed contempt, not cooperation. Spatial proximity by itself does not ensure coordinated lobbying activity. A local mechanism is needed to get workers from different firms together, even in the extreme case where they all work in the same city. In the United Kingdom, the union and manufacturing associations assume this role, although in this case to the industry's detriment. Social networks in Sheffield might have lowered the costs of communication, and specific assets have increased workers' and managements' incentives to organize, but the fragmented union structure has meant that workers are either socializing within their union (preaching to the converted) or socializing across unions with less effect. While on average, geographic concentration might lower the costs of coordination and lobbying, in the case of cutlery, fragmented unions and industrial heterogeneity forestalled the creation of a united lobbying front. Cutlery's lobbying efforts were largely ineffective (Cable 1983). Thus it still remains to be explained why cutlery gained much higher assistance than many other troubled industries did.

Electoral Concentration

Electoral concentration is an industry's spatial concentration relative to political jurisdictions;[38] is an industry geographically concentrated in a few electoral districts or dispersed over many electoral districts? An industry that is concentrated in one electoral district is probably such an important employer in that district that its representative cannot afford to ignore the industry's demands. However, only one representative cares strongly about the fate of the industry. Most scholars argue that electorally dispersed industries have more political clout; as an industry becomes more electorally dispersed, more legislators care about its fate, which makes it easier to create voting blocks and build legislative majorities (Caves 1976; Pincus 1975; Schattschneider 1935). As in the case of geographic concentration, the empirical findings on the effect of electoral concentration are mixed.[39] Scholars frequently use measures of electoral concentration as a proxy for both electoral and geographic concentration (see studies in Anderson and Baldwin 1987). Given that the predicted effect of geographic concentration is positive and of electoral concentration is negative, it is not surprising that findings are often insignificant and nonrobust. It is possible for an industry to be geographically concentrated but electorally dispersed if the region contains a large number of electoral districts (Busch and Reinhardt 1999; McGillivray 1995, 1997).

That said, there is evidence that electorally dispersed industries have political clout, particularly when industry size is taken into account (Glismann and

Weiss 1980; McGillivray 1997; Pincus 1975; Tharakan 1980). A large, electorally dispersed industry is likely to receive favorable protection.[40] Such an industry gains from both sides of theoretical debate. Being large, even though dispersed, the industry is still sufficiently important in each district that legislators care about it, and being in a large number of districts helps the industry create voting blocks. By contrast, a large, electorally concentrated industry has a single legislator who cares passionately but who is unlikely to be able to provide assistance by herself.[41] For small industries, electoral dispersion is a trade-off. If an industry is thinly spread although present in a large number of districts, its impact on jobs and the local economy is too insignificant for legislators to care. For a small industry, electoral concentration might be best since then at least one legislator might care.

The cutlery industry in Britain is electorally concentrated in the constituencies of only six Members of Parliament. It is a major employer in those districts (in 1981, approx 15 percent of the Sheffield workforce were in the cutlery and tools trade).[42] However, only about 1 percent of legislators care directly about cutlery's fate. Cutlery's electoral concentration should work against its efforts to secure trade assistance. Yet as we shall see shortly—given the electoral rule and the structure of the party system—cutlery was located in the right 1 percent of districts in the British case.

WHY DOES THE CUTLERY INDUSTRY HAVE SUCH POLITICAL CLOUT?

While there is some disagreement over the directionality and relative importance of the factors above, it would appear that a small industry with heterogeneous firms that is industrially dispersed over many firms, geographically dispersed yet electorally concentrated, is the least likely industry to receive assistance. By these standards, the U.K. cutlery industry is damned on all measures except geographical dispersion. And the benefits from geographic concentration are negligible given cutlery's heterogeneous firms and fragmented union structure. Yet, despite all these disadvantages, cutlery secures relatively high levels of government assistance versus other troubled U.K. industries, and certainly more than its rival cutlery industries in the United States and Germany.

What accounts for these differences in success? The cutlery industry is somewhat larger in Germany and the United States. It is more geographically dispersed in the United States, and the German industry is more competitive. But otherwise, the cutlery industries in all three countries are structurally very similar (Hayter 1985). Therefore, the question remains, why was British cutlery more successful in gaining assistance? Next, I argue that to understand cross-national differences in cutlery's level of government assistance, one has to look at the interactive effect of the industry's geography and political institutions.

The Interactive Effects of Political Institutions

The joint effects of an industry's geography, the electoral rule, and the strength of parties determine the political opportunities for industries such as cutlery. An industry's geography is defined as its size, its location, and its spread over electoral districts and regional locals. In the U.K. case, cutlery is a small industry, electorally concentrated over six districts and geographically concentrated in the town of Sheffield in Yorkshire. Cutlery is unlikely to have widespread parliamentary support; only six legislators directly care about the fate of cutlery. However, deriving legislators' induced preferences is only part of the story—equally important is how legislators' induced preferences are aggregated into policy decisions. In the United Kingdom, backbench Members of Parliament are not the important policy makers. Political parties are strong, and the party in government makes the policy decisions (Bailey 1979). The fate of cutlery depends on whether or not the ruling party elite cares about winning Sheffield's electoral districts. The loss of thousands of jobs in the cutlery industry would be devastating for Sheffield and the surrounding countryside in South Yorkshire. Yet why should a national party be concerned about these local effects? The answer lies in the marginality of these districts and their importance in determining which party wins the next election.

The United Kingdom is a plurality system with single-member districts. As Duverger (1954) first showed, such systems devolve to two-party competition, with the party that captures the greatest number of seats forming the government. As a practical matter, party support varies across electoral districts. Some districts, such as those in the home counties, strongly support the Conservative party, while others, such as the North of England and the West Country, strongly support the Labour party. Except under extreme conditions, it is rare for these safe seats to change hands. Other districts are party competitive; the elections are close and the seats regularly change hands. It is these latter marginal districts that are the key to electoral success.

The party in government could adopt trade and industrial policies that reward its key supporters in safe districts. While such policies might ensure that the government wins an even higher proportion of the vote in these districts at the next election, it does not help it capture or hold the marginal districts it needs to maintain a legislative majority. Alternatively, the government might target assistance to opposition strongholds in an attempt to lure voters away from the opposition. While such attempts might work, the government has so much ground to make up in opposition strongholds that it is unlikely to capture these districts. Such a policy might succeed in increasing the government's vote share but is unlikely to help it maintain its seat share. Since governments in strong-party majoritarian systems care primarily about maintaining a legislative majority, assistance is best provided to those districts where electoral support is most likely to win the election.[43] Simply put, a dollar is best spent on the district where its impact is most likely to influence who wins the district. Policies that improve the popular vote, per se, politically misallocate resources.

Vote differentials between the top two parties are the easiest way to determine which seats are party competitive. Marginal seats are commonly defined as seats that can be gained with a swing of 5 percent or less (Butler 1975; Butler and Kavanagh 1974, 1980; Butler and King 1966; Butler and Pinto-Duschinsky 1971). Another measure of key seats is the 5 percent of government seats held by the smallest majority. Although parties do not officially define what a marginal seat is, they often have lists of critical seats (Butler 1975; Butler and Kavanagh 1974; Butler and Pinto-Duschinsky 1971). A large third-party vote can obscure the identity of key seats. Contemporary newspaper accounts often provide a clear indication of which seats will be critical at the next election. Usually, these correspond to those seats with close vote totals between the two major parties.

Today's Sheffield is one of the safest, most militant Labour strongholds in the country; every seat in South Yorkshire bar Sheffield Hallam is Labour held.[44] West Yorkshire and South Wales are the regions heavily concentrated with marginal districts. Traditionally, the outer regions of Sheffield, for example, Sheffield Heeley and Sheffield Hillsborough, contained party-competitive seats. Sheffield Heeley is immediately south of the city center and was a marginal seat particularly in the early 1970s when it could be gained with a swing of 1 percent or less.[45] More generally, this region of the country gathered a large number of Liberal votes, so three-way races were common.[46] Where the Liberals drew a high third-party vote, the outcome of the election was harder to gauge. Hillsborough and Hallam—where the Liberals gained almost 20 percent of the vote—were also party-competitive seats. I argue that successive governments, both Conservative and Labour, came to cutlery's aid during the recessions of the 1970s because the industry was located in party-competitive seats. Ignoring cutlery's plight would have meant the loss of politically important marginal seats for the ruling party.

Some might want to dismiss the marginality arguments, since cutlery was distributed over only a few marginal districts and not all of Sheffield's seats were marginal. The government has less incentive to privilege such safe seats. However, such complaints fail to account for the importance of these marginal seats. In the closely run 1970 and 1974 elections, such marginal districts were seen as "make or break" for the incumbent government (Butler and Kavanagh 1974; Butler and Pinto-Duschinsky 1971). Furthermore, cutlery is a small industry, so even though some of the benefits go to the electorally less important safe districts, the cost of protecting cutlery is relatively small. No other industry allows the government to so accurately target benefits to such electorally important districts.

Changes in the political landscape since the 1970s provide further evidence. Sheffield is now a safe Labour region, and the Conservatives have little prospect of capturing seats there. Given this Labour stronghold, Conservative governments have little incentive to continue to privilege cutlery, and neither do Labour governments. Lack of government support is not the only reason the cutlery industry has waned, but the end result is that cutlery is now reduced to a cottage industry in safe Labour seats. Nowadays, it has fewer than two thousand workers.[47]

Political parties are strong in both Germany and the United Kingdom.[49] Differences in the electoral mechanism help explain why the cutlery industry gained more government assistance in the United Kingdom. Unlike the United Kingdom's majoritarian system, proportional representation (PR) systems, like that of Germany, do not have "marginal districts." Districts are multimember and seats are distributed based on the proportion of votes within each district. Germany is a mixed-member proportional representation system. Half of parliament is elected from single-member districts and the other half is selected from a list vote. Despite these single-member districts, overall the system is proportional since the overall allocation of seats in the Bundestag is decided by the nationwide party vote. Each party is awarded list seats in addition to their district seats until the total number of seats is proportional to the number of votes the party received.[49] If the ruling party in Germany loses a "marginal" single-member district seat, its votes are not wasted votes, since these votes will be used to help determine the overall distribution of seats in the Bundestag.

Which groups of voters do German parties target with policy benefits? In strong-party PR systems, the parties in government control the policy decision. Parties care about maximizing votes, since these translate almost directly into seats. The electoral process provides incentives for parties to target benefits to their core industrial supporters and to favor industries located in regional voting strongholds (even if the industry votes for another party, its fate affects the prosperity of the local economy). Whether or not cutlery wins protection in Germany depends on whether or not it supports a party in government or, at a minimum, whether the town of Solingen, where cutlery is based, is a partisan stronghold for a party in government.

Like British cutlery, German cutlery has a long historic tradition and has also been in decline for much of the twentieth century (Boche 1997; Harrigel 2000). Despite a brief comeback in the1950s, the industry struggled to compete during recessions in 1970s and 1980s (Hayter 1985). Cutlery is geographically concentrated in the town of Solingen in the Ruhr region of Germany. It is the major industry in Solingen; about a quarter of the Solingen's workforce are employed in the cutlery and tools trade (Sträter 2003). The industry was, and is, larger than that in the United Kingdom (it has also been more competitive than the British cutlery industry).[50] In Solingen in the 1970s and 1980s there were around six thousand workers and forty cutlery firms, such as Henckels, Puma-Werk, Merkur, and Trident. Nowadays, the cutlery industry in Solingen is much more reduced in size (Sträter 2003). Cutlery workers are traditional supporters of the Social Democratic party (SPD), and this region of Rhurgebiet, Solingen-Remscheid, is a strong base of support for the SPD.[51]

At the federal level, the SPD was in power through much of the 1970s. This benefited cutlery, although obviously not to the same extent as cutlery was favored in the United Kingdom. Cutlery is a small industry within the SPD's large group of industrial supporters. Given its relative size, it is perhaps not surprising that it won only limited assistance compared to British cutlery. On the other hand, because cutlery is a small industry, protecting it would have been relatively "cheap." However, the SPD was not alone in determining government policy. In the 1970s, the SPD was in government with the Free Democratic party (FDP). Most (PR) Proportional Representation governments are multiparty, and this affects how parties' preferences are aggregated. In order to form a government, the SPD needed, and still needs, malleable policy goals in order to accommodate its coalition partners' preferences. In general we should expect trade and industrial policy to be a compromise of what each party in the coalition government wants. Indeed, when the SPD was in coalition government with the Greens in 1998, the SPD cooperated on energy reforms that hurt smaller businesses, such as cutlery, to accommodate its coalition partner's desire for tougher environmental regulations.[52] This does not imply that PR systems are generally less protectionist than majoritarian systems. How parties' preferences are aggregated in coalition governments strongly affects the pattern of redistribution in the strong-party PR case.

The United States is a majoritarian system with single-member districts, much like the United Kingdom. However, unlike in the United Kingdom, the party system is weak and legislative outcomes are not determined by party elites. Instead, policy depends upon a majority coalition of legislators forming to pass legislation. Unlike the United Kingdom's or other high-party discipline systems, legislative votes are not strictly along party lines, and the coalition that forms for one bill might be completely different from the coalition that forms for another. It is these coalition dynamics that determine whether or not a legislator wins import protection for her industry. In both the United States and the United Kingdom, the majoritarian system induces similar preferences in legislators, but the aggregation of these preferences differs drastically between these systems.

In the postwar period, a small, highly geographically concentrated industry like cutlery, located largely in Connecticut and New York, found it very difficult to build the legislative majority coalition it needed to win protection. In weak-party systems, agenda-setting rules in the legislature are extremely important in determining outcomes. The cutlery industry was larger in the United States than it was in either the United Kingdom or Germany. In 1981 it was composed of about two thousand companies and around one hundred thousand workers—

however, many of these firms were in the specialized and highly competitive knife trade, concentrated in Oregon (USITC 1985). Stainless steel flatware production was clustered in parts of upstate New York and in Connecticut (USITC 1985).[53] The industry is more industrially concentrated than that of its European rivals; in 1981, the top four companies controlled 85 percent of total production in stainless steel flatware (USITC 1985). Taken together, these factors should have favored the cutlery industry with higher-than-average levels of protection. From 1956 to the early 1970s the government used escape-clause action to place on-again, off-again quotas on Japanese cutlery; however, these had little impact (USITC 1978).[54] Recessionary pressures and a flood of cheap foreign imports hit the U.S. cutlery industry in the late 1970s, and it made repeated pleas for quotas to be reinstated. In 1978 and 1983 industry appeals for quotas were denied.[55] The industry tariff remained about 5 percent—significantly lower than in the United Kingdom and Germany (Lavergne 1981).

Why did U.S. cutlery fail to get the protection it sought, and what might have helped it? Had cutlery been more politically dispersed, it would have had a presence in more legislators' districts. Unfortunately, cutlery is a small industry. If spread any thinner, its employment impact on any district would have become so small that no legislator would have cared sufficiently about it to have helped. Given its small size, cutlery's best chance would have arisen if it were geographically concentrated in the district of a representative with institutional leverage, such as the chairmanship of legislative budgetary or trade and industry committees (as we shall see in the case of footwear later). But it was not in such a district. Before a representative obtains a strong institutional position, she requires seniority. Unlike the U.K. case, where marginality helped, a representative from a party-competitive district in the United States is unlikely to develop the seniority required to gain institutional leverage. Under the U.S. political system, cutlery's political geography is part of the reason it failed to secure the financial assistance it needed to stay open.

How Does Industry Geography Matter?

The case of cutlery reveals that the relationship between industry size, spread, and location and the level of trade assistance is a contingent one that depends upon the interactive effects of political institutions. It is hardly surprising that the empirical evidence on the effect of geographic concentration or size on trade assistance is ambiguous. Depending on the type of political system, the effect of industry size is conditional on electoral spread and location or on party-industry affiliations. Geographic concentration can affect which industries win protection, but I argue it is regional, rather than spatial, concentration that matters. In the case of the steel industry, which is discussed in chapter 4, steel plants are spatially dispersed but regionally clustered in every country case. I show that, in some cases, regional concentration undermined steel firms' political struggle, while in other cases, regional concentration was the key to steel firms' political success. In PR systems, the incentives to target one region over another arise from economic and demographic differences, which structure party affiliation. Political jurisdictions by themselves are of no importance. In contrast, in majoritarian systems, political jurisdictions are everything. Within a specific region, parties compete only in those political jurisdictions where the underlying economics and demographics make the seat party competitive. I argue there is no general relationship between industry geography and political influence across all countries.

Rival Political Explanations

I argue that variance in the level of government assistance to the cutlery industry in the United Kingdom, the United States, and Germany are largely explained by differences in party strength and the electoral rule. There are, however, many other institutional variables that influence political clout and government support that I do not explore in the context of this single case. For example, Germany and the United States have federal bicameral political systems, while the United Kingdom has basically a unitary structure. The federal structure creates an extra layer of veto players—actors whose agreement is necessary to create government policy (Tsebellis 2002). It is conceivable that these veto players hindered the national government's attempts to protect the cutlery industry. U.S. individual states or German Lander might well veto trade and industrial policy that lead to an unfavorable regional redistribution of resources. This implies that regionally concentrated industries rarely win protection. On the other hand, trade and industrial policy is a multidimensional policy issue, so one could also imagine legislative bargains that buy-off coalitions of U.S. states or German Landers.

A related argument is that Germany and the United States did protect their cutlery industry to the same exent as the United Kingdom, but that I overlooked this by focusing solely on national trade and industrial policies. In federal systems, industrial assistance is often distributed at the subfederal level. Cutlery might have received much higher levels of government aid once the policies of German Lander and U.S. states are accounted for.

An alternative theoretical argument is that smaller district size in the United Kingdom made legislators more vulnerable to special interests than in the United States or Germany (Rogowski 1987). PR systems—like Germany's—tend to have geographically larger districts than majoritarian systems like the United Kingdom. These large PR districts, however, are multimember, not single-member, districts. This is an important difference. Party candidates in multimember races typically target niche groups of voters in order to win one of many seats (Cox 1990). I see no reason why these legislators are less vulnerable to special interests. I will return to this argument later in the book, when I discuss how electoral rules affect the level of protection

I do not compare the role of unions in aiding the cutlery industry to win protection. I argue that the fragmented structure of U.K. unions undermined the industry's attempts to demand protection. It is possible that the centralized wage bargaining in Germany impaired the industry's ability to effectively demand protection. Cutlery workers constitute a minuscule portion of the Metalworkers Union. It is unlikely the union would fight hard for such a tiny industry. On the other hand, it is possible that the Metalworkers Union did pressurize the government for redundancy packages on behalf of cutlery workers. Governments can use many different types of policy instrument to privilege key groups of voters. Although I do discuss the role of unions elsewhere in this book, the theoretical focus is how governments supply protection, not how industries demand protection.

Yet another explanation for cutlery's high level of trade protection in the United Kingdom is the national pride argument. There is a great deal of sympathy among the British public for the plight of the Sheffield cutlery industry and the nostalgia this conjures for industrial dominance long gone. The main express train from London to Sheffield is still called the Master Cutler. In part, this cultural resonance explains why cutlery receives higher protection than, say, shipbuilding. People are less nostalgic about British ships; they don't inherit sets of them from their grannies.[56] Protecting this kind of industry has a big electoral payoff; one that goes beyond the marginal districts in the north of England. Hence, one might argue that successive governments have protected the cutlery industry because of its cultural resonance. However, it is possible to find another industry that is as not favored with government assistance but, nonetheless, viewed wih some wistfulness (i.e., the U.K. clock industry). Nor is the national-pride argument particularly useful in a comparative context. One could argue that Germany and the United States do not offer the same levels of protection to their cutlery industries because the industry does not have the same cultural resonance in these countries. This is hard to test. It is certainly true that there is no train from Frankfurt to Solingen called the Master Cutler, yet Solingen's cutlery industry is regarded as a national symbol of German innovation and craftsmanship. These types of cultural variables undoubtedly play a role in the government's decision to supply protection. Nonetheless, in a comparative context, I argue that the variables doing most of the work are the electoral mechanism and party structure.

Throughout this chapter, the role of the cutlery case has been purely illustrative. In chapter 2, I set up the theoretical framework and derive predictions as to which groups of voters are favored with redistributive policies under each of three types of political system: strong-party majoritarian systems (like the United Kingdom), weak-party majoritarian systems (like the United States), and strong-party PR systems (like Germany). I explore how industry geography—size, spread, and location—interacts with features of the electoral system to determine which industries win protection. As the case of cutlery shows, it is important to consider both steps of this process: how industry geography affects legislators' induced preferences and how legislative preferences are aggregated into policy. This second step is as important as the first. In the case of cutlery, the initial link between industry geography and induced preferences is similar in the United States and in Britain (the geography of the industry and the electoral rule are the same); however, in the second stage, differences in how legislative preferences are aggregated into policy strongly disadvantage a small, geographically concentrated industry such as cutlery in one case, and strongly advantages it in the other.

I do not examine weak-party PR systems, of which Brazil would be an obvious case. There are several reasons for this, the primary one of which is the relative indeterminacy of predictions for this case. As Barry Ames has documented, in Brazil's weak-party system, legislators use many different tactics to get reelected. In the formal sense there are multiple equilibriums. This means that individual legislators can come to power based upon very different support groups. While in some cases these might be based on industrial groups, in other cases they are not. Although I do speculate about the Brazilian case in chapter 2, given the relative ambiguity of prediction, I do not intend to explore it in the detail I do for the other cases.

ALTERNATIVE ARGUMENTS ABOUT THE ROLE OF ELECTORAL RULES

Other scholars who use the electoral rule to explain patterns of protection offer quite different arguments from those presented here. Rogowski and Kayser (2002) argue that consumer groups are more powerful in majoritarian than in PR systems. The key feature of their argument is the greater seat-vote elasticities in majoritarian than in PR systems. This leads to greater electoral penalties in majoritarian than in PR systems (for example, a 5 percent loss in votes translates into a bigger loss of seats in majoritarian than in PR systems). Because alienating voters has higher political risk in majoritarian systems, Rogowski and Kayser predict that consumers are more politically powerful in majoritarian than PR systems. However, they roll the relationship between the electoral rule and trade policy into one step: how parties' vote share is translated into seat share. This ignores how parties' induced preferences are aggregated into policy.

In majoritarian systems, votes are not equally valuable everywhere. In the U.K. system, the most valuable votes for national parties are those in marginal seats. Aiding an industry in a marginal district is where the income effect from trade protection has the biggest impact on the government's reelection chances.

This hurts consumers, but the government can afford to lose votes in safe seats that it has either little hope of winning or little risk of losing. In the PR case, Rogowski and Kayser's argument implies that since all votes are equally helpful in obtaining seats in PR systems, the governing parties want to enrich all producer groups to maximize their support. However, Rogowski and Kayser ignore how multimembered district and coalition politics encourages parties to target niche groups of voters (Cox 1990; Myerson 1993). Party-sector affiliations and the low cost of new party entry make targeting all producer groups a risky political strategy. It is useful to construct a hypothetical case. Suppose party A typically represents farmers and party B typically represents steelworkers. If party A is in government (and B is not), then it could no doubt increase its support among its rival's traditional supporters by increasing steel protection. Yet, given steelworkers' predisposition toward party B, A's expected yield of additional votes, for each dollar of protection, is small. Further, the cost of enriching steelworkers is to harm farmers, who must pay higher steel prices. While it might well be true that PR parties are more sensitive to producer interests than consumer interests, farmers are nevertheless consumers as well as producers.[57] As such their interests are hurt by party A's attempts to lure the traditional supporters of party B. Multimembered districts allow new party entry. As party A seeks to increase its support, a new party that exclusively represents farmers' interests can make gains at A's expense. In attempting to attract additional supporters, party A risks alienating its core supporters.

So while it is true that in PR systems all votes are equally valuable, it is not true that they are all equally easy to obtain (see also Cox 1990; Myerson 1993). The electoral rule and industry geography affect which industries parties want to protect, while the electoral rule and the strength of parties also affect which industries legislators are able to protect. Which producer groups actually receive government assistance depends on the dynamics of coalition bargaining in multiparty government.

The existing work on government redistribution of transfers in the field of U.S. politics also tends to focus on one or other of these two steps. Lindbeck and Weibull (1987, 1993) and Dixit and Londregan (1986, 1998) argue that governments purchase votes by distributing money to regions teeming with swing voters. Transfers to swing voters have a bigger effect on the government's reelection chances than do transfers to their own or opposition voters. Cox and McCubbins (1986) assume parties are risk averse and argue that targeting swing voters is a risky strategy. Parties will, first and foremost, target policy to benefit the party loyal. Hence, governments purchase votes by investing in regions where they already have high support. However, both arguments assume parties are strong. I assume that U.S. parties are weak. In the U.S. case, the key policy makers are coalitions of individual legislators. I contend that the Dixit and Londregan swing-voter argument is better suited to a strong-party majoritarian system, like the United Kingdom's. In contrast, the predictions of the Cox and McCubbin model, where parties reward loyal voters, are a better fit for the strong-party PR case. However, Cox and McCubbins's argument is quite different from the one I propose. I do not assume that parties are risk averse in one type of electoral system and risk acceptant in the other. Although in the PR case, parties' induced preferences make them act as if they were risk averse. The ease of new party entry makes it least costly to target groups within your own set of party supporters.

The basic theory is about redistribution, not trade. Restated to refer to all types of government transfers, my thesis is that the government weighs the costs and benefits of using policy to buy votes to win reelection. In PR systems with strong parties, one vote is as good as any other vote. The least costly votes to buy are those from individuals who are ideologically predisposed to vote for you in the first place. Hence, parties are predisposed to gaining votes within their traditional constituencies. In majoritarian systems with strong parties, one vote is not as good as any other vote. Votes in marginal districts are more valuable, since winning the marginal districts is the key to winning the election. It costs more to buy off these voters, but it is worth the expense because their votes are more valuable. In both cases it is extremely costly to lure away voters who have strong opposition-party loyalty. In PR systems it is cost effective to target loyal core voters; in majoritarian systems it is cost effective to target voters in marginal seats. While governments in PR systems appear risk averse and governments in majoritarian systems appear risk acceptant, this behavior is shaped by the structure of the political system.

THE DYNAMICS OF TRADE POLICY: SHIFTING INFLUENCE

An industry's political clout does not always remain constant over time. As discussed earlier, cutlery's political influence diminished once the electoral landscape changed and Sheffield's electoral districts became safe Labour seats. Here I explore the dynamic aspects of industry protection and ask what political factors change trade and industrial policy.[58]

As the Sheffield case suggests, in strong-party majoritarian systems a change in the marginality of districts affects an industry's political influence. Empirically, marginality is reasonably stable in the medium term. Yet voter realignment—such as occurred in Canada in the 1980s—can cause a major shift in marginal districts. While such sudden changes are rare, economic development and shifts in the salient political issues produce gradual shifts in the distribution of marginal seats. In both Australia and the United Kingdom textiles have maintained their privileged positions because their semirural locations have remained party competitive throughout the postwar period. Other industries have seen their fate change. Austin-Rover, a United Kingdom automobile producer, was concentrated around Birmingham in the Midlands region. In the

1980s, its largest plant, Longbridge, employed about fourteen thousand workers.[59] Not only was it the biggest plant in the Rover group, it was also the biggest employer in Birmingham. For various reasons, the firm operated at a loss for decades, but successive governments supported Austin-Rover with massive bailouts (Marklew 1995). By 1984, British Leyland, Austin-Rover's owner, had absorbed $3 billion in subsidies. Given the scale of the plant, closure would have devastated not only the local economy but economic conditions throughout the Midlands. In addition to the fourteen thousand Longbridge workers, around fifty thousand workers were employed in subsidiary companies that supplied Longbridge.[60]

Allowing Longbridge to fail for a long time posed too high a political liability, and successive governments sought to save it. Yet in the late 1980s, after almost a decade of heavy public backing, Thatcher's Conservative government drew the line at future bailouts.[61] While the case of economic hardship remained unchanged, the political costs had lessened. Longbridge was on the southern edge of Birmingham, and its surrounding electoral districts were a mix of middle-class semirural housing and council estates. In the 1959, 1964, 1970, 1974, and the 1979 elections these districts held the key to victory.[62] In an area so rich in marginals, no government could risk harming it; whether the government was Labour or Conservative, it bailed out Longbridge.[63] Yet shifts in marginality undermined Longbridge's privileged position. The marginals of the 1980s were the East Midlands, South Wales, Northwest England, and Outer London. By 1986, only eight of seventy-seven Conservative held marginals had significant motor interests (marginals here are generously defined by majorities of less than 10 percent in the 1983 general election).[64] Without its dependence on these districts, the government felt safe to break up and sell off Austin-Rover.[65] In a strong-party majoritarian case like this, it is a change in marginality that strongly shifts the pattern of protection.

In a weak-party majoritarian case, a change in the agenda-setting power of the industry's representatives affects the level of protection, as does a change in the industry's coalition partners. For example, the U.S. footwear industry's fate depended upon the agenda-setting power of its representatives. Until the 1990s, footwear was relatively protected from imports.[66] A small industry, it was largely located in Maine and Missouri; however, it was part of a coalition with textiles and apparel, which extended its geographic influence. Part of the reason footwear was a valuable coalition partner was that its representatives had political clout. The heart of its power lay in the important committee assignments held by the senators from Missouri and Maine (McGillivray and Schiller 1998; Schiller 1999). Senator Danforth (R-MO) was chair of the Finance Subcommittee on Trade from 1981 to 1986. Senator Mitchell (D-ME) was a member of the Finance committee and then Senate majority leader from 1989 to 1994. These legislators were able to block legislation that damaged the footwear industry. With the departure of these institutional leaders, footwear lost its political clout, and it was deserted by its coalition partners (textiles and apparel) since it no longer had anything to offer. Political analysts commented, "Having Mitchell as a majority leader was crucial. Mitchell would block the tiniest footwear provision, it would never get through because of him. They really lost their champion when they lost him."[67] Today, Missouri's shoe industry is almost completely gone, its production moved overseas.[68]

In PR systems a change in the party composition of a coalition government shifts the distribution of protection. Parties have incentives to target niche groups of voters,[69] and tend to have ties to particular industries. For instance, in Ireland, Fianna Fail is associated with the construction industry, while the German textile industry is associated with the Christian Democratic Union (CDU). When the CDU left office in 1969, political support for textiles bottomed out (see chapter 6). Similarly, the Swedish paper and pulp industries won substantial subsidies in the late 1970s and early 1980s because the party they supported, a small center party, moved into government.[70] Of course, if the same parties continually remain in government, such as the Christian Democrats in Italy or Belgium, then the industries that support them should see their assistance remain largely unchanged.

Different political systems suggest different dynamic patterns in how assistance changes over time. I exploit these differences to derive additional hypotheses and new dependent variables. In particular, I focus on how a change in government affects redistributive policy. These dynamic implications of the theory are explained in greater detail in chapter 2.

WHO PROTECTS MORE: PR OR MAJORITARIAN?

Which states are the most protectionist? This is a common question in trade politics. While most efforts have compared autocratic with democratic regimes (see, for example, Mansfield et al. 2000), some attention has been paid to the role of the electoral rule. Although, as I shall argue, some of the emphasis placed on this question is misguided, it is worth exploring the logic behind arguments before considering the empirical evidence.

Magee, Brock, and Young (1989), Rogowski (1989), and Mansfield and Busch (1995) suggest PR systems are less protectionist than majoritarian systems because they are characterized by larger electoral districts.[71] Since larger districts are more likely to be industrially heterogeneous, legislators representing such districts must weigh a wider array of interests, which isolates them from parochial interests. The following example captures the gist of the argument. Suppose industry A has 100 workers. In a constituency of 1,000 voters, industry A represents 10 percent of the electorate. In a constituency of 100,000 voters, industry A represents only 0.1 percent of the electorate. Refusing to protect 0.1 percent of her electorate is unlikely to affect a politician's reelection chances. Refusing to protect 10 percent of her electorate is much riskier. In this way, the large districts that characterize PR systems insulate PR governments from industry demands. Along similar lines, Magee, Brock, and Young (1989) argue that in the United States, the president, whose constituency is the whole country, is less protectionist than senators, who in turn are less protectionist than congressmembers. While this argument has much to commend it, it focuses only on the desires of individual legislators to protect industries and says nothing about whether they can influence policy.

Rogowski and Kayser (2001) predict that producer groups are more powerful in PR systems. This implies that PR systems are more protectionist than are majoritarian systems. The model developed here says nothing about whether PR or majoritarian electoral systems are characterized by higher average levels of protection. Because the relationship between the electoral rule and industry geography is a contingent one, the level of protection in strong-party majoritarian systems depends on how many districts are marginal and how industries are dispersed across these districts. In PR systems, parties do not maximize the welfare of a large constituency; rather, they target niche groups of voters. In weak-party majoritarian systems, the level depends on how industries are dispersed across districts and how much institutional clout the representatives from each district have. Industries' geography and the political system interact to determine the distribution of protection. Within this context, the average level of protection is vastly insufficient to describe the range and extent to which different industries receive assistance. We might, for example, find that a few industries get lots of protection in majoritarian countries (a small number of industries in marginal districts with high protection), but that many industries get lower levels of protection in PR countries (from multiple parties bargaining in a coalition government). Within this conception, it is unclear that the average level of protection is a useful statistic with which to compare very different distributions of trade protection. Even if the mean protection level is regarded as the appropriate measure for deciding whether nations are more or less protectionist, such claims cannot be directly attributed to the electoral system since the average level of protection depends, for example, on the number of marginal districts and how industries are distributed across them.

Recent work by Shigeo Hirano (2002) on the impact of electoral reform in Japan (in particular, in moving from multimember to single-member districts) also speaks to this issue. Under the old multimembered district system he finds that legislators targeted and drew their support from a subsection of constituents in the electoral district. Following reform and the introduction of single-member districts, legislators want to target and draw support more broadly from within what are generally smaller electoral districts. The overall effect of the electoral system on protection is ambigouous.

The empirical evidence is mixed. The majoritarian countries in Europe, France, and the United Kingdom were, until recently, regarded as the most protectionist countries in the EU. The smaller countries, such as Italy and the Netherlands, tend to be more free-trade oriented. Table 1.2 contains the averages for the 1980s for a variety of trade measures (Dutt and Devashish 2002). Looking across the table at the different measures of trade assistance, no clear pattern of protection emerges for any one country. True, on average, Canadian tariffs are higher than Belgian tariffs, but quotas are more common and subsidies (as a percentage of the GDP) tend to be higher in Belgium. Overall, Belgium has larger trade flows ({exports + imports}/GDP), but this is not surprising.[72] Small countries tend to be heavily dependent on their export trade and have stronger incentives to support free-trade policies. Since many of the PR countries in Europe are small, their free-trade position could have more to do with their size than with their type of electoral system. Nonetheless, this does not stop PR countries from bending the rules and finding other ways to support their domestic industries. While some countries appear free-trade oriented within Europe, they use nontransparent policy instruments to help struggling industries on their home turf. Among the Italian political parties, there is a widespread consensus that free trade is preferential to protectionist policies (Grilli and La Noce 1983). However, as a percentage of the GDP, Italian industrial subsidies are frequently higher than those in Germany, the United Kingdom, the United States, Australia, and New Zealand.[73] Federal countries, like Germany or Canada, are accused of only sounding free-trade oriented because they know the sub-federal-level states will step in to help industry. In Germany, Lander (state level) and city governments often step in to aid industry.[74]

Table 1.2 lists different measures of trade assistance for various countries in the 1980s. New Zealand has the highest average tariffs (Switzerland, the lowest); the highest subsidies (as a percentage of the GDP) are in Sweden (the lowest in the United States);[75] quotas are most heavily used in Portugal (least used in Canada); the highest import duty as a percentage of imports are in Australia (lowest in Germany); Belgium makes the most extensive use of NTBs (lowest NTB coverage in Norway); however the highest trade flows are in Belgium (the lowest are in the United States).[76] It does appear that the majoritarian countries tend to prefer to use tariffs, while PR countries often prefer to use subsidies.[77] Although this is not true across the board; the United Kingdom has some of the lowest tariffs and quotas.[78] The fact that there are so many different ways a government can privilege an industry begs the question as to why certain governments tend to favor one form of policy instrument over another. Mansfield and Busch (1993) find that PR countries tend to have more NTBs than majoritarian systems; however, this does not necessarily mean that PR systems are more protectionist. It could mean governments in PR systems prefer to use NTBs rather than other policy instruments, such as tariffs, to assist industries (although tariffs and NTBs tend to be correlated

TABLE 1.2
Different Measures of State Assistance in Twenty-two High-Income
OECD Countries, Averages for 1980s

	Average Tariff[a]	Quota Coverage Ratio[b]	Import Duty (% of imports)[c]	Size of Trade Flows (relative to GDP)[d]	Industrial Subsidies (% of sectoral GDP)[e] 1980–1984	Nontariff Barriers Extent of Coverage,[f] 1983	Electoral Rule
Australia	n.a.	n.a.	8.481	28.058	1.6	24.1	Majoritarian
Austria	0.047	0.021	1.706	62.350	2.7	6.0	PR
Belgium	0.036	0.112	n.a	118.602	4.4	33.9	PR
Canada	0.046	0.019	3.873	45.937	3.1	n.a.	Majoritarian
Denmark	0.042	0.112	0.093	72.941	3.2	15.9	PR
Finland	0.059	0.067	1.485	61.153	n.a.	9.2	PR
France	0.019	0.050	0.064	43.979	2.9	28.1	Majoritarian
Germany	0.039	0.119	0.014	47.045	1.6	18.3	PR
Greece	0.041	0.142	n.a.	20.506	n.a.	23.2	PR
Italy	0.021	0.069	0.057	35.484	2.6	14.6	PR
Japan	0.020	0.058	2.643	21.034	1.1	16.9	PR
Netherlands	0.040	0.126	n.a.	98.426	2.6	28.0	PR
New Zealand	0.176	n.a.	5.625	36.284	1.2	n.a	Majoritarian
Norway	0.014	0.041	0.843	78.034	4.4	5.8	PR
Portugal	0.047	0.194	3.141	36.778	n.a	n.a	PR
Spain	0.042	0.123	5.220	29.066	3.8	n.a	PR
Sweden	0.033	0.028	1.011	73.463	7.5	n.a.	PR
Switzerland	0.012	0.176	3.855	104.573	n.a	23.6	PR
U.K.	0.018	0.044	0.121	42.846	2.4	17.5	Majoritarian
U.S.	0.020	0.123	3.432	15.825	0.5	17.3	Majoritarian

Sources: Dutt and Mitra 2002. Their data is generously made available at www.arts.ualberta.ca/~econweb/ dutt/data.xls. As detailed below, the data set includes data drawn from UNCTAD compilations, World Bank's Development Indicators, and Barro and Lee 1994.

[a] Average for 1980s, where each import category is weighted by a fraction of world trade in that category (includes all import charges). Barro and Lee 1994.

[b] A coverage ration for nontariff barriers to trade. Average for 1980s. Barro and Lee 1994.

[c] Average for 1980s. World Bank's Development Indicators.

[d] (exports + imports)/GDP, average for 1980s. World Bank's World Development Indicators.

[e] At market prices. Ford and Suyker 1990, table 3.

[f] The amount of own imports covered by NTBs in 1983, excluding fuels. Nogues, Olechowski, and Winters 1986, table 1c.

[Rodrik 1995]). At the end of the book, in chapter 6, I discuss the endogenous choice of policy instrument. I argue that the strength of the party system affects whether governments prefer to use geographically blunt policy instruments, like tariffs, to redistribute, or geographically targetable policy instruments, like subsidies. However, leaving aside for the moment the question of why governments choose different policy instruments, table 1.2 reveals that in both PR and majoritarian countries, governments find ways to privilege their favored domestic industries.

THE EMPIRICAL TESTS

As the previous section revealed, lack of policy transparency makes it difficult to measure how governments redistribute public assistance to industries.[79] In part, this is because trade and industrial policy is multidimensional. Not only can government provide different levels of assistance to each industry, but government can also use different policies such as tariffs, quotas, subsidies, tax breaks, procurement, or regulation to assist each industry. Comparing the monetary value of subsidies versus tariffs, or procurement policies versus low-interest loans, is extremely tricky. As table 1.2 revealed, looking at only one of these policies can cause serious bias in the results. Today's governments use a complicated mix of different types of assistance. If we look just at subsidies, we risk ignoring other forms of assistance. Although international agreements often restrict or limit the amount of assistance, nations have become adept at bending the rules and finding different ways to privilege industries. For example, governments might resort to bureaucratic harassment. Britain taxes French perfumes at the same high rate as alcohol. The French make Japanese videos travel to the town of Poitiers in central France for customs clearance.[80] Research and development support has replaced subsidies as the most popular form of state aid—in large part because it is geographically flexible.[81] In Germany, research and development subsidies are a popular way to target benefits to specific regions through the creation of industrial parks.[82] Within the EU, it has become particularly hard to measure which countries are pushing for which particular industries because the decision-making process is nontransparent. While we do get slivers of information—for instance Britain pushed for textile protection within the EU, yet it fought the hardest against a sensitive label (excluded from tariffs) for carpets under the Generalized System of Preferences (Cable and Rebelo 1980)—it is extremely difficult to know who is helping whom.

To test the hypotheses derived in chapter 2, what I ideally need is clear, comparable measures of the total assistance granted to each industry. Unfortunately, such measures are hard to come by. Tariffs are probably the easiest protection to measure, but even calculating the effective tariff from the nomi-

nal tariff is a complex task.[83] The quantitative analysis of NTBs is very difficult. We have data on the presence of NTBs across industries. However, we
do not have comparable data on the degree of NTBs across industries.[84]

Price differentials offer an innovative and promising way to measure industry
protection. If we ignore problems of transportation costs and economies of
scale, if truly free trade exists, then arbitrage should ensure that prices in every
country are the same. However, barriers to trade distort these prices. Rogowski
and his colleagues (1999; Rogowski with Kayser 2002) use deviations from
average world prices as measures of protection for different products across the
world. They find evidence that trade is more open in majoritarian systems. One
advantage of this method is that it provides a measure of all the different types
of government assistance to industry in comparable units. Of course, its biggest
limitation is that it probably reflects other factors that have nothing to do with
barriers to trade, such as transportation costs, market size, and demand. Controlling for these other effects is tricky (Rodrigez and Rodrik 2000).[85]

Our inability to accurately measure levels of assistance severely limits our
ability to test our theories. I propose several solutions to overcome these problems. I use two different types of dependent variable to test the theory outlined
in chapter 2. The first dependent variable is a direct test of how much income
from tariffs goes to industries and electoral districts in Canada and the United
States—two majoritarian countries with strong and weak parties, respectively.
While I have argued that tariffs make up only one means of assistance, I use
tariffs from the 1970s, when they were still the predominant tool for protection.
Additionally, I limit the statistical analysis to Canada and the United States,
neither of whose tariff policy was subverted to a customs union at the time. By
the 1970s, tariff levels within much of Europe were regulated by the European
Economic Community or European Free Trade Area.

One advantage of this empirical setup is that I am able to test the interactive
effects of industry size, location, and electoral concentration. In Canada I find
that, as expected, industries highly electorally concentrated in marginal districts receive the most favorable levels of protection. In the United States,
industries located in safe districts receive more favorable levels of protection
than industries located in marginal districts; large, electorally dispersed industries are able to secure the most favorable levels of protection. This analysis
helps unravel the mixed findings in the literature on the effect of geographic
and electoral concentration on the level of industry protection. Busch and Reinhardt (1999) argue that this is largely a measurement issue.[86] I argue that the
effect of electoral or geographic concentration on political clout depends on
the interactive effect of institutional variables.

While the results in chapter 3 support the arguments for majoritarian systems, they do not provide a test of the predictions for strong-party PR systems. Neither do they control for government assistance through other policy
instruments.

Much of the extant literature has dealt with the problem of multiple policy instruments by either ignoring the problem or attempting to construct indices of protection. While the latter attempts are potentially rewarding, I prefer another tack. The second dependent variable is an indirect measure of the value of government assistance to an industry—industry stock prices. In chapter 5, I test auxiliary hypotheses about the effect of government change on redistributive policy using the relative price of industry stock prices in PR and majoritarian systems.

Stock market data provide a valuable and, I believe, a much underused measure of government policy.[87] Actors in stock markets, particularly large institutional investors, have incentives to, on a case-by-case basis, examine the impact of government policy and bureaucratic regulation on an industry's profitability at a level of detail impossible for a political scientist looking at many industries across many countries to duplicate. What is more, stock markets aggregate each investor's assessment and report the information in comparable units across all industries and across all nations—namely, the value of an industry.

The French government's rebate plan of 1994 provides an excellent example of the stock market's ability to capture the value of protection. In 1994, the French government offered a rebate to consumers willing to trade in their old cars for new, less-polluting models. The stated goal of the rebate was to help the environment. However, because it was tied to the purchase of French automobiles, the rebate also helped French automakers. One way of measuring the value of the government subsidy to Peugeot-Citroen is to estimate how much the rebate affected Peugeot-Citroen sales in 1994. It is estimated that about 7 percent of Peugeot-Citroen's increased sales in 1994 were due to the government subsidy.[88] Alternatively, we could look at what happened to the price of Peugeot-Citroen's stock on the French stock market—did it rise with the news of the government rebate? Private investors are highly efficient at incorporating this type of information into their expectations about industry share prices. If the future profits of an industry are expected to change because of an alteration in trade or industrial policies, then the value of equities in that industry will adjust accordingly. Further, a comparison of stocks allows us to compare the impact of very disparate policies. For example, were the rebates to Peugeot-Citroen more or less valuable than the research and development subsidies awarded to the French chemical company Rhodia? Comparing these two policies without an intimate knowledge of both markets is like comparing apples and oranges, yet stock prices provide directly comparable, although admittedly noisy, measures. Since monetary units or percentage changes in market capitalization are easily compared, stock-market data makes it possible to compare the value for Chrysler when the Austrian government pays a third of the cost of a new Chrysler factory, to the value of the grants to Volkswagen from the

German state of Saxony, to the value of the French government's rebates on trade-ins for Peugeot-Citroen cars.[89]

Unfortunately, stock-market-based measures are not perfect, since many factors other than the value of government policy affect stock prices. This volatility makes the measure noisy. Despite this noise, there is considerable evidence that financial markets react as expected to shifts in party government and to changes in domestic industrial policy or trade shocks (Quinn and Jacobson 1989). Using U.S. stock prices, Mahdavi and Bhagwati (1994) find that the announcement of Voluntary Export Restrictions does increase the stock price of affected industries. Herron, Lavin, Cram, and Silver (1999) found that the profits of different industry sectors in the United States reacted as expected to anticipated political change in the 1992 presidential election.[90]

I exploit the efficiency with which stock markets incorporate information to test the dynamic implications of the model. In addition to predicting which industrial groups are likely to receive protection as a function of the electoral system, the theory also predicts how the winners and losers of the competition for industrial assistance change in response to political change. For example, in PR systems, trade and industrial policy represents a bargained compromise between the parties in government. When the government changes, so will the nature of this bargain, with issues that the outgoing parties cared about being dropped and the issues of the incoming parties being incorporated. With such a change, the winners' stock prices should rise while the losers' fall. In majortarian systems, a change in marginality (with strong parties) or a change in the agenda-setting power of legislators (in weak party systems) produces policy changes.

An event analysis of investors' changing valuation of Peugeot Citroen stock is one way to assess the policy impact of government change in France.[91] However, such a direct test is problematic over a wide range of industries because it requires a detailed knowledge of which industries are associated with which parties or legislators. Such information can be readily compiled for a particular industry in a particular country—for example, from newspaper accounts and political contributions (where relevant)—but for a cross-national, cross-industry study coordinating, this data is impractical. This data constraint prevents me, in a large N setting, from assessing who the winners and losers are from a policy change. Yet a policy change produces winners and losers. The winners' stocks should rise and the losers' stocks should fall: a divergence in stock price accompanies policy change. I create a measure of stock-market price dispersion by asking how much price changes for individual industries vary from the average market price change. Since this dispersion measure increases with policy changes, it provides a means to assess policy change, and I regress this measure on political change.

It is critical to recognize that in these tests it is not the average market price, per se, that I care about, but rather the extent to which industries deviate from the market average. Following a change in government there might be a 1 percent increase in the average market price. This average change is not of interest here. Rather, is this 1 percent change the result of all industry groups experiencing a 1 percent gain or are the winners from a change in industrial policy gaining 11 percent, while the losers are losing 9 percent? The former implies no redistributive implications from the change in government, while the latter suggests a change in the set of industries privileged from trade and industrial policy. I assess how the dependent variable "price dispersion," responds to political and economic change in both PR and majoritarian systems across fourteen stock markets, from 1972 to 1996.[92] While it is not a direct assessment of the quantity of assistance provided to each industry, the comparison of stock data allows me to test an auxiliary hypothesis derived from the theory.

In between the two empirical chapters, 3 and 5, I provide a test of the causal plausibility of the theory using another type of dependent variable. It is traditional in the trade literature to think about competition between industries. In most cases this is appropriate, since most assistance policies affect all firms in an industry equally. Yet this is not always the case. The theory I advance concerns redistribution, and it asks under what conditions government chooses to privilege one group over another. While I couch the theory in terms of industries, the theory is equally applicable at a subindustry level. In chapter 4, I examine the government's role in plant closures within the steel industry in Australia, Belgium, Germany, Sweden, the United Kingdom, and the United States.

By the early 1980s the steel industry in each of these countries was under immense pressure from cheap imports and a falling price for steel. In each county it was clear that the steel industry needed urgent restructuring, which in all cases meant closing some plants. In most cases the government played an active role in choosing which plants remained open and which were closed: a redistributive choice. Steel manufacturing involves massive plants that typically dominate the employment in the areas where they are situated. The choice of which plants to close has enormous redistributional consequences, since plant closures result in high levels of unemployment and economic stagnation for the local economy. As I shall demonstrate, the decision to keep certain plants open and others close was not a decision based on economic efficiencies. The decisions were primarily political.

For example, in the early 1980s, the U.K. Conservative government implemented a radical restructuring plan for the steel industry. The plan called for the closure of steel plants in both Wales and the Northeast of England, while the Ravenscraig plant in Scotland was kept open. Such a plan was clearly not formulated on an efficiency basis: the Welsh plants were far more efficient than Ravenscraig. Indeed, the British Steel Corporation (the nationalized industry that ran steel) and a parliamentary select committee both opposed keeping Ravenscraig open. Politics holds the key as to why the government imposed the economic misery on communities in the Northeastern England rather than in the far greater loss-making plant in Scotland. While the regions of Wales and Northeastern England strongly support the Labour party, Ravenscraig to the Southeast of Glasgow near Motherwell included the few remaining seats that the Conservatives held in Scotland. As we shall see in chapter 4, the Ravenscraig case demonstrates how governments in majoritarian systems with strong parties redistribute in favor of marginal districts.

In a PR system, the theory predicts that governments will favor the party faithful. The restructuring of Belgium steel illustrates this well. In December 1981, a Catholic-Liberal coalition took over from the socialist-center government. This new coalition was dominated by northern, Flemish interests. Unlike the previous government, it pushed for reform of the steel industry. Specifically, the new government restructured and closed southern (Wallonian) steel plants (Bain 1992; Capron 1986). Although the government provided public funds to the southern plants, the one-shot subsidies were designed to speed their closure and put a stop to their long-term drain on the public purse. Closing the older Wallonian steel plants and redistributing assistance as a reward to Flemish constituencies in the north was both economically and politically rational for the new government.

The steel case studies emphasize the centrality of redistribution to understanding trade and industrial policy. Given the policy instruments at its disposal and the geographic distribution of industrial groups relative to political jurisdictions, government privileges those groups upon whom they depend for political success. Chapter 4 demonstrates that, given its choice of policy instrument, the government privileges groups to maximize political ends. However, this begs the question of why certain governments tend to favor one form of policy instrument over another. I discuss this endogenous choice of policy instrument in the final chapter of the book, chapter 6.

CONCLUSION

The purpose of this book is to show how governments use trade and industrial policy for political goals. In particular, governments use these policies to privilege certain groups. As such the pattern of trade protection and industrial assistance depends upon how an industry is distributed and what political system is in place. Who wins and who loses from trade and industrial policy depends upon a two-stage mapping. First, the geographic distribution of an industry relative to political jurisdictions determines which industries legislators wish to help. Second, the electoral system and the strength of parties determine how these induced preferences are aggregated into policy. It is not enough to simply have legislators that want to help your industry; you need legislators who can also convert their preferences into policy.

In the next chapter I provide a detailed exposition of the theory. In particular I analyze how the industry geography required to obtain government assistance varies according to the strength of political parties and the electoral rule.

CHAPTER 2

Who Are the Decision Makers and
What Motivates Them?

IN THIS CHAPTER I set up my theoretical framework and derive predictions as to which groups of voters are favored with redistributive policies under each of three electoral systems: strong-party majoritarian, weak-party majoritarian, and strong-party proportional representation. The theory is one of redistribution that has implications about which type of industry and which regions of the country are favored by government assistance to industry.

As a brief summary of the results to follow, I argue that in strong-party majoritarian systems, parties target the redistributive policies of trade and industry toward rewarding those in marginal districts (districts where the vote between rival parties is close). Hence, I predict industries located in such districts receive greater state assistance than industries located in safe seats. In strong-party PR systems, each party in the governing coalition wants to target redistributive rewards toward their core supporters. Parties reward their electoral base because of the possibility of new-party entry. The resulting trade policy is a compromise of what each governing party wants. This compromise generates a trade policy that is in flux, dropping policies targeted toward the supporters of parties that leave office and incorporating policies directed toward supporters of parties entering government. In weak-party majoritarian systems, a coalition of individual legislators is necessary to pass legislation. In such systems, specific institutional features, such as which legislators have agenda control and seniority, strongly influence which legislators receive protection or assistance for the industries in their constituency. Beyond these specific features, industries spread over numerous electoral districts provide the basis for a natural coalition among legislators. Government assistance is given to industries widely dispersed over numerous electoral districts.

The theory is primarily about redistribution. Since trade and industrial policy allows governments to reward one group at the expense of others, the formation of this policy is shaped by domestic political incentives. An industry's geography matters, because whether an industry is a suitable instrument to target rewards to key groups of voters depends upon its geography: its size, spread, and location.

THE THEORETICAL ARGUMENT

In the theoretical framework, the institutional properties of the electoral system are incorporated as determinants of the endogenous formation of trade policy. The electoral system has two key components, the electoral rule and the strength of parties (electoral cohesiveness). The building blocks for the theoretical argument are the electoral rule, the strength of parties, and industry geography. These factors affect the derivation and aggregation of legislators' preferences. The electoral rule and industrial geography affect which industries legislators want to protect. The electoral rule and the strength of parties affect which legislators determine policy outcomes and, hence, which legislators' induced preferences get represented. I propose a two-step link between geographic location and trade policy:

1. The electoral rule maps industry geography into legislators' induced preferences over which industries to protect or assist.
2. The electoral rule and strength of party aggregate legislators' induced preferences into policy.

I examine three stylized forms of electoral system: strong-party majoritarian systems, strong-party proportional representation systems, and weak-party majoritarian systems. Strong-party majoritarian systems are characterized by single-party majority government. In this case, the ruling party elite de facto chooses policy. PR systems, on the other hand, are typically characterized by multiparty government. In strong-party PR systems, policy choices represent compromises and bargaining between parties in the government and in the legislature. In weak-party majoritarian systems, a majority coalition of legislators (not necessarily along party lines) determines policy. I use these three stylized systems to reveal the incentives afforded politicians in different electoral systems.

I do not examine weak-party PR systems. Most weak-party PR systems use open-list rather than party-list ballots. In the latter, voters get to vote for a party, and candidates are allocated seats through their party. In open-list PR, voters vote for a candidate, who is typically affiliated to a party. In large part this is why parties are weaker in the open PR case. I do not study these cases because of the relative indeterminacy of predictions for this case. In Brazil, national parties are weak and there are multiple legislators per district. Individual legislators use many different tactics to target the niche groups of voters they need to get reelected (Ames 1993, 2001). These legislators can come to power based upon very different support groups—in some cases industrial groups, in other cases ethnic groups or social groups or issue-based interest groups. Agenda setting and legislative rules are key in determining how individual legislator's preferences are aggregated. Later in this chapter I do speculate about the Brazilian case. We might expect that representatives redistribute in favor of industries that are highly concentrated in geographic localities. However, given the relative ambiguity of prediction and the uniqueness of each weak-party PR case, I do not intend to explore it in detail as I do for the other types of political systems.

The electoral rule and the strength of parties are treated as fixed, exogenous variables. While real political systems are obviously more complicated than these stylized examples, I can focus on the underlying differences between systems considering the "perfect limiting" cases. Having derived predictions in each case, I explore the interactive effects of industry geography—size, spread, and location—on the theoretical predictions. Given an industry's geography, I predict which industries are the winners and losers in trade and industrial policy based upon their geographical distribution relative to political jurisdictions.

DEFINING ELECTORAL SYSTEMS: THE ELECTORAL RULE AND THE STRENGTH OF PARTIES

Electoral Rule

The electoral rule is defined as having three components: ballot structures (i.e., n alternatives, pick one or rank); electoral formula (PR or majoritarian);[1] and district magnitude (number of representatives per district) (Rae 1971). There is a large literature on how these features of the electoral rule affect political representation (Duverger 1954; Grofman and Lijphart 1984; Huber and Powell 1994; Lijphart 1984, 1990, 1994; Powell 2000; Rae 1971, 1995; Taagepera and Shugart 1989). I characterize the key differences between PR and majoritarian systems as follows. In PR systems, seats are assigned to parties in proportion to votes (using one of the PR formulas: D'Hondt, Sainte-Lague, Hare, etc.). In majoritarian systems, electors vote for individuals and, depending on the electoral formula (i.e., plurality or majority rule), the candidate with the most (or majority of) votes wins the seat. Across the board, majoritarian formulas are much less proportional in terms of electoral outcomes than are PR formulas. There are differences in the proportionality of PR formulas; for example, the Sainte Lague is more proportional than the D'Hondt formula (Cox 1997; Monroe 1995). However, these differences within PR systems are smaller than the differences between PR and majoritarian systems (Benoit 2000; Rae 1971; Sartori 1986; Taagepera and Shugart 1989).[2] PR systems have multimember districts, while majoritarian systems typically have single-member districts. Hence PR systems are characterized by a few large electoral constituencies, while majoritarian systems are characterized by many small electoral constituencies.

Most theorizing in comparative politics about electoral rules has concerned the causal linkages between these political system characteristics and effective representation in the legislature. PR systems are widely regarded as a fairer representation of aggregated individual preferences because of the closer relationship between party votes and number of legislative seats. (Gallagher, Laver, and Mair 1992; Lijphart 1990; Rae 1971; Rustow 1950; Sugden 1984).[3] The higher district magnitudes associated with PR systems partly explains their greater number of small, niche parties (Rae 1971, 1995). Whereas most majoritarian systems have a district magnitude of one, district magnitude in PR systems varies from 2 to over 150 legislative seats per district. If the district magnitude is one, a single seat is awarded to the party that receives the most votes, typically political parties with a broad base of support. Yet, as district magnitude increases, parties representing more specific or particular interests can win a seat. For example, if a particular party represents the interests of a specific 5 percent of the population, then it will rarely defeat broader-based parties in a majoritarian system where it needs to win a plurality of the vote to win the district seat. Yet such a party becomes increasingly likely to obtain a seat as district magnitude increases; a smaller fraction of the vote is necessary to win a seat. Appeals to voters become increasingly "narrow" as each party seeks the niche of voters it needs to win a seat (Cox 1990, 1997; Myerson 1993). Hence, minority groups are often able to win representation.

In contrast, majoritarian systems severely penalize third-place parties in terms of parliamentary representation (Rae 1971). Duverger (1954) observed that majoritarian formulas encourage two-party systems. Minority groups are often shut out of the legislative process.[4] Not surprisingly, the choice of electoral formula has the biggest effect on representation in electorates with strong minority groups: ethnic, religious, social, or political (Amorim, Neto and Cox 1997; Gallagher, Laver, and Mair 1992; Levin and Nalebuff 1995; Ordeshook and Shvetsova 1994). In electorates that are highly homogenous and consensual, the choice of electoral system makes little difference as to who wins representation.

Recently, scholars have argued that representation is affected by more than the mapping of party votes to legislative seats (Laver 1997; Baron and Ferejohn 1989; Schofield 1993, 1996, 1997). Although individuals vote for parties, they do so given their preferences over what government will do. Rather than judge an electoral system solely on the proportionality with which it allocates legislative seats, it is important to examine whether or not the electoral system gives voters the policy outcomes they want (Austen-Smith and Banks 1988, 1991; Powell 2000). Multiparty PR systems are typically characterized by multiparty government. Two-party majoritarian systems are characterized by single-party government. In majoritarian systems, a majority of votes is not necessary to win a majority of seats in the legislature. As long as there are an odd number of legislative seats, one of the two parties forms a majority government. In PR systems, a majority of votes is generally necessary to win a majority of seats in parliament. The high level of party competition makes it difficult for one party to get a majority of the votes. Hence, PR governments are typically multiparty coalition governments and are often minority governments (Strom 1990b).[5]

These features of party competition influence representation through a number of channels. Parties are strategic actors, and their choice of policy positions anticipates the policy positions that they will be able to enact after forming a government. There is a large and growing literature on coalition formation in PR systems. In it, the electoral rule and the nature of party competition shape the electoral strategy parties take and the postelection bargaining they engage in (see Laver and Schofield 1990; Laver and Shepsle 1994; McKelvey and Schofield 1987; Riker 1962; Schofield 1993, 1997; Strom 1990a, b). Recent modeling attempts suggest that the number of parties formed, the policy positions parties adopt, and the government formation process are all interrelated (Baron and Diermeier 2001; Diermeier and Feddersen 1998; Kalandrakis 2000). Theory suggests that parties tend to adopt dispersed policy positions in PR systems. Because parties anticipate making compromises in multiparty coalition government, they adopt more extreme policy positions to pull the policy outcomes closer to their party's ideal point (Cox 1990; Baron 1993; Myerson 1993).

In contrast, in majoritarian systems most governments are single-party majority. Parties have incentives to adopt policy positions closer to their preferred policy because they do not have to bargain with another party over policy issues while in government (Cox 1990, 1997; Myerson 1993). Downs (1957) predicts that in a two-party system, vote-maximizing parties in a unidimensional vote space will converge toward the median voter (Osborne 1995). However, empirically we often observe parties adopt divergent policy positions (Budge and Laver 1993). There may be institutional barriers that prevent parties "converging" in policy positions (Strom 1990b). For example: parties are not unitary actors; party activists may make it impossible for the party to move to the center of the policy space (Francis et al. 1994; Schlesinger 1991; Strom 1990b; Tsebelis 1995).[6]

There is a growing literature on the policy effects of these features of PR and majoritarian systems. For example, they affect the stability and the duration of government (Mershon 2002); the level of inflation and the amount of trade protection (Grilli, Masciandaro, and Tabellini 1991; Rogowski 1987); the size of the budget deficit and the amount of redistribution (Lizzeri and Persico 2001; Milesi-Ferretti, Perotti, and Rostagno 2001; Persson and Tabellini 1999; Tsebelis 1999, 2002; Roubini and Sachs 1989). I focus on how government policy is redistributed between voters in majoritarian and PR systems.

I integrate the insights of the coalition bargaining literature in setting up the model of the stylized cases for both PR and majoritarian systems. A key aspect to understanding the role of the electoral rule is that it does more than map votes into seats; it also influences the number of parties, their policy positions, the process of government formation, and bargaining—all of which affect redistributive politics. In majoritarian systems, single-party governments use redistribution to maximize the probability of the government retaining power. In contrast, the redistributive policy of coalition governments is less focused, with each coalition member wanting to privilege different groups. Unfortunately, formally modeling the impact of these different pulls is difficult (Laver and Schofield 1990). Nonetheless, it is possible to derive hypotheses for multiparty PR systems and two-party majoritarian systems using a simple informal framework that incorporates the intuitions learned from the coalition-bargaining literature.

The Strength of Parties

The strength of parties determines which political actors set policy. In reality there is a continuum of party strength; parties are stronger in the United Kingdom than in France, stronger in France than in the United States, stronger in the United States than in Brazil. However, the key theoretical distinction is whether the voter is choosing a party with an associated package of policies or the voter is choosing an individual who will enter the bargaining process to further constituency interests. Parties are defined as weak or strong based on this criteria.[7]

In strong-party systems, the public votes for parties rather than for individual candidates, and the electoral organization is controlled by parties, not by individual candidates. Representatives toe the party line, voting with the party when it demands. In majoritarian and PR systems with strong parties, the political actor is the party (or parties) in government. In contrast, in both majoritarian and PR systems with weak parties, individual legislators are more important in policy formation. Additionally, when parties are weak, legislators are much more beholden to their constituency's wishes for their political survival than is the case when parties are strong. Bawn, Cox, and Rosenbluth (1999) describe the latter as electoral cohesiveness: "the extent that the electoral fate of legislators from the same party are tied together" (1999, 330).[8] This concept is closely related to the strength of parties; both are strong when politics is nationalized and partisan, and both are weak when politics is localized and personal (Bawn, Cox, and Rosenbluth 1999).

There are two institutional features that greatly affect the strength of parties: party discipline and legislative agenda-setting power. The electoral rule, party organization, campaign finance rules, procedural rules for the legislature, and historical precedent influence the level of party discipline (Cox 1987). PR systems tend to foster high party discipline. Most PR countries use a list system in which parties present a list of candidates in each constituency. In some countries, the ranking order of candidates cannot be altered by voters; it is fixed by the party. The party punishes candidates who do not obey the party leadership by placing them lower down on the list. There are, however, PR systems with open-list rules. This encourages weak-party systems; Brazil is such a case. It is the number of votes a candidate receives and not the party ordering that determines how high a candidate is ranked on the list for her constituency (Ames 2001; Mainwaring 1999). The open-list rule is, however, atypical. The list system in most PR systems fosters strong party discipline.

Majoritarian systems tend not to sustain as high levels of party discipline. In parliamentary majoritarian systems local party members select district candidate nominations (Bowler, Farrell, and McAllister 1996). This decentralized form of party control tends to be less effective than centralized control over party lists at maintaining party discipline; nonetheless, local parties can ultimately deny reselection (Epstein 1994; Norton 1978). For this reason, many majoritarian systems—Canada, Australia, and the United Kingdom, to name a few—have high party disciplines.

However, not all majoritarian systems have highly disciplined parties. In the United States, a low-party-discipline majoritarian system, candidates are nominated by direct primaries. The party organization has only limited influence on candidate nominations—for example, providing campaign service or campaign funds.[9]

Party discipline is not the only institutional feature that empowers parties. In parliamentary democracies, the cabinet government controls the agenda and uses legislative rules and restrictive procedures to preserve bargains within the cabinet (Indridason 2002; Laver and Shepsle 1994). Even when dissenting backbenchers and opposition parties form a majority, it is difficult for them to pass a bill against the cabinet government's wishes. The cabinet government has a host of restrictive procedures with which to kill the bill. Agenda control also gives the government considerable power to push legislation against the will of opposition parties and backbenchers. The government can repackage the vote; if an issue is multidimensional, it can divide a vote into two votes, months apart. It can also use the vote of no-confidence to pull dissenting backbenchers back into line (backbenchers vote for the government rather than risk an ill-prepared election campaign) (Huber 1996). Backbenchers do have some control over leaders. For example, they can use a vote of confidence to depose the party leader, but in many respects, their power to discipline leaders is limited.

In contrast, in a presidential democracy, the legislature typically controls the agenda. Legislative support is not cohesive, in part because the president does not require it to remain in office. Vetoing executive bills does not risk the dissolution of the legislature and a subsequent untimely election campaign. The United States is the key example of a presidential majoritarian system with weak parties.[10] Brazil is an example of a presidential PR system with weak parties.

In the theoretical argument, party strength determines whether the party elite or individual legislators are the key actors in determining policy outcomes. The strength of parties is treated as exogenous, and in the empirical section of the book, it is defined as a dichotomous variable: strong or weak. As stated earlier, I do not use a continuum of party strength because the key theoretical distinction is whether the voter is choosing a party with an associated package of policies or the voter is choosing an individual who will enter the bargaining process to further constituency interests.

In summary, I argue that the strength of parties—an institutionalized feature of party behavior—interacts with the electoral rule to determine which legislators get the policy they want.[11] The electoral rule and the nature of party competition also shape the electoral strategy parties and legislators take and the postelection bargaining they engage in. Next, I outline the general assumptions in the model.

GENERAL ASSUMPTIONS

To make comparisons between electoral systems possible, I make similar assumptions about the motivations of parties and legislators in strong- and weak-party systems. By using the same basic assumptions for each of my three stylized cases, I control for extraneous factors and examine how the differences in institutional configurations predict different patterns of protection and assistance.

Before listing the assumptions in detail, I will briefly run through the argument for strong-party systems. This should help provide some context for the statement of the assumptions to follow. The government knows that when voters go to the polls they consider both the government's ideological position relative to their own and the real income they receive as a result of the policies the government pursues. Although the party leadership is constrained by the mass membership of the party from altering party ideology, the leadership has considerable freedom of choice in other policies that are not as tied to the left-right dimension. Leaders use this policy discretion to choose policies that maximize their probability of retaining office. Policies such as trade assistance allow leaders to privilege certain electoral districts relative to others. At election time, the voters simply vote for the parties they think will benefit them the most. More formally the political and economic assumptions are as follows:

1. Politicians seek reelection. Political parties want to form a government.[12]
2. Political parties have fixed ideological positions on all issues but trade and industrial policy. As parties have fixed ideological positions, individuals are

simply biased toward one party or another. This is a natural starting point for posing the question: holding all other policies fixed, how does trade policy affect a politician's chances of reelection?[13]

3. Voters care about two things: income and ideology.[14]

4. Income is generated by a government's ability to run the economy, but it is also redistributed through trade and industrial policy. The model predicts how governments redistribute income through the instrument of trade assistance.

5. Political systems have either strong or weak parties.[15]

6. Trade assistance generally lowers average real income nationally.[16] Everybody cannot simultaneously be made better off. However, trade assistance can be used to redistribute income.

7. Factor mobility is sufficiently low that changes in relative prices do not lead to the immediate redeployment of factors.[17] If factor mobility is low, as trade assistance increases for an industry, then income for labor and capital in that industry increases. The benefits are concentrated in the industry that wins assistance, while the costs (i.e., increased prices) are spread over all industries and consumers. If the constituents of an electoral district are employed or have capital in the district's major industry, the political cleavage is between electoral districts rather than between labor and capital or between import and export industries.

Working with these basic assumptions, I derive hypotheses about how the electoral rule and party strength determine which industries are winners and which are losers with respect to trade policy. I initially develop the arguments in terms of the competition between industries; which groups receive government assistance under different political arrangements? While I use the term *industry* in the exposition of the theory, the political competition is between geographically distributed groups. To the extent that trade and industrial policy allow governments to distinguish between firms within an industry, similar arguments apply. In the context of the steel industry, I will subsequently expand my arguments to intraindustry competition and examine how and why governments influence which plants close and which remain open. I next examine the three stylized electoral system cases.

MAJORITARIAN SYSTEMS WITH STRONG PARTIES

Two-party competition with single-party majority government characterizes majoritarian systems with strong parties. Legislators are elected from single-member districts. To build the arguments, suppose the system has five constituencies, a ballot structure of one vote for two-alternative candidates, plurality rule, and a district magnitude of one. The party in government controls the policy decision and is interested in maintaining a legislative majority rather than maximizing the vote share, which in this case means winning three districts. To make the simplest assumption possible, suppose each electoral district contains a single major industry.[18]

Suppose that the five electoral districts, A, B, C, D, and E, differ in the positions of their median voters. The median voter is highly biased toward the governing party in districts A and B and biased toward the opposition party in districts D and E. These districts are labeled "safe." District C is labeled "marginal" because the median voter is indifferent between supporting the government or the opposition party. To survive in office, the government needs to retain three electoral districts. The governing party must decide which, if any, industries it wants to privilege, knowing that doing so enriches the district with the protected industry at the expense of citizens in the other districts.

Suppose the government uses trade policy to privilege the industries located in districts D or E. This protection improves real income in these districts at a cost to all other districts (A, B, and C). The income effect in these districts improves the governing party's electoral prospects in districts D and E. Since these districts are heavily biased against the government, however, the income effect from protection is not sufficient to capture these seats. Alternatively, the government could target protection to industry in districts A and B as a reward to loyal voters. Winning more votes in districts A and B does not help the government's reelection chances. In fact, rewarding loyal voters actually harms the government's probability of retaining office, since it reduces the welfare of voters in district C, whose support the government needs to maintain.

The government already holds districts A and B by a large majority. However, the support of district C is more fickle, since on ideological issues the district is evenly divided between the parties. The government targets the industry in C because the income effect from protection will have the biggest electoral effect. The marginal district is cheaper to buy off than either of the opposition's safe districts, D and E. The government is prepared to sacrifice total vote share in the "party loyal" districts A and B to maximize its probability of retaining three seats, districts A, B, and C.

Under single-member district systems, governments target redistribution toward marginal, or party-competitive, districts.[19] It is these districts that determine which party will win the next election and, as such, governments want to ensure their support. Yet which districts are targeted does not depend upon which party is in office. Both parties want to privilege the marginal districts at the expense of their own, and the opposition's, basis of support.

Voter Motivation

By assumption, voters care about ideology and income, with income being a shorthand for economic welfare. Ideological differences between voters means

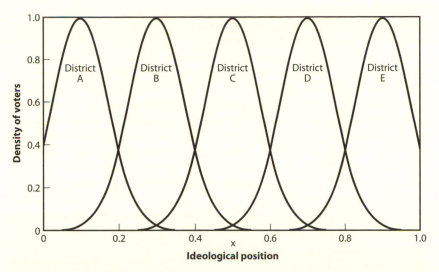

FIGURE 2.1. The Distribution of Voter Ideal Points on the Left-Right Dimension.

that, controlling for income effects, some voters prefer the left to the right party and vice versa. While from an ideological standpoint a voter might prefer the left to the right, if the right offers her substantially greater income, she might shift her vote. In my stylized case, the extent to which the median voter in each district was predisposed to one party over the other differs. In districts A and B, I assume that a majority of the voters strongly prefer left to right. This is not to say that these districts could not be persuaded to vote for the right, just that the income differential between the two parties would have to be high. In contrast, I assume voters in district C are more centrally distributed, so the median voter in this district is relatively indifferent between left and right. Figure 2.1 shows this pictorially. In this figure, the distribution of preference is represented as normally distributed, although from the median voter theorem we know that the shape of the distribution is unimportant; only the position of the median voter matters (Black 1948; Downs 1957).

The justification for assuming radical differences in the ideological positioning of voters in different districts is empirical. As a practical matter, districts often have strong ideological affiliations. For example, in the United Kingdom many safe Labour seats are located in Scotland, the North of England, Wales, Cornwall, and Devon. In contrast, the South and the home counties typically vote Conservative. As a region, the Midlands is composed of many marginal districts and, as such, is often a political battleground since the party that wins these seats, when combined with their safe seats, will have a majority. It is a political reality that safe districts exist. As my father-in-law is apt to say about voting in Melton Mowbray, the town where he grew up, "If they had dressed up a tea-pot as a Conservative, people would have voted for it."

An implicit assumption of the theory is that everyone in a district receives the same shift in income from protection. Obviously this is a simplification, but it can be justified. Although those associated directly with a protected industry benefit most, the income effects are passed on to others in the district. For example, increased demand from wealthier workers translates into improved welfare for those in subsidiary or local service industries. The closure of a local industry can cause a regional recession: house prices tumble, retailers shut up shop, and the local tax base declines. Local residents do not benefit as much as industry workers from protection; nonetheless, they indirectly benefit from the continued presence of the protected industry in their district.

While I have specified what voters care about, I have yet to characterize the informational assumptions about voters. In part this is because, as I hope to explain, the same predictions hold whether voters are assumed to be naive or sophisticated. Modern political science is replete with arguments about the sophistication of voters (Austen-Smith 1991), which are based on the extent to which voters can disentangle the origins and implications of policy. We might suppose the government influences an individual's income in two ways. First, government competence and ability to regulate and manage the economy affect overall income levels. Second, redistributional policies increase the income of some citizens at the expense of reducing the income of others. Of course, the object of this book is to ask how the political system influences who wins and who loses from such redistributions. Unfortunately, the question arises as to what extent do citizens reward the government for a rise in their income. The answer depends upon the sophistication of the voters and their information. Fortunately, the predicted redistributional policy of the government—namely, targeting marginal districts—does not depend on the level of voter sophistication.

Initially, suppose that voters are extremely naive and do not recognize that income could be derived from either economic competence or redistribution. Such voters reward governments that increase their income but support the opposition otherwise. Under these circumstances, the government targets marginal districts with redistribution since these are the "cheapest" districts to buy.

Suppose instead voters are completely sophisticated. In this setting, voters in marginal districts know the government has incentives to channel resources toward them through redistribution. Therefore, they do not attribute all the rise in their income to the government's economic competence. Also, they do not credit the government for favoring them over other voters, since they know that the opposition parties would also target them for redistribution. In this setting, the government gains nothing from redistribution, and the voters can differentiate the economic competence of the government. Nonetheless, the government still has incentives to target redistribution to marginal districts. Although the government gains no electoral advantage from redistribution, it suffers electorally if it fails to do so.

First, suppose voters observe the impact of trade policy. If the government fails to target redistribution to marginal districts, it will lose votes to the opposition parties who are willing to redistribute in favor of marginal districts. Alternatively, if the voters cannot disentangle trade policy, which is probably the more realistic assumption, then the government's failure to redistribute causes a reduction of income in marginal districts, leading sophisticated voters to infer that the government is poor at running the economy, and as a result, the government will lose votes. To illustrate more explicitly, suppose redistribution targeted toward marginal districts results in an effective income shift of 3 percent. If this redistribution is removed, voters in marginal districts will see their income fall by 3 percent. Of course, this increases income in the remaining districts, but since these districts are either already progovernment or need extremely large shifts in income to change their vote, this does not benefit the government. If the voters only observe local income levels but are politically sophisticated such that they anticipate a 3 percent redistribution in their favor, then the withdrawal of redistribution is interpreted by the voters as economic policy failure, with the overall economy seen to do 3 percent worse than it actually has. If the voters observe income in all districts rise, then a 3 percent decline in their marginal district reveals the government is no longer targeting them. However, since they know the opposition party would target marginal districts, their support for the incumbent declines. The key is that whatever the assumed sophistication of voters, governments target marginal districts.[20]

In summary, assumptions about the sophistication of the voters and their access to information influences the logic behind the result; fortunately, it does not alter the underlying prediction that governments in strong-party majoritarian systems target marginal districts. This result is shown formally elsewhere (McGillivray and Smith 1997). The importance of marginal districts has been pointed out in country studies of the United Kingdom and Australia (Cable and Rebelo 1980; Conybeare 1984). In the real world, of course, majoritarian political systems deviate from this stylized political model. I address the case of multiparty majoritarian systems in appendix 2.1. The predictions remain unchanged.

PR SYSTEMS WITH STRONG PARTIES

Next I consider the case of a multiparty PR system with strong parties. Electors vote for parties in large multimember districts. Although the details differ slightly by system, seats are allocated in proportion to the national vote for each party.[21] To construct the simple stylization, I assume a single nationwide constituency, a ballot structure of one vote for n-alternative candidates, and vote share converting directly into seat share. In such systems, a multiparty coalition government is the normal state of affairs. Following the allocation of seats, party leaders attempt to form a coalition government. Typically, the competition to form a coalition is regulated by some rules as to which party— often the larger party—has the first opportunity to form a coalition (Kalandrakis 2000; Warwick and Druckman 2001; Diermeier and Merlo 2001).

If a majority coalition forms, the parties in government control the policy decision. Given that parties are strong, once decisions are made at the cabinet level, they are supported at the legislative level. In the case of minority governments, the parties in government must form coalitions with other parties in the legislature to pass legislation. In the majoritarian case, I assume that the government wants to maximize its probability of retaining power. Unfortunately, since it is rare for a single party to attain a majority in a PR system, specifying the motives of the multiparty government in PR systems is somewhat trickier.

In PR, as in majoritarian systems, parties want to maximize their probability of being in government, however, parties also want to increase their influence within the coalition government. There is a broad correlation between seat share and distribution of cabinet portfolios in coalition governments (Gallagher, Laver, and Mair 1992; Schofield and Laver 1985). This correlation suggests that parties should want to increase their vote share since this translates into seats, which in turn translates into cabinet positions and, hence, influence.

Unfortunately, the dynamics of coalition formation suggest that the probability of inclusion in the government is not monotonically increasing in seat share. For instance, suppose that party A has 35 percent of the seats and forms a coalition with party B, which has 16 percent of the seats. This gives the coalition a legislative majority, with party A being the senior party. Now suppose that party B fares much better at the next election, gaining a vote share of 30 percent. Now, assuming A retains 35 percent, B is no longer a junior partner and might expect a much larger share of the spoils of office. As a result A might find another party a more attractive coalition partner. As an example, in Germany (with the exception of one brief period of grand coalition) all governments have been a coalition between the first and either the third or fourth largest parties. Hence, it is unclear that increasing vote share and becoming the second largest party is advantageous for smaller parties.[22] Despite this, as a working assumption, I assume parties want to at least maintain their voter share, since this maximizes the probability of multiparty government maintaining a legislative majority. Given this caveat regarding the incentives of parties, I analyze trade policy using a simple stylized model.

Suppose a PR system with one electoral district, multiple legislators, and three parties: A, B, and C. For simplicity, suppose that the economy is composed of only three sectors: steel, textiles, and farming. Suppose that steelworkers represent the core supporters of party A. Similarly, suppose that the parties B and C typically draw their supporters from textile and farmworkers, respectively. The question I pose in this hypothetical system is, if the only tool at the government's disposal is a redistributive policy such as trade, which voters does it target?

As an initial supposition, let parties B and C be in government together. I claim that such a coalition government would provide redistributive benefits to textile and farmworkers, the support base for parties B and C, but that they would provide little assistance for supporters of party A (steelworkers).

Parties B and C would like to attract the support of steelworkers, traditional supporters of party A, and perhaps could do so by targeting protection to the steel industry. However, the costs of protecting steel are borne by textiles and farmworkers, who pay higher prices as consumers. There is also the additional risk of losing valuable export markets for agricultural and textile products because of foreign retaliation. If parties B and C neglect their core supporters and pander to different constituencies, then new parties might emerge that could split off the textile and farming vote. For example, if party B started endorsing policies designed to attract A's supporters, a party representing only textiles workers' interests could siphon off some of B's support. This scenario is possible because of the low costs of new-party entry in PR systems. High proportionality means that parties with a small vote share can still win representation. In majoritarian systems, parties can afford to compete over the same voters and neglect their core constituencies, since new parties have no incentive to enter (and voters have no incentive to support them) because the voting rule allocates seats to the single party receiving the most votes in numerous small districts. The threshold for obtaining legislative seats is much lower in PR systems (Rae 1971).

Instead of protecting steel, parties B and C could protect jobs for textile and farmworkers at the expense of steelworkers. The benefits from protecting textile- and farmworkers are concentrated among textile and farmworkers. The costs are dispersed over all three groups. The net effect on the income of textile- and farmworkers might be a positive one; the net effect on the income of steelworkers is negative. Parties B and C will choose to protect textile and agricultural goods; they won't win new votes, but it will prevent new parties from syphoning off their current supporters. I argue that in strong-party PR systems, the parties in coalition government target trade and industrial policy to reward their electoral base. This prediction also holds for PR systems with multiparty competition but single-party government (see appendix 2.1).

In coalition governments in PR systems, redistributive policy is a compromise between policies the supporters of each governing party want. Party B wants to enrich textile workers. Party C wants to enrich farmworkers. Yet to pass legislation and implement policy, each coalition partner needs the support of the other and so must be prepared to compromise. The electoral system shapes policy via the two-step mapping discussed earlier. First, the electoral rule determines which industries the legislators want protected—in this case legislators want their party's traditional niche group of supporters protected. Second, the electoral rule and strength of parties determines how legislators' induced preferences are aggregated. In this case, the parties in the coalition government must compromise on redistributive policies, giving each member party (or if a minority government, various parties in the legislature) some of what it wants, in order to form a legislative majority.

The ability to buy off opposition parties by using redistributive policies to privilege particular groups also helps explain minority coalitions. My explanation thus far focused on majority coalitions, yet in reality many governments in PR systems are minority coalitions. In such settings, the government requires legislative support from outside the coalition. Such support can potentially be raised by helping particular groups via industrial policy. A first step to fleshing this out requires an explanation as to how voters assess and reward parties in the legislature and the government. This is a poorly understood process (see Laver and Schofield 1990), and underlies the discussion in the next section.

Voter Motivation

In the above discussion of the majoritarian case, I showed that whether voters are assumed to be politically naive or politically sophisticated did not affect the predicted trade policy (although it did affect the extent to which voters responded to favorable policies). Unfortunately, in the PR case, the situation is somewhat more complicated because policy formation depends upon coalition dynamics. Unlike the clear-cut strong-party majoritarian case, it is ambiguous how voters attribute credit and blame (Powell 2000; Powell and Whitten 1993). I will work on the assumption that voters hold the parties in government accountable for success and failure. However, an argument can be made that supporters of a particular party hold their party liable even when out of government (Gallagher, Laver, and Mair 1992; Laver and Schofield). Given my working assumption, parties in government target trade and industrial policy to reward their core supporters, whether we assume voters are politically sophisticated or naive.

Politically naive voters benefit from favorable trade and industrial policies and attribute their gains to the parties in government. If voters are politically sophisticated, they realize that changes in their income are not purely a function of the government's handling of the economy. Yet since only the party that represents their group's interest targets protection for their industry, voters continue to support their party in order to keep their party in the government and hence their protection in place. If voters observe parties shifting redistribution away from their industry/region, they will be susceptible to the appeals of emerging parties that promise to redistribute in their favor. Voting for a small party is not a wasted vote; parties that win more than 5 percent of the vote win seats in the legislature,[23] and as I discussed earlier, small parties can be pivotal members of a coalition government. While parties seek to maximize their vote share, switching policy to target industrial groups outside of their core constituency is politically unwise.

District Marginality

Although PR systems frequently have more than one district, the concept of marginality makes little sense. Seats are divided up proportionally in multi-party constituencies on the basis of national vote. The party in government is interested in maximizing expected votes. Votes are valuable everywhere, and there is no reason to favor particular districts on the grounds of marginality.

That said, some PR systems have small district magnitudes and so could potentially be classified as marginal districts. Suppose, for instance, a PR district has a district magnitude of two. The first seat will be won by the largest party, but the second seat is contested between a number of parties. Obviously, marginality will also depend on regional political characteristics and the size and number of parties. Nonetheless, it is feasible that when district magnitude is small, PR systems can have marginal districts. PR systems with small district magnitudes are less proportionate and, so not surprisingly, are characterized by majoritarian features—a few large parties and marginal districts. In practice, however, most PR systems have complex multitiered voting rules that drastically diminish the marginality created by small district size. These multitiered rules mean that even if district magnitude is low, the final allocation of seats takes place on the basis of all votes.[24] In Germany, Denmark, Belgium, Norway, and Sweden, "unused" votes are redistributed at a higher tier of districts. The upper tier increases proportionally, whatever the district magnitude of the lower tier. The lower the number of upper-tier districts and the higher their district magnitude, the more proportionate the outcome. In Denmark, the 18 lower-tier districts have an average magnitude of eight: the single upper tier has a magnitude of forty.[25] Lijphart (1990) argues that the upper tier is decisive in terms of proportionality. What this means is that even if district magnitude on the lower tier is low, the district is not "marginal." This is because the overall allocation of votes are divided proportionately at the second tier. Parties have incentives to target total vote share, since this is largely equivalent to seat share.

Germany is an interesting case of a mixed electoral system. Half of the Bundestag (the German parliament) is elected from single-member districts, the other half from the list vote. However, the overall allocation of seats in the Bundestag is decided by these list votes. Each party is awarded as many list seats as is needed until the total number of seats is proportional to the number of votes that the party received. Lower-tier districts, which are decided by plurality rule, might appear "marginal," but since the overall allocation of votes is decided by PR, parties target overall votes, not particular seats. By targeting marginal seats, parties could lose the support of core supporters to new parties. In strong-party majoritarian systems, parties can afford to lose votes from core supporters in safe seats, if it means they can pick up votes in marginal districts.

MAJORITARIAN SYSTEMS WITH WEAK PARTIES

Although the United States is a majoritarian system with a large number of single-member districts, the structure of representation is different from the strong party case. While single-member districts induce the same preference for individual legislators, the aggregation of these preferences differs drastically in the absence of the strong parties characteristic of parliamentary systems. This difference highlights the importance of both steps in the mapping between geography and policy outcomes.

In the weak-party majoritarian case, representatives want to redistribute trade policy in favor of their district or geographical base of support. Legislators know that if they do not provide benefits for their constituents, then a challenger will. Hence, to survive in office—a politician's basic goal—legislators enrich their constituents. In the U.S. context, benefits targeted toward a specific district are called "pork," and the American politics literature abounds with its importance.[26]

In the strong party case, legislative outcomes are controlled by the majority party. As the U.S. case demonstrates, individual legislators play a larger role in weak-party majoritarian systems. Political parties exist in the United States, but, at least in a comparative context, are much less important (Diermeier and Fedderson 1998; Mayhew 1974). Legislative votes often cross party lines and outcomes are determined by a majority coalition of legislators—not political parties. Unlike the British case in which the government and opposition party almost perfectly split on every issue, in the United States who supports each bill varies across different bills. Without strong parties, a successful bill needs the support of a majority of legislators. Yet, many coalitions can be formed, so the question becomes which ones actually do. As scholars of American politics are aware, agenda-setting procedure, seniority, and committee membership all play an important role (see Baldwin 1985; Box-Steffensmeir et al. 1997; Conybeare 1991; Epstein and O'Halloran 1996; Finger, Hall, and Nelson 1982; Lohman and O'Halloran 1994). I do not explicitly consider different agenda-setting procedures here since they are idiosyncratic to the political system and unrelated to industry geography (although given that the United States is my only case of weak-party majoritarian system, it would do no harm). Instead, I focus on how industry geography influences the cost of coalition formation.

Suppose that there are five electoral districts, A, B, C, D, and E, each containing a different industry. Protection or assistance to the industry in district A benefits district A, with the costs borne by all five electoral districts. In other words, the benefits from protection are concentrated in one electoral district, and the costs are dispersed over all five electoral districts. All else equal, district A's legislator wants the industrial assistance, but the legislators representing B, C, D, and E do not.

Independently, district A's legislator cannot form a majority coalition. However, every time legislator A gets another legislator to join the coalition, the aggregate benefits to A's district decline. Bringing B into the coalition brings A one step closer to a majority, but the net gains to A's district are less because they bear some of the cost of protecting the industry in district B. Yet in order to get a majority, A still needs to add another member to the coalition. Suppose A and B consider courting C. The benefit of doing so is that they get to form a majority coalition and win protection for the industries in their districts. Unfortunately, A now suffers the cost of protecting both B's and C's industries. As the number of industries needed in the coalition increases, the costs of forming a majority coalition rise. Sometimes it may be worthwhile for A and B to include C as part of the coalition. At other times, the costs outweigh the benefits, and A and B will not want to form a coalition with C.

The natural question arises of which industrial geographies encourage coalition formation and which do not. Suppose that instead of each district having a single industry, some industries are spread over several districts. Dispersion over numerous districts provides a natural basis for coalition membership. In the discussion above, we saw that districts A, B, and C might have incentives to coalesce to protect the industry in each district. However, such a coalition is difficult to establish and maintain, particularly as rival coalitions exists and as there is little reason for legislators A, B, and C to pick this coalition arrangement over the others available. Yet, if an industry has a significant presence in districts A, B, and C, the coalition formation is simplified. Attaining the support of three legislators does not require any negotiations; they all want the same thing. This suggests that the pattern of industry dispersion across districts influences the costs of coalition formation.

According to demand-side theorists, an industry that is highly spatially concentrated is best organized to demand protection (see chapter 1). Furthermore, the legislator who represents the district desires to provide assistance to local industries. Yet preferences are not aggregated by intensity but by the number of yes votes in the legislature. The district's legislator really cares about the fate of local industry but can do nothing alone. This example demonstrates the importance of considering the two steps required in mapping industrial geography into policy. Considering only the first step, how geography induces legislators' preferences, one might erroneously infer that the concentrated industry would be protected. Extremely concentrated industries might indeed shout the loudest, but only one legislator is listening.

At the other extreme, highly dispersed industries also find it difficult to win assistance. Some industries or sectors have a small presence in nearly every district. For example, we might consider supermarkets. Every town has one; they are present in every district. This potential gives supermarkets lots of supporters for a coalition, yet they are not a politically powerful industry. Demand-side explanations suggest that dispersion makes it difficult for the industry to organize. Supply-side reasons suggest that no legislator wants to protect this industry. First, since supermarkets are approximately evenly spread across the country, the costs and benefits of assistance are also approximately evenly distributed. Since, on aggregate, economic protection is inefficient, the cost outweighs the gains, and each district would on average be a net loser. Second, since supermarkets are so widely spread, the impact of assistance in each district is extremely small. Extremely dispersed industries fail because no legislator wants them protected.

Successful industries, those that receive the assistance they desire, are dispersed across numerous, but not all, districts and are large enough that their impact in each of the districts in which they are located is significant. These industries are the winners. Of course, in reality no industry is perfectly located in half the electoral districts plus one, but dispersion across a number of districts forms the perfect basis for forming coalitions with other industries.[27]

These concepts are perhaps best clarified by looking at some simple examples. Consider table 2.1, below. For the case of five electoral districts, A through E, it examines different hypothetical industrial geographies. I assume that each industry is of unit size and that the numbers in each cell indicate the proportion of industry located in each district.

Industry Z demonstrates the ideal geography to attain protection. A majority of legislators each want to protect or assist industry Z. In contrast, industry Y is too dispersed to attain protection. Each district gains equally from its protection, but each must also pay costs. On average, protection of Y is a net loss to all districts and so it has no supporters. Industry X has a different problem: legislator E intensely wants protection but is not in a position to form a coalition. Industry W has two supporters, legislators A and B, but is still unable to form a majority legislative coalition. However, having a presence in multiple industries, W has a natural base from which to form a coalition. For instance, industries W and V might very effectively lobby to gain the support of legislators A, B, and C. Note that legislators A and B don't want to protect industry V, since V is outside their district and thus protecting V is a costly to their constituents. Similarly, legislator C does not want to protect industry W. Yet a

TABLE 2.1
Hypothetical Industrial Geographies for Five Electoral Districts

Industry	District				
	A	*B*	*C*	*D*	*E*
Z	1/3	1/3	1/3	0	0
Y	1/5	1/5	1/5	1/5	1/5
X	0	0	0	0	1
W	1/2	1/2	0	0	0
V	1/5	1/5	3/5	0	0

bill protecting both V and W together is supported by A, B, and C. Other pairs of industries do not exhibit this natural coalition.

Obviously such simple examples do not capture the complexities of assembling legislative coalitions, but they do illustrate how industrial geography can help or hinder coalition formation.[28] The United States—the case I examine—is even more complex because the passage of legislation requires approval by two legislatures, the House of Representatives and the Senate. In addition, the executive has influence over the formation of trade legislation. These factors mean industries must form a coalition that will receive support under multiple political jurisdictions (McGillivray and Schiller 1998). Since these factors are particular to the United States, I postpone discussion until the next chapter.

Voters' Motivation

How do voters react to an increase in protection for the industry in which they are employed? Politically naive voters will be "bought off" with a simple rise in income. Sophisticated voters use income to deduce that their legislator is competent. In the weak-party setting, a legislator's competence is the ability to bring income to their district (pork). Sophisticated voters realize their legislator is one of many legislators trying to win pork. If income falls in their district, the sophisticated voter assumes that the legislator is incompetent and that other districts are reaping the benefits of pork. If income rises, the sophisticated voter assumes that the legislator is not incompetent. Again, as in the previous cases, regardless of what assumptions of political sophistication we make, legislators want to increase income to their districts through trade and industrial policies.

District Marginality

Does district marginality affect policy outcomes in weak-party majoritarian systems? Suppose electoral districts A, B, C, and D are safe districts. District E is marginal. In a low-party-discipline system, a marginal seat is a competitive seat without long-term incumbents. District E's legislator is more concerned about changes in district income level than are the other legislators. The legislator tries to engage in coalition building frequently, and he can be brought into coalitions more cheaply than other legislators. However, district E's legislator is unable to vote-trade as effectively as other legislators because legislators in marginal seats are less likely to be able to reciprocate the vote trade in the next term of office. Marginal legislators can be brought into coalitions more cheaply, but they will not be able to extract as much. Furthermore, since more senior members of legislatures typically have greater agenda control, party-competitive districts by nature are unlikely to have senior legislators and thus are less likely to receive favorable legislation. Given these handicaps, industries located in marginal (party-competitive) districts should receive the least favorable levels of protection.

PR SYSTEM WITH WEAK PARTIES

PR systems with open lists tend to generate weak-party systems. In the case of Brazil's open-list PR system, it is the number of votes candidates receive and not the party ordering that determines the ranking of candidates on the constituency list. Brazil's campaign finance laws and strong presidential system also undermine party strength. Brazil has multimember districts and, as Barry Ames (2001) and Scott Manwairing (2002) have shown, legislators use many different tactics to get the votes they need to get reelected. Individual legislators can come to power based upon very different support groups. While in some cases these groups might be based on industrial groups, in other cases they are issue groups or racial groups.

These differences in local incentives makes it harder to be definite about legislative coalition formation. As in the U.S. case, agenda-setting rules and the costs of coalition building are important in determining how legislators' preferences are aggregated. We might expect that, as in the U.S. case, the least costly coalition will consist of legislators with common industrial linkages. In the postelection coalition bargaining, we should perhaps expect that large and dispersed industries get highest level of protection (as in the United States). But Brazil is in other ways nothing like the United States.[29] It lacks a seniority system in the legislature, and committee composition is unstable. There is a generally high level of turnover from one election to the next; key individuals are shuffled back and forth between the two houses and in and out of the executive branch (Albano Franco from the Chamber to the Senate and to the governorship back to the Senate).

It appears that firms pressurize ministers more than legislators. Firms tend to lobby high-profile ministers (Alysson Paulinelli for agriculture, Albano Franco for heavy industry) rather than committees in Congress. My intuition is that the prediction "decentralized industries are favored" will not be the case. Rather, highly industrially concentrated, wealthy industries will wield the most political clout. These hypotheses are highly speculative. I do not test them empirically, in large part because it is ulnlikely that the theory will yield many useful results in this case.

THE ELECTORAL TARGET HYPOTHESES

In summary, the electoral target hypotheses for the three stylized types of political system are as follows:

> **H1:** In strong-party majoritarian systems, redistributive policy is targeted to marginal districts.
>
> **H2:** In strong-party PR systems, redistributive policy is targeted to government supporters.
>
> **H3:** In weak-party majoritarian systems, redistributive policy is targeted to safe districts.

The theory is one of redistribution. Whether an industry is a suitable candidate to give rewards to voters depends upon its geography: its size, spread, and location. Next, I consider how the structural characteristics of an industry affect its level of trade assistance in the three political system types.

INTERACTIVE EFFECTS OF INDUSTRY SIZE AND GEOGRAPHY

Strong-Party Majoritarian Systems

In strong-party majoritarian systems, governments have incentives to target redistributive policy toward voters in marginal districts. Given the political motivation to reward marginal districts, which industries get protected? Whether an industry is a suitable candidate to provide rewards to marginal districts depends on its size, spread, and location. Size is often cited as a variable affecting an industry's success at securing protection.[30] Extant arguments predict competing effects: too small and no one cares sufficiently about the industry's fate; too large and the industry faces a large antiprotectionist coalition. Yet, these arguments neglect how size affects the political distribution and breakdown of the industry.

In strong-party majoritarian systems, the marginal effect of industry size on the level of protection is ambiguous. The cost of protecting a small industry is low, yet in political terms the benefits can be high if the industry is concentrated in a marginal district. Yet, if the same industry is located in a safe seat (either for the government or the opposition), there are few political rewards, and so the costs of protecting that industry will probably outweigh the benefits. An advantage of protecting a large industry is that the magnitude of the redistribution is high enough for politicians to provide large rewards. Unfortunately, it is more likely that a large industry is spread over both safe and marginal districts. While the political benefits are high in the marginal districts, redistribution to safe districts has low political efficacy.

Whether the benefits are worth the costs depends on how many marginal districts the large industry is spread over. Hence, while the theory predicts the effect of size in conjunction with location, size by itself should have an indeterminate effect on interindustry levels of tariff protection. The same is true for geographic and electoral concentration.

Whether or not geographically or electorally concentrated industries win protection depends on whether or not the industry is spatially concentrated in marginal districts. This is where the income effect from protection has the biggest impact on the government's reelection chances. Industries electorally concentrated in marginal districts will receive higher levels of protection. There is also a spillover effect: industries that are geographically concentrated in regions rich with marginal districts will receive higher levels of protection—even if the actual plants or firms are located in safe seats. The livelihoods of many voters are associated with the welfare of local industries: redundancies and plant closures have adverse economic consequences for house prices, retail owners, and local tax revenues outside of the electoral constituency. If industrial decline in a party-competitive region leads to a local recession, this will undermine the party's reelection chances.

Size and concentration by themselves do not matter. It is the ability to privilege marginal districts that is important. Despite this we might suspect that certain kinds of electoral and geographic concentration might be associated with higher protection, not because these geographic distributions influence trade policy, but rather because such distributions make it likely that an industry could provide a vehicle to reward marginal districts. For instance, a widely electorally dispersed industry is unlikely to be a good candidate for assistance, since it is likely to have a wide presence in many safe districts. In contrast, the most highly protected industries are likely to be electorally and geographically concentrated. Although the majority of such industries are concentrated in safe districts or in regions with few marginal districts, a concentrated industry has the possibility of being concentrated in a region rich with marginal districts. Although on average, concentrated industries will not be winners, the winners are more likely to be concentrated industries.

Strong-Party PR Systems

In PR systems, the government targets redistributive policy to reward its core supporters. Given the political motivation for parties to reward their electoral base, which industries get protected? As in the previous case, whether an industry is a suitable candidate to provide rewards to core supporters depends on its size, spread, and location.

Size has an ambiguous effect in PR systems. In PR systems the government targets the voters who have a predisposition to vote for them (core voters). Which industry gets protected depends on which party is in government. A large industry full of militant socialists is expensive for a right-wing coalition to buy off. It is unlikely to try to do so. More generally, larger industries contain more votes, but the benefits and costs of protecting one large industry are roughly the same as protecting two half-sized industries. Small industries can occasionally exert a high level of political influence within the coalition if they support a pivotal party. In Sweden, the pulp and paper industries won substantial subsidies in the late 1970s and early 1980s because the party they supported—a small center party—controlled key ministerial positions in the right-center-liberal coalition (in power from 1976 to 1981).

Geographic concentration still matters in PR systems. We should expect parties to favor regions that are party strongholds. The livelihoods of many voters are associated with the welfare of local industries; redundancies and plant closures have adverse economic consequences for house prices, retail owners, and local tax revenues. If industrial decline in a regional party stronghold leads to a local recession, this will undermine the party's base of support. As such, geographic concentration matters in both PR and majoritarian systems. There are differences, however. In PR systems, the incentives to target one region over another arise from economic and demographic differences that structure party affiliation. Electoral jurisdictions by themselves are of no importance. In contrast, in majoritarian systems, electoral jurisdictions are everything. Within a specific region, parties compete only in those political jurisdictions where the underlying economics and demographics make the seat party competitive.

Weak-Party Majoritarian Systems

In weak-party majoritarian systems, common industrial linkages make it easier to form a majority coalition. Which type of industries get protected? The earlier examples show that electoral and geographic dispersion increase an industry's political clout. The more legislators who care strongly about the fate of an industry, the easier it is to form a coalition in the legislature. In the U.S. case, legislation needs the approval of a bicameral legislature. Smaller states are overrepresented in the upper house; hence regional, as well as electoral, dispersion helps an industry's legislative clout.

Does size affect the policy outcomes? Earlier I argued that size has an interactive effect with both electoral and geographic dispersion. Large, electorally dispersed industries are more likely than small dispersed industries to employ a large proportion of workers in a large number of districts. The least costly protectionist coalitions (for those involved) are those that coordinate a coalition of electoral districts that support the same large industry. I predict that, on average, large electorally dispersed industries find it "easier" to form protectionist coalitions than small dispersed industries.

In systems where decisions are taken by a coalition of legislators, outcomes are sensitive to agenda-setting procedures as well as to the costs of coalition building. The theoretical model concentrates on the costs of coalition building, predicting that large, electorally dispersed industries win the highest levels of protection. Unfortunately, not all the agenda-setting hypotheses coincide with the costs of coalition hypotheses. There are circumstances where being electorally concentrated is advantageous for an industry. In the U.S. case, if that industry is concentrated in an important legislator's district—for example, the district of a legislative committee chair—that legislator has the power at the committee stage to influence outcomes and at the legislative stage can also better employ logrolling to engineer outcomes. Footwear is a small industry, located largely in Maine and Missouri. However, these states' senators chaired important trade and finance committees in the 1980s and were able to win import protection for footwear throughout that period (McGillivray and Schiller 1998).[31]

INDUSTRY STRUCTURE AND MONEY

Thus far the focus has been on which types of industries are the best vehicles through which to target voters with policy benefits. I have ignored the role of money in politics. There are many ways that governments can choose to redistribute between groups of voters. Instead of targeting trade policy to privilege an industry in a marginal district, a government could use money to buy additional media coverage in marginal districts and instead target policy to those industries that donate the most money. In the United States, trucking is a geographically dispersed industry: however, it makes high political action committee (PAC) contributions, perhaps as an attempt to compensate for its politically unfavorable geography (Grier, Munger, and Roberts 1994). However, outside of the United States, private money plays a much smaller role in party politics.[32] In the case of cutlery in Germany and the United Kingdom, money certainly had little political role. Even in the United States, the role of money on the outcome of elections and the content of government legislation is ambiguous (Zardkoohi 1988). Nonetheless, it is certainly true that if an industry is not favored by the legislature with protection, it will find another route to win aid. For example, the cutlery industry in the United States repeatedly applies for administered protection with the U.S. International Trade Commission. It is too politically concentrated to be influential in the U.S. legislature, but its geographic concentration means that as an industry it can lobby alongside its state members for administered relief through the USITC (Finger, Hall, and Nelson 1982).

THE INDUSTRY-LEVEL HYPOTHESES

In summary, the link between industry geography and political influence depends on the complex interactive effects of the electoral system. In the three stylized types of electoral system, the types of industries that are useful vehicles to redistribute benefits to key groups of voters are as follows:

H4: In strong-party majoritarian systems, politically favored industries are electorally concentrated in marginal districts.

H5: In strong-party PR systems, politically favored industries are traditionally linked with the party in government.

H6: In strong-party PR systems, politically favored industries are geographically concentrated in regional strongholds of the party in government.

H7: In weak-party majoritarian systems, politically favored industries are large and geographically dispersed.

The discussion of size, electoral concentration, and geographical concentration suggests that all three of these variables might be correlated with assistance even if none of them has a direct effect. As I discussed in chapter 1, despite numerous direct tests, the literature has been unable to pick a clear winner between these variables and policy outcomes. This is unsurprising. As the above discussion showed, even if electoral concentration were the only determinant of assistance—a claim much stronger than I make—other measures of size and geographic concentration would still be correlated with assistance. When combined with the problems so prevalent in measuring the size of assistance, it is not surprising that no dominant theory can be picked from the competing arguments. However, my argument does have testable implications for differences in the variance of political outcomes between electoral systems. These auxiliary hypotheses are laid out next.

DYNAMIC IMPLICATIONS: HOW POLITICAL CHANGE
AFFECTS REDISTRIBUTION

Political change has a different impact in each of the stylized cases. In each case, a change in party government is expected to lead to a change in the industries that receive protection. However, in each case, the immediacy and the extent of the impact differs.

Strong-Party Majoritarian Systems

Single-member district systems encourage governments to target redistribution toward marginal, or party-competitive, districts. Since both parties want to privilege the same districts, a change in party government might be expected to have little effect on redistributive policies. This suggests that changes in party government in strong-party majoritarian systems produce few changes in trade and industrial policy.

Of course, the above prediction is derived by assuming the simplest of industrial distributions. In practice, there are usually several industries in an electoral district. The political motivations imply that both parties want to target favorable policies toward marginal districts. Yet the prediction did not specify that the parties would use the same policy instruments or even target the same firms within these districts. On the basis of different ideological or other policy stances, each party might prefer to reward the marginal districts via different industries. In my stylized example, I assumed a single industry in each district: this, of course, is rarely the case. Suppose marginal district C contains two industries, i and j. Both left and right parties want to target district C, but, perhaps for ideological reasons, the left party might prefer to enrich district C through industry i while the right party prefers to use industry j. Hence, while assistance to C continues despite a change in government, the channel of assistance might change. In addition, underlying changes in demographics and economic development lead to shifts in voter ideology and affect the voting characteristics of districts. Some districts may cease to be marginal, while new marginal districts may emerge. Since elections provide an assessment of these changes, we might expect some change in redistributive policy following elections.[33]

Strong-Party PR Systems

In PR systems, parties target redistributive policies toward their core supporters. If redistributive policies are a compromise between the members of the coalition, with each wanting to privilege their core supporters, then political change implies a change in trade and industrial policy. Suppose that the coalition of parties B and C breaks up (perhaps, but not necessarily, as the result of an election) and a new coalition government forms between parties A and C. This political change alters the redistributive priorities of the government. Suppose that steelworkers are associated with party A, textiles workers with party B, and farmworkers with party C. Prior to the political change, the government's core support was composed of farm and textile workers. Following the political change, no member of the government cares about textile workers, party B having been displaced by party A. While the details of the coalition bargaining might be complex, we should expect a policy shift away from the interests of textile workers toward those of steelworkers. This tactic will not win votes from supporters of party B; however, by rewarding their supporters, parties A and C prevent the entry of new parties who could siphon off support from disenchanted voters. Political change is predicted to lead to a change in which industries win trade assistance.

In stark contrast to many theories that suggest policy is relatively fixed in PR systems (Roubini and Sachs 1989; Rustow 1950), my theory predicts that trade and industrial policy alter with political change. Given the sharp difference between my prediction and those of extant theories, I pause to consider the extent of disagreement. Often veto players are cited as the impediment to policy change in coalition government (Bawn 1999; Tsebelis 1995, 1999 2002). Although these ideas are persuasive and much evidence has been offered to support them, the predictions typically refer to low-dimensional ideological policy spaces rather than the high-order dimensionality of trade policy. Unlike ideological issues, such as the traditional left-right split where policy changes are along a single dimension, trade offers a huge variety of policies. Trade policy determines the extent to which each industrial group is privileged. We might further subdivide industrial policy to allow the targeting of specific firms within each industry, as I consider in chapter 5. Additionally, groups can be privileged via numerous instruments: tariffs, quotas, regulation, and the like. However, it is sufficient to think of trade and industrial policy as having as many dimensions as industrial groups. This high dimensionality makes policy fungible. To a much greater extent than traditional policies, redistributive policies provide a transferable good, which in the context of the veto-player argument, can be used to buy off opposition. Indeed I believe that there is a strong complementarily, rather than a contradiction, between veto-point arguments and the theory advocated here. Trade and industrial polices play a key role in targeting benefits to specific groups. This allows governing elites to buy off veto players and enables at least limited movement on ideological issues.

Weak-Party Majoritarian Systems

Industry geography serves as the basis for coalition formation in weak-party majoritarian systems. Each legislator wants to protect the industries with a significant presence in her district but does not want protection for industries outside of her district. As such, political change in terms of who holds a seat should have little impact on the induced preferences of legislators. In contrast, political changes through redistricting might have much larger effects. Unfortunately, the ease of coalition formation is not the only important variable in the passage of legislation. Seniority, committee assignment, and agenda control alter with political change. A junior legislator does not receive the same powerful committee appointments that her senior predecessor held. For example, Senator Danforth of Missouri was chair of the powerful Finance committee (from 1981 to 1986) and later the Senate Majority Leader (1989 to 1994). He helped protect the footwear industry—most of which was located in Missouri and Maine. Since the 1990s, the footwear industry has lacked a powerful ally in Congress. Much of the industry has subsequently moved overseas (McGillivray and Schiller 1998; Schiller 1999). Through such agenda control processes, political change alters the redistribution of trade and industrial protection. In summary, the model generates the following hypotheses:

> **H8:** Political change is predicted to lead to a change in the distribution of protection in all types of electoral system.
>
> **H9:** In strong-party majoritarian systems, change in the pattern of protection occurs because either (*a*) parties enrich marginal district via different industries or via different policy tools or (*b*) there is a change in which districts are marginal (perhaps as the result of some underlying economic change).
>
> **H10:** In strong-party PR systems, shifts in government lead to a reformulation of the trade policy bargain and hence a change in trade policy. However, due to the bargaining process, the impact of political change is less immediate than in strong party majoritarian systems.
>
> **H11:** In weak-party majoritarian systems, changes in seniority and agenda-setting power shift trade policy.

SUMMARY OF THEORETICAL MODEL

In all three theoretical models, the government wants to protect those industries that maximize its reelection chances. I have argued that which interests get represented by government depends on a two-step mapping of legislators' induced preferences and industry geography. The electoral rule affects which industries legislators want to protect. The electoral rule and the strength of parties affects which industries legislators are able to protect. I derive testable implications for three stylized cases: strong-party majoritarian systems, strong-party PR systems, and weak-party majoritarian systems. I explore how deviations from the stylized cases affect the predictions—in particular how variations in industry size and geographical concentration affect the model's implications.

The theoretical model yields a number of hypotheses, which are grouped by industry, electoral district, and political change. The remainder of the book sets about testing these hypotheses. In the next chapter, I use industry tariff rates in Canada and the United States to test electoral target and industry hypotheses for strong-party majoritarian and weak-party majoritarian systems. In particular, I test for the complex interactive effects between industry geography and political institutions. In chapter 1, I discussed the problems using tariffs as the sole measure of government assistance. Tariffs are not the only policy tool governments can use to aid industry. Where they are used, tariffs are some weighted combination of domestic and foreign preferences. However, the tariff data used in chapter 3 is from the 1970s: I argue that tariff rates in this period are more representative of the domestic structure of protection than are those in later periods. However, I do not attempt to test the PR system hypotheses using tariffs, in part because most developed PR countries were part of the EU in the 1970s, and the Common External Tariff (CET) reflects some European average of social and political forces.

Instead, I use a case study to examine hypotheses 1 through 6 for the three types of political systems. In chapter 4, I study how governments distributed industrial aid between steel plants/firms during the 1980s steel crisis in Belgium, Germany, Sweden, the United Kingdom, and the United States. In chapter 5, I move away from testing the rather complex relationship between industry geography and electoral systems, and test the model's implications for differences in the variance of political outcomes between electoral systems. I test how political change affects redistribution, using industry stock prices, for all three systems.

DEVIATIONS FROM THE STYLIZED MODEL

MULTIPARTY MAJORITARIAN SYSTEMS

The model assumes two-party competition and a single-party government. The majoritarian system severely penalizes third-place parties in terms of parliamentary representation (Rae 1971, 1995). However, most majoritarian systems have experienced periods of multiparty competition. Small parties whose support is concentrated regionally can do well in majoritarian systems. If the competition is multiparty, then the government will continue to target the seats it won by the narrowest of winning margins or the seats where it came a close second. In principle, third parties can make it difficult to determine which seats are marginal. Yet in practice, third parties often have regional strongholds and typically represent similar ideological positions to one of the major parties. For example, in Australia, the Labour party represents the left wing, while the right wing is composed of the National and Country parties. Yet, these parties rarely compete with each other at the district level; the Country party represents the political right in rural areas and the National party takes precedence in nonrural areas. Despite the close association between farmers and the National party, it is unclear that farmers fare any better when the National party is part of the government than not. Indeed, the fate of farmers has remained remarkably stable and has changed little with switches in governments. However, when farming seats in West Australia became hotly contested marginals, agriculture became the beneficiary of government policy.[34] Similarly, in Canada the Quebeçois represent the right in Quebec province but have little or no presence in other provinces. France is somewhat different in that the right-wing parties of Gaullist RPR and UDF typically compete in every district as do the communists and the socialists. Sometimes, however, these sets of parties would negotiate single candidates for the first round of voting. Unlike the plurality rules of first-past-the-post seen in most other majoritarian countries,[35] France has a strictly majoritarian system. If no party receives 50 percent of the vote in the first round, then a second runoff election occurs between the leading contenders.[36] Under such runoff systems, multiple right-wing parties do not harm the political right, since in the second round, all the right-wing support typically coalesces around the more successful candidate from the first round, and the two right parties, which occupy similar ideological positions, form a coalition government.[37]

These arguments preserve the logic of the stylized two-party case. Nonetheless, in circumstances where there are genuinely three competitive parties in a majoritarian system, such as the rise of the British Labour party and its slow displacement of the Liberals as the main rivals of the Conservatives in the first half of the twentieth century, then the predictions require modification. Fortunately, the dominant pattern in majoritarian systems is two-party competition (Duverger 1954). For the empirical cases to follow, the assumption of two functioning parties appears tenable.

SINGLE-PARTY PR SYSTEMS

Multiparty coalition governments in PR systems typically represent a heterogeneous group of industries. I predict these multiparty coalition governments will protect their industrial vote base. They do not want to provide an opportunity for a new party to emerge and syphon off disgruntled industries' voters This prediction holds for PR systems with multiparty competition but single-party government. Most single-party governments in PR systems are core parties. These large, centrist parties frequently dominate coalition governments (de Swaan 1973; Laver and Schofield 1990; Schofield 1998). Core parties tend to have big, industrially heterogeneous support bases. For example, the Peoples' Party in Austria is a federation of the Austrian Farmers Association, the Austrian Business Federation, the Austrian Workers and Employees' Federation, and the like. Core parties also tend to be internally fractionalized. Like the multiparty coalition government, the core party protects all its industry supporters because the government fears alienating any single industrial faction. Again, this is because the low cost of entry in PR systems makes it cheap for an industrial faction to break away from the core party and support a competing party.

In the extreme case, where the core party or coalition government contains all industries, the government will chose to protect all industries rather than adopt free trade. This is despite the fact that free trade would have increased aggregate wealth and improved all supporters' incomes.[38] The following example explains this decision: suppose a country has only three industries: steel, textile, and agriculture. A core party is in government. It draws support from all three industries. If the core party adopts free trade, steel prefers to split from the party and form a new party pursuing protection for steel. In order to maintain a legislative majority (or at least prevent a majority from defeating it) the former core party might need to form a coalition with its former faction, the steelworkers' party. This party is likely to demand some protection for steel as a price for joining the coalition. If, however, the former core party protects steel, it imposes costs on agriculture and textiles. This increases the probability that the agricultural and textile industries will split from the core party and form new parties. Anticipating this vicious circle of events, the core party gives all three industries protection. Yes, the nation's aggregate wealth would be higher under free trade, but the economic costs are irrelevant. What matters are the political costs.

CHAPTER 3

Party Strength as a Determinant of Industry Tariffs

THE EMPIRICAL TESTS in this chapter focus on the institutional features of parties in determining industry tariff levels in majoritarian systems. The strength of parties plays a vital role in determining how industry geography influences trade policy. The interactive effects are complex but empirically testable. Unfortunately, while there is a large body of empirical work on the effects of industry structure on industrial tariffs, there is limited research on the effect of political institutions.[1] There is a tendency for scholars to assume that political systems outside the United States, such as Canada, function just like the United States. For instance, Caves (1976) uses Canadian data to test the argument that electorally dispersed industries receive more protection because they have more representatives per industry. Having more representatives makes it easier to create voting blocks and build legislative majorities. Pincus (1975) found evidence of this effect in the United States, but rather puzzlingly, Caves found no evidence of the vote-adding argument in Canada. However, once you consider the differences in how legislators' induced preferences are aggregated in the United States and Canada, this ambiguous result is unsurprising. Where parties are weak, as in the United States, a majority coalition of legislators determines policy outcomes. In this case, the more legislators that support an industry, the better the chance of forming a winning coalition. Where parties are strong, as in Canada, the ruling party elite determine policy outcomes. In Canada, parliamentary MPs are relatively unimportant actors in the policy process. Differences in how legislators' preferences are aggregated into policy strongly advantage an electorally concentrated industry in one case and strongly disadvantage it in the other. How geography matters—the size, spread, and location of the industry—depends on the electoral rule and the strength of parties.

In this chapter, I test the electoral system and industry geography hypotheses for the strong- and weak-party majoritarian systems using industry tariff data for Canada and the United States.[2] For instance, I ask, do industries located in marginal districts receive more favorable levels of protection than industries in safe districts? The theory predicts a positive relationship between district marginality and industry protection in the Canadian case and a negative relationship in the U.S. case. Do electorally concentrated districts receive higher levels of protection in Canada than electorally decentralized industries? The theory suggests that the opposite holds in the U.S. case. Does the interactive effect of size and electoral concentration matter as predicted in the U.S. and Canadian cases?

There are a number of reasons for choosing this pair of countries and for selecting this slice of time. Tariff rates in the 1960s and 1970s are more representative of the domestic structure of protection than those of later periods. Industry tariffs are used to test—among other things—whether being electorally dispersed is more advantageous for an industry in the United States than in Canada and whether marginal districts secure more favorable levels of protection in Canada than in the United States. The dependent variable approximates how much money is distributed through tariffs to each electoral district in Canada and in the United States (strong- and weak-party majoritarian systems, respectively). Data on industry employment by electoral districts in 1977 in the United States and 1971 in Canada are matched with industry tariffs from 1979 and 1970, respectively. I test for the interactive effects of industry size, electoral concentration, and political location.

The empirical focus of this chapter is the role of party strength in the choice of tariffs. Canada is an example of a strong-party system, and the United States of a weak-party system. Both countries are majoritarian systems. Neither Canada nor the United States was part of a larger trading block in the period I study (although in 1965 Canada signed an Auto Pact with the United States, allowing free trade in automobiles). Tariffs reflect national preferences. There are, however, other economic and political variables that vary across these two countries that could affect the predictions—such as the structure of the federal system or the effect of presidentialism. These variables are not discussed in the theory chapter; however, in the discussion of the U.S. and Canadian cases, I consider the effects of political and economic variables outside of the model presented in chapter 2. These are discussed next.

THE POLITICAL ECONOMY OF TRADE POLICY IN CANADA

The structure of Canada's political system has remained stable in the postwar period, and the institutional context in which tariffs are set has changed little over time. Canada has a two-tiered system of party government: the House of Commons and the Senate. Unlike House of Commons MPs, who are elected for a five-year term, Senators are appointed by the governor-general and serve until retirement. Although Queen Elizabeth II is the formal head of state, the governor-general serves as the Queen's representative in Canada.

Compared to the House of Commons, the Senate is a minor legislative body; it can delay legislation from the House of Commons for only a year. Although the legislature's assent is needed for new legislation, neither the House nor the Senate is actively involved in the formation or implementation of policy.

Party discipline is strong in the bicameral Federal Parliament. Franks (1987) argues that on the floor of the house, "party, party lines and party discipline count for everything and the autonomy of the individual MP is negligible." The prime minister and his cabinet direct and formulate policy. The tariff-setting process has remained centralized in the Federal Cabinet within the Department of External Affairs, the Department of Finance, and the Department of Industry, Trade, and Commerce.[3] Ministerial positions are typically filled from the House of Commons, and the prime minister is elected from a parliamentary party caucus (Johnston 1986). Although, MPs in the House of Commons can, in principal, veto any tariff settlement negotiated by the government, as a practical matter defection rates from party lines are extremely low and defection typically occurs only when it will not seriously damage the government's incumbency (Franks 1987). Those MPs that vote against their party can be punished by their local party organization, who can refuse to allow them to run for reelection, and by the party leadership, who can prevent promotion from the backbench to the government ranks.

The strong-party system extends through the legislative committee system. Despite various reforms, committees have a strong partisan component and little independent impact on outcomes. The position of a committee chairman is a stepping stone for advancement within the party. The strong-party system isolates the MP from industry pressure in his constituency by taking away his accountability for his legislative voting record.

Until the late 1970s, election results swung back and forth around the "normal vote" (Franks 1987), where the normal vote is the relatively fixed cleavage between left and right in the population. In any given election, the vote swings around this, the "expected value" of the election. District marginality is relatively stable in the medium term. It is reasonable to assume that underlying marginality is constant (Johnston 1986). This is important. Tariffs change incrementally and at discrete intervals. If marginality is volatile, then comparing marginality and tariff rates at a single point in time is a futile exercise. The analysis I undertake uses political data from the 1970s. It would be more difficult to analyze later periods; more regional separatist parties have entered the political arena, and elections have become more volatile and less predictable. In the 1993 election, the Progressive Conservative party lost its parliamentary majority, retaining only two parliamentary seats. When voting is this volatile, all seats are marginal, and the concept of targeting marginal districts has little meaning.

The Liberal government made a substantial number of tariff concessions during the Kennedy Round, from 1963 to 1967.[4] The Liberals held on to government by a narrow margin throughout this period. I hypothesize that Canadian tariffs in 1970 will reflect the pattern of marginality during this earlier decade. In 1963 and 1965, the Liberals were in government but were four and two seats short of a majority, respectively. In both cases, the opposition parties

were in organizational disarray and feared the electoral consequences of forcing an early election. The absence of only a few opposition members during a
vote was enough to ensure government success in the House, and this—not
third-party support—allowed the government to maintain power. In 1968, the
Liberals swept into power with a large majority under Pierre Trudeau. On
average, the Liberals were a full 9 percentage points ahead of the next best
party in each electoral district. This extraordinarily large victory created a new
set of marginals. However, I identify those seats that were "underlyingly marginal" during this period: seats that would be marginal if the election were
close. It is hypothesized that tariffs are likely to favor industries in underlyingly
marginal districts.

In Canada, a strong-party majoritarian country, it is predicted that industries
electorally concentrated in marginal districts will receive higher levels of protection than industries electorally concentrated in safe districts and industries
that are electorally dispersed. While it is unambiguously best for an industry
to be electorally concentrated in a marginal district, we might expect that on
average, concentrated industries are more likely to win higher levels of protection. The most highly protected industries are likely to be electorally concentrated. Although on average, concentrated industries will not be winners, the
winners are more likely to be concentrated industries. There is no institutional
advantage to being large and electorally dispersed in the Canadian system.

The Political Economy of Trade Policy in the United States

Unlike Canada, the executive and legislative branches of government are separate institutional bodies in the U.S. political system. The leader of the executive
branch, the president, is elected for a four-year term by the electoral college.
The delegates of the electoral college are voted for in state-level elections,
and the number of delegates per state is determined by population size. The
legislature is a two-tiered system: the House of Representatives and the Senate.
In each state, two senators are elected for a six-year term. Members of the
House of Representatives are elected for two years from a single-member constituency, in first-past-the-post elections. How many House representatives
each state has depends on population size.[5]

The United States has essentially a two-party system, the Democratic and
Republican parties. However, "party government" in the United States is very
different from that in Canada. Control of the House, Senate, and presidential
offices are frequently divided. Even if party government is unified over both
branches of government, legislative proposals supported by the president are
often defeated in Congress. Legislative support is not cohesive because
the president does not require it to remain in office. Vetoing bills favored by
the executive does not risk the dissolution of the legislature and a subse-

quent untimely election campaign. Congressmembers are held accountable by the electorate for the well-being of their constituency more than the well-being of their nation. Party still matters, but not to the same extent as the Canadian case.[6]

Since the New Deal in the 1930s Democrats have tended to take protectionist stances more often than Republicans (Baldwin 1985; Lavergne 1981). However, this is in large part because Democrats are more likely to represent unskilled, low-wage-industrial workers than are Republicans.

The most important institutional difference between the United States and Canada is that the United States is a presidential, rather than a parliamentary majoritarian, system. The U.S. president plays an important role in the formation of trade policy. The president and Congress face different institutional constraints and are predicted to target different constituencies. Industries must form coalitions that will receive support under multiple jurisdictions.

The head of the executive branch, the president, has traditionally been regarded as free trade in orientation (Baldwin 1985; Milner 1988). Magee, Brock, and Young (1989) argue that this is because the nation is the president's constituency and he increases his reelection chances by maximizing the national welfare. The president, however, is not elected by direct popular vote. He is elected from an electoral college filled with state delegates. In his first term, the president has incentives similar to that of the incumbent government in a strong-party system, that is, to target states that are marginal and that have a large number of electoral college votes. President Bush—an avowed free trader—slapped on steel tariffs of up to 30 percent on many products.[7] One reason was to ensure votes in the industrial midwest—a cluster of party-competitive states with relatively high numbers of electoral votes.[8] The president is not driven by reelection motives in his second term of office because he cannot get elected to a third term of office. Perhaps this is why presidents sometimes appear free trade in orientation.

Under current fast-track rules, Congress must vote either for or against trade agreements negotiated by the president. Any settlement reached by the president therefore is structured so as not to alienate possible protectionist coalitions in Congress (S. Smith 1988). I predict that large, decentralized industries provide a focal point for coalition formation in Congress. Although the president has an important independent effect on outcomes, he will avoid making agreements that aggravate the large, electorally decentralized industries.

One reason large, electorally decentralized industries win more favorable levels of protection is that they are more likely to be receive support in multiple jurisdictions. The bicameral structure of Congress affects how industry geography matters. In the United States, the presence of an industry in several House districts may act as a focal point for coalition formation in the House of Representatives. However, an industry also needs to be spread over a number of states if it is to influence more than two representatives in the Senate. Those states with many congressional seats are underrepresented in the Senate. Because of the different method of distribution of seats in the House and Senate (population versus geography) states with many house seats are likely to be under-represented in the Senate. Depending on their economic geography, industries tend to be "powerful" in either the House and Senate.

To illustrate, suppose the United States has two industries, A and B. Industry A is spread over thirty Californian congressional districts. It is represented by thirty seats in the House and two seats in the Senate. While industry B, which is spread over Dakota, Vermont, and Wyoming, has three seats in the House and six seats in the Senate. Legislators need to coordinate across chambers of Congress to secure protection for these industries. Import-competing industries, therefore, tend to be powerful in either the House or the Senate. For example, the sugar industry is extremely powerful in the Senate; it wields little influence in the House, however. The opposite is true of the automobile industry (Destler and Odell 1987). Whether an industry that is spread over a large number of states receives more favorable levels of protection than an industry that is spread over a large number of House districts, depends on how legislators themselves coordinate among state delegations and across the Chambers of Congress to secure protection for these industries. The evidence points to the Senate as being influential in determining trade policy outcomes (Baldwin 1985). In large part, this explains why farming interests are so powerful in the United States. Less than 4 percent of the United States population is in farming. Farm votes are crucial for only 10 percent of legislators in the House of Representatives. However, every state has some farming, which means every senator has an interest in the fate of American farming.[9]

There are circumstances in which it is beneficial for an industry to be electorally concentrated. In chapter 2, I hypothesize that marginal (party-competitive) House or Senate districts receive the least favorable levels of protection because their legislators likely lack the seniority they need to make reciprocal arrangements.[10] Vote trading plays an important role in lowering the costs of coalition formation. Without seniority, legislators are unlikely to be on powerful committees where they have control over agenda setting. Given these handicaps, legislators in marginal districts are less likely to be able to protect their district's industries. In contrast, electoral districts represented by legislators who are appointed to important committees receive more favorable levels of protection. Examples of important committees are the House Ways and Means Committee and the Senate Finance Committee. These committees have the ability to influence policy outcomes both at the committee stage, when legislation is developed, and at the legislative state, strategies such as logrolling can be used to engineer outcomes.[11] In the House, the Ways and Means Committee has primary jurisdiction over trade policy involving tariff barriers and reciprocal trade agreements. In the Senate, this task is assigned to the Finance Committee. The congressmembers on these committees are influential as "agenda setters." In addition, since 1962, two members of the Ways and Means and the Finance committees have been a part of the U.S. multilateral trade delegation. Other committees, such as the Committee on Interstate and Foreign Commerce also have influence over some aspects of trade policy. It is hypothesized that a district whose representative is on the Ways and Means Committee (or the Foreign State and Commerce Commission receives more favorable levels of protection. Furthermore, it is hypothesized that a state whose representative is on the Finance Committee receives more favorable levels of protection. It is similarly hypothesized that industries dispersed over a large number of electoral districts will receive higher levels of protection in a majoritarian system with low party discipline.

In sum, unless an industry (like textiles) is very large and electorally dispersed over House districts and U.S. states, it is unlikely to receive widespread support in both the House and the Senate. Industries that are thinly dispersed are unlikely to be a strong voting force in any single district. A congressman is unlikely to go out of his way to offer these industries his support.[12] It is hypothesized that in the United States, a weak-party majoritarian system, that large, electorally dispersed industries will receive more favorable levels of protection than large, electorally concentrated industries. Small, electorally dispersed industries will receive the least favorable levels of protection.

EMPIRICAL TESTS

Two sets of empirical models test these hypotheses. These tests differ according to the unit of observation: electoral district versus industry structure. In the first set of tests, I focus on the level of protection at the electoral district level and use a dependent variable devised by Conybeare (1984)—average tariff for each electoral district—which approximates how much money is distributed through tariffs to each electoral district. To construct this measure, for each district, I calculate the proportion of the district's workers within each industry. I then weigh the tariff for each industry by these proportions to generate a district's average tariff. Hence for district j the average level of tariff protection $= \sum_{i=1}^{I} t_i (E_{i,j} / E_j)$ where t_i is the tariff for industry i, $E_{i,j}$ is the number of workers in district j that work in industry i, and E_j is the total workforce in district j. The summation is over all industries. The data on industry employment by electoral districts in the United States in 1977 and in Canada in 1971 is matched with industry tariffs from 1979 and 1970, respectively.[13] These tests examine the extent to which industrial and electoral characteristics of a district influence the level of protection it secures. Among the economic effects that I control for are the electoral district's unemployment levels and the import-competitiveness of its industries.

In the second set of tests, the unit of analysis is industry, and the dependent variable is nominal tariff rates for each industry. As before, the industry tariff data are from 1970 for Canada and 1979 for the United States.[14] I examine how aspects of industry's industrial geography and its electoral distribution affect the level of protection it receives. The independent variables are industry electoral concentration and other industry electoral characteristics. Industry size and the import competitiveness of the industry are operationalized as control variables.

In both the electoral district and the industry level models, it is assumed that tariff rates adjust quickly to a change in the political market, such that the rate of protection is a reflection of government and industry preferences at that point in time. We might suspect that there is institutional lag. Major tariff changes are enacted after years of bargaining in international negotiation rounds; incremental changes are not implemented continuously. However, major shifts in tariff rates occurred in 1970 and 1979, at the end of the Kennedy and Tokyo GATT rounds. It is hypothesized that these tariffs are largely a product of the 1968 Canadian parliamentary government and the 1976 U.S. House of Representatives, respectively. The findings for both models are discussed next.

THE ELECTORAL DISTRICT MODEL

This model considers the amount of protection that is directed toward each electoral district through tariff policies. The dependent variable is the district's average level of tariff protection. The findings for Canada and the United States are presented in table 3.1 as unstandardized coefficients. Variable means and standard deviations can be found in appendix 3.1.[15] The empirical findings for Canada and the United States generally support the hypotheses for majoritarian systems with weak- and strong-party systems. Nonetheless, the level of protection an electoral district receives is not solely determined by the political characteristics of the electoral district. The industry characteristics of the electoral district also affects its level of protection. These findings are discussed first.

The Industrial Characteristics of Electoral Districts

One of the few general findings in the literature is that comparatively disadvantaged industries receive the highest levels of tariff protection (Chen 1974; Helleiner 1977). These industries face the severest displacement costs when trade barriers are lowered. This implies that electoral districts containing industries facing stiff import competition receive higher levels of protection. A control for this effect indicates the degree to which industries in each dis-

TABLE 3.1

The Electoral District Model for Canada (1970) and the United States (1979)

	Electoral District Level of Protection	
Independent Variables	*Canada* *1970*	*United States* *1979*
District comparative disadvantage[a]	.0405*** (.0041)	.1105*** (.0027)
District marginality[b]	.0138** (.0079)	−.0006** (.0002)
Number of districts in state[c]	.0140*** (.0021)	−.0015*** (.0001)
District party representative[d]	−.0147 (.0159)	−.0002 (.0002)
District represented by a minister[e]	.0092 (.4913)	—
Marginal districts represented by a minister[f]	.0339 (.1473)	—
District unemployment[g]	.0304** (.0141)	.0008*** (.0003)
Seniority of representative[h]	—	.00153** (.0011)
Member of Ways and Means Committee[i]	—	.0003 (.0003)
Member of Foreign and Interstate Commerce Committee[i]	—	.0006** (.0002)
Intercept	1.691*** (.2315)	.00137* (.0009)
Number of cases	257	425
Adj. R^2	.53	.83

Note: Figures are unstandardized beta coefficients; standard errors are in parentheses. Regression with Huber standard errors.

[a] District comparative advantage coded as Σ_i (imports$_{i,j}$/exports$_i$)/E_j, where i = industry and j = electoral district.

[b] District marginality in United States coded as − | %vote for Democratic party$_j$ − %vote for Republican party$_j$|; in Canada coded as − | %vote for Liberal party$_j$ − 9% − %biggest vote for rival party$_j$ |.

[c] For each district, the total number of electoral districts in its province (or state).

[d] In the United States, coded 1 if legislator is a Democrat, 0 otherwise; in Canada, coded 1 if district is Liberal, 0 otherwise.

[e] Cabinet MPs from 1968–70 are coded 1, otherwise 0.

[f] An interactive term, district marginality$_j$ × minister's district$_j$.

[g] Unemployment ratio, in Canada (district employment/district population), in United States, (unemployed/total workforce).

[h] Seniority coded as log | 1980 − year legislator in district j first elected to Congress|.

[i] Coded 1 if a legislator is on the committee, 0 otherwise.

$*p < .10; **p < .05; ***p < .01$, all one tailed tests.

trict are declining. The Comparative Disadvantage in district j equals $\sum_{i=1}^{I}$ (imports$_i$ / exports$_i$) ($E_{i,j}$ / E_j), where the ratio imports$_i$/exports$_i$ is the ratio of imports to exports within industry i, $E_{i,j}$ is the number of workers in district j that work in industry i, and E_j is the total workforce in district j. The summation is over industries. The impact of the variable is positive, statistically significant and large in magnitude in both the Canadian and the U.S. models.[16] As expected, electoral districts containing industries facing high import competition receive protection in both Canada and the United States.

The unemployment level in the electoral district may also affect the electoral district level of protection (Cassing, McKeown, and Ochs 1986; Magee, Brock, and Young 1989). The displacement-costs argument is frequently used by politicians to defend economically "hard hit" areas from additional cuts in protection. Although the magnitude of the effect is not large, the positive, significant coefficients in both the Canadian and U.S. models support the hypothesis that electoral districts with higher levels of unemployment receive more favorable levels of protection.[17]

The Political Characteristics of Electoral Districts

As expected, the Canadian government not only targets those districts containing comparatively disadvantaged industries; it also targets those marginal districts necessary to retain government. The more marginal a district is, the greater its average tariff.

I use vote differentials to determine which seats are safe and which seats are marginal. If the Liberals win a seat by a large majority, then that district has low marginality. Similarly, if the Liberals are far from winning the seat, then the district too has low marginality. Several measures of marginality were tested in the Canadian case.[18] The measure reported in Table 3.1 controls for the Liberal landslide victory in 1968. The Liberals won by a 9 percent margin in terms of popular vote share. Given this swing, the Liberals captured several opposition districts that they would not normally have expected to take, and they held the underlying marginal seats by a much higher vote seat than normal.[19] Given the massive swing, the vote was not close in underlying marginal seats. These are the seats the government needs to hold if it wants to maintain power. In defining marginality for Canada, I control for this landslide victory by subtracting off the 9 percent swing and calculating which seats would have been marginal if the vote share had been close. It is these seats that determine whether the government wins or loses the next election. Formally, for Canada marginality in district j equals $-$ | %vote for Liberal party$_j$ $-$ 9%$-$%biggest vote for rival party$_j$ |. For the U.S., marginality of district j is measured as $-$ | %vote for Democratic party$_j$ $-$ %vote for Republican party$_j$|.

For Canada, the positive and significant coefficient suggests that as the marginality of a district increases, so does the average level of protection for industries in that district. Specifically, a 10 percent shift in the vote differential in a district (the Liberal's margin of victory or margin of defeat changes by 10 percentage points) accounts for roughly 10 percent of the variance in the level of protection supplied to a district.

In contrast, representatives from marginal seats in the 1978 U.S. Congress receive lower levels of protection than do representatives from safe seats.[20] District marginality is statistically significant and negatively signed as predicted. This implies safe seats win higher levels of protection—although the effect is not large. A measure is included to account for the number of years a representative has been in the House. The coefficient for seniority of representative is positive and statistically significant, although the effect is small. Nonetheless, this result implies that representatives with seniority are able to get more protection for industry in their district than newer representatives can.

Both the United States and Canada are federal systems, but with different federal institutions. States have different forms of political representation in Canada and the United States. A control variable, the number of districts in a state, captures the population size of the state in which the electoral district is located. The number of districts variable is statistically significant in both country models, although positive in the Canadian case and negative in the United States. In Canada, highly populated provinces receive higher levels of protection than do less-populated provinces. In the United States, less-populated states receive higher levels of protection than more populated states. One explanation is that the Canadian Senate does not overrepresent the interests of less-populated states as the U.S. Senate does.[21] In Canada, senators are not elected; they receive lifetime appointments by the governor-general. In the U.S. Senate, each state elects two representatives. This skews tariff protection in favor of less-populated states. This interpretation is supported by similar findings by Baldwin (1985) and Lavergne (1983) for the United States.

A number of other political control variables are included in the U.S. and Canadian models. "District party" is a dummy variable, taking the value of 1 for Democrats in the United States and 1 for Liberals in Canada. It is insignificant in both country regressions. In Canada, this is an interesting result, given that the Liberals were in power for the larger part of the postwar period. If Liberals had been interested in targeting their loyal party supporters instead of marginal electorates, they had plenty of opportunity to do so.

In the Canadian parliamentary system, one could argued that cabinet ministers win higher levels of protection for industries in their districts than backbenchers do, particularly if they are in marginal districts. There is no empirical evidence of this; both the dummy variable for ministerial districts and the interactive term for marginal ministerial districts are insignificant.

In the U.S. model, dummy variables are used to capture whether members of the Ways and Means Committee or the Interstate and Foreign Commerce Committee receive higher levels of tariff protection in their district. There is no evidence in the U.S. model that members of the Ways and Means Committee represent districts with higher levels of tariff protection. While the dummy variable indicating membership of the Interstate and Foreign Commerce Committee is positive and significant, the magnitude of this effect is negligible.

To summarize the electoral district results, the single best predictor of electoral district protection is the degree to which industries in electoral districts are comparatively disadvantaged. Nonetheless, the political characteristics of the electoral district also affect which electoral districts receive more favorable levels of protection. As predicted, marginal districts receive higher levels of protection in Canada, and safe seats, whose representatives have seniority, receive higher levels of protection in the United States. A control variable, proxying for differences in federal institutional structure, indicates that highly populated states receive higher levels of protection in Canada, while less-populated states receive higher levels of protection in the United States. These results are entirely consistent with theoretical predictions.

THE INDUSTRY LEVEL MODEL

I now switch the unit of analysis to the industry and ask how electoral geography influences the level of tariff protection an industry receives. The findings for Canada and the United States are presented in table 3.2 as unstandardized coefficients. As with the electoral district model, variable means and standard deviations are provided in appendix 3.1.[22] Generally, the empirical findings support the industry-level hypotheses. However, a number of controls have important effects on the industry level of protection. These findings are discussed first.

The Industrial Character of Industry

Consistent with earlier findings, such as those of Reidel (1977), the variable with the greatest explanatory power is industry comparative disadvantage. Industry comparative disadvantage is measured by the ratio of imports to exports for each industry. The positive and significant parameter estimates indicate that the industries facing high levels of import competition receive favorable levels of protection in both Canada and the United States.

The theory predicts that industry size matters only in the United States. In weak-party systems, large industries find it easier to create protectionist coalitions. The ability to build coalitions is not an important industry feature

TABLE 3.2

The Industry Level Model for Canada (1970) and the United States (1979)

Independent Variables	Industry Tariff Levels	
	Canada 1970	United States 1979
Industry comparative disadvantage[a]	.1718***	.135***
	(.0486)	(.033)
Industry size[b]	−.0044	.286**
	(.0228)	(.144)
Industry electoral concentration index[c]	.4119**	.185***
	(.019)	(.064)
Industries concentrated in marginal districts[d]	.1762*	—
	(.1418)	
Large, decentralized industries[e]	.0506	.1819**
	(.0812)	(.0983)
Intercept	7.38***	8.78***
	(2.28)	(.78)
Number of Cases	107	419
Adj. R^2	.19	.07

Note: Figures are unstandardized beta coefficients; standard errors are in parentheses.

[a] Industry comparative advantage is coded imports$_i$ /exports$_i$.

[b] The size of an industry is coded as total employment in industry i.

[c] Industry concentration across electoral districts is coded as $\sum_j (E_{i,j} / E_i)^2$, where i = industry and j = electoral district.

[d] $\sum_j, (E_{i,j} / E_i)^2 \times$ district marginality (see footnote b in Table 3.1)

[e] An interactive term, − (industry concentration$_i$ /industry size$_i$)

*$p < .10$; **$p < .05$; ***$p < .01$. All one tailed tests.

in strong-party systems. A variable is included that measures the total number of employees in an industry. As predicted, this variable is insignificant in the Canadian regression but positive and significant in the U.S. regression.

The Political Character of Industry

As expected, electorally concentrated industries receive more favorable levels of protection in Canada. An electoral concentration index measures industry employment in each district as a share of total employment in that industry, squared and summed over all districts.[23] Electoral concentration in for industry i equals $\sum_{j=1}^{J} (E_{i,j} / E_i)^2$, where $E_{i,j}$ is the employment in industry i in district j and E_i is the total employment in industry i. The summation is over all electoral districts. If an industry is concentrated in only one electoral district, then it has an electoral concentration of 1. If this industry is evenly divided over ten electoral districts, then it has an electoral concentration of $10 \times (0.1)^2 = 0.1$. The coefficient is positive, significant, and large in magnitude, suggesting that in Canada electorally concentrated industries receive more favorable levels of protection.

A variable is included to distinguish industries that are electorally concentrated in marginal districts. Industries electorally concentrated in many marginal districts take the highest values, and industries that are electorally dispersed over many safe districts take the smallest values. This variable equals $\Sigma_{j=1}^{J}$ $(E_{i,j} / E_i)^2 \times$ *district marginality*. In the Canadian model this variable is positive and significant at the 10 percent level in a one-tailed test. Although barely significant, the magnitude of this effect is nontrivial. This finding weakly supports the hypothesis that although electorally concentrated industries receive more favorable levels of protection, the most favorable levels of protection go to industries electorally concentrated in marginal districts.

In the United States, I predicted that electorally decentralized industries receive more favorable levels of protection than electorally concentrated industries do. As in Canada, however, electorally concentrated industries in the United States receive higher levels of protection than electorally dispersed industries. This finding does not support the predictions. Instead, the results appear to support the standard pressure group model discussed in the introduction.

In the United States, however, it is hypothesized that size has an important interactive effect with the level of electoral concentration. The argument predicts that large, decentralized industries receive the most favorable levels of protection in the United States. No such effect should be present in the Canadian case. The variable—large, decentralized industry—is calculated as − (industry electoral concentration/industry size) and takes the largest values for large, decentralized industries and the smallest values for small, centralized industries. This interactive term for size and electoral concentration is insignificant in Canada, as expected. However, the positive, significant parameter in the U.S. model indicates that large, decentralized industries receive higher levels of protection in the United States. In the U.S. case, there is mixed support for the theoretical predictions. Electorally concentrated industries receive higher levels of protection, on average, than electorally decentralized industries. However, large, electorally decentralized industries are able to secure favorable levels of protection. It would appear that the ability to shout loudly, the willingness of legislators to listen, and the ability of legislators to form coalitions determines which industries win protection.

To summarize the industry-level results, the highest levels of protection go to industries that are comparatively disadvantaged. Nonetheless, the findings support the hypotheses that in both Canada and the United States, electorally concentrated industries receive higher levels of protection than industries that are electorally decentralized. The standard pressure-group model argues that these concentrated industries received protection because they find it less costly to organize and press their demands. My theory, however, makes an additional prediction. In Canada, I predict that industries electorally concentrated in marginal districts receive the highest levels of protection. In the United States, but not Canada, I predict that large, electorally decentralized industries are able to secure highly favorable levels of protection. The interactive effects predicted in chapter 2 are supported in the findings.

NO SMOKING GUN

It would certainly appear from the tests above that the pattern of trade protection in majoritarian countries fits the predictions. Although the tests examine tariff data from the 1970s, in terms of testing the theory, the evidence is lacking in two regards. First, the hypotheses for proportional representation systems are not examined. By the 1970s most industrialized PR nations were members of the EU, which imposed common external tariffs. Within the EU, tariffs represented a bargain over what each country wanted. Countries within the European Union that wanted to assist an industry had to rely upon means other than tariffs. This is the second problem with these tests: can tariffs be relied on to accurately represent redistributive policy toward industries?

The traditional tool of protection was the tariff. Tariff protection is transparent and a clearly observable form of protection (Bhagwati and Feenstra 1982; Laird and Yeats 1990). Following the Second World War, successive GATT rounds have successfully decreased tariff barriers and increased trade—particularly since the late 1970s. Unfortunately, a reduction in tariffs does not ensure free trade, and nontariff barriers (NTBs) and economic assistance have become the dominant forms of protection. In the United States during the 1990s, the trade debate was expressed in terms of competition between *free trade* and *fair trade*. Fair-trade supporters insisted that other nations should use a level playing field. For example, Japan came under much criticism because of the difficulties foreign firms had breaking into the Japanese sales market. In part, cross-ownership of shares among Japanese suppliers, producers, and distributers, as well as the strong vertical and/or horizontal integration of firms was blamed. However, vertical constraints are often the most efficient way for producers to get their goods to the market. It is difficult to assess whether steep vertical integration is a reason for Japan's success or is a device to restrict U.S. access to Japanese markets.

Unfortunately, modern forms of protection are all too often hidden in the fine print of regulation or other nontariff barriers. The assessment of the value of protection is no longer simply a debate about the appropriate method for converting between nominal and effective tariffs (see Caves 1976; Helleiner

1977; Lavergne 1981), but is instead a debate about whether a regulatory measure is a protectionist measure or cultural trait or a quirk of the importing country. As an example, U.S. farmers are quick to complain about their inability to gain access to the Japanese rice market. The price for a pound of rice in Japan is around three times as expensive as in the United States. The Japanese contend that supporting Japanese agriculture is important for both national security and to preserve the cultural life of the Japanese countryside. While it is clear that the massive, highly mechanized farms in the United States are more efficient than the tiny, typically handworked, terraced fields of Japan, the Japanese can legitimately counterclaim that part of the reason the United States grows rice so cheaply is subsidized water. Particularly in the Southwest, where water is scarce, agriculture receives water at prices far below market rates. While farmers would claim this as a legitimate property right, the Japanese might view it as an illegal subsidy. It is too easy for both side to cry foul and demand "fair trade" on a level playing field. Even from an objective viewpoint, it is hard to see what such a playing field looks like.

Many scholars still use tariffs to assess the extent to which an industry is protected. Historically, this is a useful measure of which industries won protection.[24] U.S. and Canadian industry tariffs in the 1970s are a reasonable measure of which industries were more or less protected. However, the same cannot be said of U.S. and Canadian tariffs in the 1990s. As I discussed in the introduction, in recent work scholars employ cross-national measures of industry NTBs (Mansfield and Busch 1995). All of these approaches are legitimate attempts to assess the level of state aid.[25] However, rather than simply looking for direct measures of protection, the innovation in this book is to find complementary evidence of the distribution of trade protection across countries. Using the deductions of my theory as a guide, in the next two chapters I look at two new dependent variables to test the theory: how governments choose between groups within an industry and how political change influences changes in redistributive policy as measured through stock-price dispersion.

TABLE 3A.1
Summary Statistics: Canada

Variable	Mean	Standard Deviation
District comparative disadvantage (10^{-2})	2.53	4.92
District marginality	−13.56	9.84
Number of districts in state	55.8	33.2
District party representative (10^{-1})	5.49	4.98
District represented by a minister	.095	.293
Marginal districts represented by a minister	−2.47	10.02
Unemployment in district (10^{-1})	−3.81	2.14
District level of tariff protection	1.82	1.25
Industry comparative advantage	6.07	12.92
Industry size (10^3)	42.68	42.44
Industry concentration across electoral districts (10^{-2})	9.94	3.24
Industries concentrated in marginal districts (10^{-1})	−2.05	6.18
Large, decentralized industries (10^{-6})	−7.46	13.51
Industry tariff levels	11.66	6.70

TABLE 3A.2
Summary Statistics: United States

Variable	Mean	Standard Deviation
District comparative disadvantage (10^{-2})	.024	.033
District marginality ($10^{2)}$	−.390	.291
Number of districts in state (10^2)	.181	.129
District party representative	.635	.482
Seniority of representative (10^2)	.705	.075
Member of Ways and Means Committee	.0823	.284
Member of Foreign and Interstate Commerce Committee	.089	.285
District unemployment (10^1)	.536	.298
District level of protection	.0034	.0043
Industry comparative advantage	.0583	.0883
Industry size (10^4)	3.305	4.871
Industry electoral concentration index	.0315	.0486
Large, decentralized industries (10^{-3})	−.006	.032
Industry tariff levels	.0576	.0619

CHAPTER 4

Restructuring and Redistribution in the Steel Industry

THE THEORY IN THIS BOOK is about redistribution. The logic of the theory tells us under what conditions the government chooses to privilege one group of voters over another. While I couch the theory in terms of industries, the theory is equally applicable at the firm or plant level. This chapter offers a comparative analysis of how governments supplied trade and industrial policy among steel plants in the 1980s. Which steel plants are privileged depends upon their geography—particularly their regional location—and the structure of the electoral and party system in their country.

The economic woes of the steel industry have been a high-profile political issue in most industrialized countries. I remember from childhood the dominant presence of the Ravenscraig steel plant, its smokestacks dominating the view of the Clyde valley from my home. Today they are completely gone. Yet in the early 1980s Ravenscraig was more than a physical presence. Ravenscraig symbolized the decline of working-class industrial jobs in the Clyde valley. The boom years had passed; the shipyards of the Clyde were mostly silent; Ravenscraig stood alone as a solitary reminder of Glasgow's postwar industrial prosperity.

From an economic perspective Ravenscraig had no right to exist. Ravenscraig was a wide strip mill with six processing plants scattered over a twelve-mile radius of Motherwell, to the southeast of Glasgow, Scotland. Such decentralization meant huge inefficiencies. Between each stage of processing the steel had to be cooled, transported to the next site, and reheated. Transportation costs for the finished sheet steel added to Ravenscraig's price disadvantage. Most of Ravenscraig's customers were located in England. In addition, Ravenscraig's port was located far from the plant and was not in deep water. By 1983, Ravenscraig's losses added up to 50 percent of the British Steel Corporation's weekly deficit (Hudson and Sadler 1989). Keeping Ravenscraig open was clearly not economically rational. Neither was it good management. Indeed, early in the 1970s the British Steel Corporation (BSC) proposed closing Ravenscraig in favor of Port Talbot and Llanwern (Beynon and Sadler 1991; Dudley and Richardson 1990). The decision to keep it open was political.

Why did Margaret Thatcher's Conservative government thwart the microeconomic reforms that dominated its policy making of the early 1980s to keep open a large, inefficient plant—an action that cost tax payers almost $200 million per year? (Bain 1992). The short answer as to why Thatcher closed

Corby, Normanby Park, and Scunthorpe plants but kept Ravenscraig open, is that the political implications of closing a steel plant in a region with marginal Tory districts—one of Scotland's few regions with any Tory seats—made Ravenscraig's closure politically unacceptable.[1] Only after the government privatized BSC was the strip mill at Ravenscraig finally shut down in 1992. While the causes of steel's decline lie in economics and while government policy cannot ignore these realities, governments do have considerable say over which plants are modernized and which are closed.[2] These choices are political, not economic, as the United Kingdom's former chancellor of the exchequer Nigel Lawson (1993) recognized: "Quite apart from the persistent tendency to attempt to shore up failing industries, governments have a pretty poor record in trying to pick winners. Moreover, in both cases, political considerations inevitably loom large, with marginal seats counting more than marginal costs."

The British steel industry was not alone in suffering in the 1980s. As I shall detail below, by the 1980s, the steel industries of many Western nations were in turmoil. Although Western countries had invested huge amounts into steel in the 1960s, by the end of the 1970s most Western steel plants were antiquated compared to those in such industrializing nations as Taiwan and Japan. When combined with a fall in world demand for steel, this increased supply drove down the price of steel. Across much of the industrialized world, steel firms were either going bust or were being propped up by government subsidies. The growing indebtedness of firms eventually forced governments to restructure their steel industries. As the Ravenscraig case shows, these decisions were not always made on an economic basis. I examine the restructuring of the steel industries of Belgium, Germany, Sweden, the United Kingdom, and the United States in the 1970s and 1980s as a test of the causal plausibility of the arguments laid out in chapter 2.

Throughout the OECD, steel is a heavily protected industry. Bilateral quota agreements, limiting steel imports are widespread (see table 4.1). However, the nontariff barrier (NTB) aggregates in table 4.1 do not convey the focused impact of selective assistance measures. Governments have also used cheap loans, exchange rate policy, research and development grants, redundancy payments, antipollution legislation, debt write-offs, union legislation, regional policy, subsidized inputs, loan guarantees, and tax concessions to assist the industry (Duchene and Shepherd 1987; Meny and Wright 1986). In some countries, steel firms argued that the level of aid should be discounted because the government rigged input prices (i.e., energy) and forced firms to keep open unprofitable plants. Although it is widely recognized that the French and Italian steel industries had been heavily subsidized, there is strong disagreement about how they rank up against the West German or British steel industries (Ford and Suyker 1990; Morgan 1983). While it is difficult to tell which government gave steel the most trade assistance, it is easy to observe which steel plants remained open and which closed. Governments played an im-

TABLE 4.1
Nontariff Barriers to Iron and Steel Products, 1983, Selected Countries

	Iron and Steel, NTB, Coverage Ratio	Manufacturing, NTB, Coverage Ratio	Iron and Steel, NTB, Frequency Ratio	Manufacturing Frequency Ratio
Australia	55.6	23.6	14.4	17.9
Austria	0	2.4	0	0.9
Belgium and Luxembourg	47.4	33.6	17.8	8.9
France	73.9	27.4	56.6	21.9
W. Germany	18.5	53.5	19.5	11.1
Italy	48.6	9.3	21.2	8.4
Netherlands	35.5	17.8	16.2	10.2
United Kingdom	42.1	14.8	16.9	12.3
United States	37.7	17.1	22.8	6.9
European Union	52.6	18.7	23.4	12.0

Source: Nogues, Olechowski, and Winters (1986) tables 1C and 1F. The NTB coverage ratio represents the amount of trade flow that NTBs affect. The frequency ratio indicates the number of items involved.

portant role in determining how the industry was restructured. Although across countries the ownership of firms and the structure of labor unions differed, indebtedness made practically all steel plants beholden to government, and, as we shall see, the government chose which plants would survive the crisis and which would not.

The main thesis in chapter 2 is that the distribution of industrial assistance and protection depends upon an industry's geography—its size, spread, and location—and the nature of the electoral system. Yet while the theory was expressed in terms of competition between industries, the argument could just as easily be applied to distinguishable industrial groups. In the context of the steel industry, these groups are the different plants. Most studies of the distribution of industrial protection focus on competition between industries. Since many groups aggregate at the industry level as a political unit, this often makes sense. Yet, as I shall show for the case of the steel industry, competition between groups can take place at the subindustry levels. I argue that the extent to which intraindustry competition exists depends upon the government's chosen policy instrument.

This chapter explores how governments supply trade and industrial policy among steel firms. It asks, what are the incentives of politicians in different political systems to privilege one steel plant relative to another? Does a change in party government affect which steel plants are privileged? The dependent variables are the distribution and change in distribution of assistance to firms or plants within the steel industry. I examine government response to the steel industry's demands for assistance in five industrialized countries: Belgium, Germany,[3] Sweden, the United Kingdom, and the United States. The sectoral and geographical characteristics of steel are similar across the six cases: steel firms are characterized by fixed assets and regional concentration. However, three of these countries have PR systems and two are majoritarian systems, one with weak parties. In each of these countries, the government was involved in the fundamental restructuring of domestic steel firms in response to the plunge in world steel prices in the late 1970s and early 1980s. In the period under study, opposition parties swept into office in each of the six countries. To a large extent, these new governments directly chose which steel plants remained open and which closed. While economics dictated that some plants would close, politics determined which ones remained open. The effect of the industry's geography—its size, spread, and location—is conditional on the type of political system.

In each country, the government's response to the decline in the steel industry supports the hypotheses advanced in chapter 2. In PR systems, as parties move in and out of coalition, the distribution of representation for firms within an industry changes. Those firms that win trade assistance in proportional representation systems represent a compromise of the policy goals of the parties in coalition government. In PR systems, the incentives to target one geographic region over another arise from the economic and demographic differences that structure party affiliation. Geographic electoral jurisdictions by themselves are of no importance. However, because the closure of industries can adversely affect local economies, parties sometimes have incentives to target firms in regional voting strongholds. For example, in Belgium, a change in multiparty government in 1981, from a socialist to a Catholic-liberal coalition dominated by northern (Flemish) interests, led to the restructuring and closure of southern (Wallonian) steel plants. In Germany, a right-wing coalition took over government in September 1982, when a no-confidence vote expelled the socialist-led coalition from office. Despite the coalition's market-oriented ideology, regional incentives induced the government to target industrial policy toward steel firms in the Ruhr and Saarland regions of Germany. In Sweden, the center-right coalition that replaced forty-four years of social democratic rule targeted aid to their core constituency by buying out small businessmen in struggling steel firms.

In majoritarian systems with strong parties, both major parties target industrial policy to the same group of firms. In particular, since capturing marginal districts determines the outcome of elections, whichever party is in office targets assistance to those firms in marginal districts. BSC's decision to delay the closure of the Ravenscraig steel works in the early 1980s was tied to its dependence on government handouts, and the importance of the plant to the Conservative's electoral fate in Scotland. In contrast, in majoritarian systems with weak parties, firms dispersed over safe seats receive the most favorable levels of protection both because there are lower costs to coalition formation and because their legislators are more effective agenda-setters. In the United States, the steel industry's geographical concentration in the heavily populated midwestern states meant that successive presidents were responsive to steel's demands, while the geographical spread of the steel union helped explain the strong support for steel in Congress.

In each of these five cases, industry geography and sectoral party alignments affect the pattern of government assistance. Governments use redistributive industrial policy to privilege those groups that further their survival in office.

WHY STUDY STEEL?

In the United Kingdom, in May 1979, the Labor party government was voted out of office and the Conservative party was elected to government. The market-oriented Conservative government had promised to restructure Britain's nationalized dinosaurs, and the steel industry was a particularly large dinosaur.[4] The domestic market for basic steel had collapsed, and the British Steel Corporation (BSC) had been in serious trouble since 1974. By the early 1980s, British Steel's losses amounted to more than $2 million each day.[5] Plans to restructure the steel industry were initiated under the Labour government; although most plant closures and job layoffs occurred under the next, Conservative, government. The British Steel Corporation began closing smaller, older facilities and concentrating production at five coastal sites. Among others, steel plants in Corby, Consett, and Scunthorpe were closed. About 200,000 workers were employed in the steel industry in the mid-1970s. By 1990, that number had been reduced to about 50,000 (see table 4.2).

While eradicating almost half the steel jobs in the United Kingdom might appear a radical move, in the comparative context, the British government's steel policy resembled those adopted by other countries (see table 4.2). Between 1974 (the boom year in worldwide sales) and 1990, almost 75 percent of steel jobs in the United States were lost and almost 50 percent in Belgium, Germany, and Sweden. In the 1980s steel industries across all of the industrialized world faced tremendous pressure from new competition and changes in technology. Only fifteen years earlier, states had been overly optimistic in their projections for steel demand and had encouraged new investment in the industry. By the 1980s the highly capital intensive integrated steel mills were already becoming antiquated and could no longer compete with newer, more efficient plants in such countries as Mexico, Japan, South Korea, and Venezuela (Pearce, Sutton, and Batchelor 1985). The labor productivity figures in table

TABLE 4.2
Employment in the Iron and Steel Industry, Various Years, and Labor Productivity, 1984, Tones per Emplyee per Year, Selected Countries

	Employment 1974	Employment 1979	Employment 1984	Employment 1990	Labor Productivity 1984
Australia	43,000	43,000	30,000	30,000	200–250
Belgium	64,000	49,000	37,000	26,000	300–350
Canada	53,000	53,000	48,000	53,000	300–350
France	156,000	125,000	87,000	46,000	200–250
Germany	231,000	204,000	157,000	125,000	250–300
Japan	324,000	282,000	265,000	305,000	350–400
Netherlands	24,000	21,000	19,000	17,000	300–350
Spain	89,000	87,000	70,000	36,000	100–150
Sweden	51,000	45,000	31,000	26,000	n.a.
United Kingdom	198,000	162,000	62,000	51,000	200–250
United States	521,000	479,000	267,000	204,000	300–350

Source: ILO (Iron and Steel Committee) 11th Session, 1986. "Productivity Improvement and Its Effects on the Level of Employment and Working Conditions in the Iron and Steel Industry" (Geneva: ILO), tables 1.5 and 2.2. Employment figures for 1990 from the International Iron and Steel Institute 2001 "World Steel in Figures" (Brussels: IISI).

Note: Employment is rounded to the nearest thousand. Productivity is measured in tons per employee per year.

4.2 show how Japan dominates other OECD countries in the labor productivity of its steelworkers. At the same time as supply increased, the pattern of demand also shifted. Consumers increasingly wanted specialized products, rather than bulk quantities of low-grade steel. For example, the automobile industry, long a staple consumer of steel goods, reduced its dependence on raw steel products, utilizing instead new plastics, aluminum, and specialized steels. In 1972, the BSC produced 25 million tons of steel and forecast an increase in demand. Ten years later, the BSC was struggling to sell 8 million tons of steel per year.[6] Across the industrialized world, there were strong economic pressures on the steel industry to restructure and reduce capacity (Meny and Wright 1987).

Unfortunately, closing a steel plant had dire consequences for the surrounding regions. Steel factor assets are highly specific, and integrated-technology steel plants are large and geographically concentrated. Indeed, steel plants are often located in "one-industry towns," and in some cases, plant closure created ghost towns (see Esser and Vath 1986; Meny and Wright 1986).

Additionally, steel plants are often located in depressed areas that already have high regional unemployment (Bain 1992). The unemployment considerations meant that restructuring steel had heavy political overtones and that governments played a major role in shaping the fate of the steel industry throughout the industrialized world. For this reason, the steel industry has been a major focus in the study of industrial policy.[7] The focus of the industrial policy literature has been to explain the nature of government-industry relations and to rate the success of government intervention in the steel industry. The approach in this book differs. Rather than looking at the extent or the success of government's, capital's, and the union's role in restructuring, I look instead at the distribution of government intervention between plants within the industry. Unions were largely inconsequential actors in the regional conflict over which plants closed. I shall discuss how internal dissension within the unions, whether they be fragmented or all-encompassing, prevented labor from coordinating on the choice of plant closure.

While steel policy has been an important case study in the field of industrial policy, it is often treated as an outlier in the trade-policy literature. Steel is highly protected across OECD countries, in part perhaps because the fate of the industry is tied to national security issues. A viable domestic steel industry is widely regarded as an important component of security preparedness. However, in this chapter I do not explore why steel is heavily protected vis-à-vis other industries. Rather, I seek to explain how governments redistribute resources within the steel industry. These choices are not tied to issues of national security but to economic efficiency and political expediency.

In contrasting the PR systems of Belgium, Germany, and Sweden with the majoritarian cases of the United Kingdom and the United States, I simply ask, if the government needs to close one of two steel plants, which one does it close? Does a change in party government affect which steel plants are privileged? The dependent variables are the distribution and change in distribution of assistance to firms or plants within the steel industry.

The Structural Characteristics of Steel

Although the structure and geography of steel varies across the five cases, the similarities outweigh the differences. The size of the steel industry differed across the five countries under study. Of these cases, the United States had the largest worldwide production in the 1980s (approximately 80,000 tons per year) and Sweden the smallest (approximately 11,000 tons per year) (Hudson and Sadler 1989). However, steel was a relatively large, important industry in all of the five countries studied (see employment figures for selected countries in table 4.2).

In all five countries, the steel industry is a declining industry that is asset-specific, industrially concentrated, spatially dispersed and regionally concentrated. Steel production has large economies of scale; for example, labor levels remain static as the size and productivity of integrated plants increase (Bain 1992). Hence, as an industry, steel tends to be industrially concentrated. In the United Kingdom, there is one dominant firm (BSC). In Belgium, the United States, Sweden, and Germany, the steel industry consists of several large firms. Even in the German case, the least industrally concentrated industry, 94 percent of crude steel was produced by seven firms in 1979 (Esser and Vath 1986).

Integrated steel mills are large, multifunction complexes (furnace, steelworks, and rolling mills). There are six different plants in the Ravenscraig complex, and these are all within a twelve-mile radius of Motherwell in Scotland. Steel complexes are often clustered together within a region, in part because there are cost advantages to being close to natural resources, rivers, and ports. In Germany, most steel firms are located along the Rhine, although there are also large firms in the Saarland and Bremen. In the United Kingdom, the largest steel plants are located at several coastal sites across the country, although the bulk of the industry is located in Wales and the northeast of England. The industry is geographically dispersed. Busch and Reinhardt (1999, 2003) define geographic dispersion as a function of the physical distance of plants to the midpoint of an industry. The industry is spatially dispersed, yet, it is also characterized as regionally concentrated; plants are clustered in a small number of regions. It is on this geographic feature of the steel industry that I focus. The political division between plants within the industry is expected to lie along firm and regional lines.

Given that most steel plants are large and regionally clustered, they tend to be a big, if not the biggest, employer in a region. Most steel towns are basically one-industry towns—for example, Corby or Consett in the United Kingdom.[8] Steelworkers don't have skills that transfer easily to other industries, making it difficult for them to switch jobs, even if other jobs are available. The closure of steel plants can lead to serious, permanent unemployment problems (Meny and Wright 1989). For example, Duisburg, in the Ruhr in West Germany, had an unemployment rate of 13.5 percent even before major cutbacks began in the 1980s.[9] More generally, the closure of a steel plant can have a devastating effect on the regional economy. In the short term, it can also mean job losses for subcontractors and service industries, boarded-up shops and malls, and the collapse of housing prices for local residents.

In all five countries, the steel industry has the distinction of being both regionally concentrated and electorally dispersed. It is a very large industry that tends to be located in heavily populated areas. In most electoral systems, legislative seats are distributed to political jurisdictions based on population size. This is particularly important in the U.S. case, where steel is both regionally concentrated and electorally dispersed across the industrial Midwest. It is an important employer in several highly populated states; hence, many legislators care strongly about the fate of the industry. Given these characteristics of steel's geography, the choice facing each government was the same; which region of the country would suffer the costs of plant closure and which region would get a reprieve.

Another important feature of steel is the type of firm ownership. In some countries, steel firms were state-owned (the United Kingdom); in others there was a mix of state and domestic private firms (Germany, Belgium, Sweden); and in yet other countries the steel industry was composed of private domestic firms (Australia and the United States). This is an important difference in the structure of government-industry relations. For example, it affects the options firms have for funding restructuring. There are limited cases of cross-country ownership of steel plants, for example, Arbed had plants in Luxembourg, Germany, and Belgium (Morgan 1983). Nonetheless, whatever the structure of firm ownership, in each case the government heavily influenced the path of restructuring. The worldwide crisis in the industry had left both nationalized and private firms deeply in debt—both types of firms needed loans and subsidies to restructure. Cockerill steel in Belgium, Usinor in France, Italsider in Italy, BSC in the UK, even Thyssen-Gruppe in Germany were losing millions of dollars a year (ILO 1986; Morgan 1983). Governments were forced to choose which plants to close and in which to subsidize production. They faced this choice whether or not the industry was nationalized or in the hands of private capital.

In all five countries, steel unions were big, powerful, and well organized. The unions' strength is hardly surprising, given the structure of the industry. Assets are highly specific, and as such we should expect labor to lobby alongside capital (Alt et al 1996). However, there are important differences in the political organization of unions across countries, both in the structure of the unions and their approach to collective bargaining. Sweden and Germany are at one extreme, having highly centralized unions that bargain collectively with the government. The United Kingdom is at the other extreme, with highly fragmented unions engaged in localized bargaining (Freeman and Medoff 1979). However, only in the United States did the unions strongly unite with steel firms to fight plant closures. In Western Europe, there were divisions between and within trade unions in the steel industry—whether the union was highly centralized or fragmented in structure. In part, this infighting was because the form of government assistance favored by many countries—subsidies, redundancy payments and low-interest loans—could be targeted at specific plants. The government had to choose which plant to close, which to subsidize, and which to modernize. This pitted one steel plant against another. For example, keeping Ravenscraig open would eventually mean job loses at two Welsh strip mills in the United Kingdom. Hudson and Sadler (1989, 75) describe the conflict.

Llanwern union leaders launched a campaign to protect their works, to prevent it becoming a victim of Scottish political pressure to keep Ravenscraig open. They submitted evidence to the same Select Committee which compared Llanwern's profits to Ravenscraig's losses and claimed far greater customer satisfaction with the quality of Llanwern output. The committee finally recommended that, for the present, no works should be closed, but the damage to national trade union organization had been done.

The chairman of the Joint Union Committee at Shotton told Ravenscraig workers, "Back off and leave Wales alone. Stand on your own feet—we won't be part of your fight" (Hudson and Sadler 1989, 81). In Sweden, the issue of whether jobs should be lost at steel plants in Domnarvet or Lulea divided the industrial union. In Germany, government assistance to firms in the Saarland would mean job losses in Duisburg or Dortmund in the Ruhr. The industrial confederation was "immobilized" by infighting. If the unions were fragmented along regional lines, the unions were divided over closures (for example, Belgium). If the unions were united in a confederation, they were immobilized because of dissension among members (for example, Sweden).

External pressure from the EU to cut back on overcapacity exacerbated the conflict regarding plant closures. In the 1980s, the EU implemented formal production quotas to encourage a reduction in the number of steel plants and the production of steel.[10] Although production quotas applied to companies, closure of one plant took pressure off the others to cut production. For instance, in Belgium, Flemish steel plants gained from the closure steel plants in Wallonia. Similarly, at the international level, the closure of plants in one member state took pressure of the other member states to reduce capacity. To some extent, governments used state aid in a game of chicken; using aid to infuse life into their steel industry while pushing other countries to bear the burden of plant closures and job loss. Later, I argue that the closure of the U.K. Ravenscraig steel plant was delayed in the early 1980s because it was located in a politically sensitive region of the country. However, Dudley and Richardson (1990) argue that Ravenscraig's closure was delayed by the British government because other EU countries had yet to close more inefficient steel plants. This was certainly the political spin the government put on the decision. However, this argument for keeping the Ravenscraig complex open does not fully explain why the government was willing to close steel plants in other parts of the country. I argue domestic political concerns were the root cause of Ravenscraig's stay of execution.

Outside of the EU, governments had more flexibility in their choice of policy instruments to aid the industry. EU member countries were unable to act unilaterally on tariffs and quota agreements—not so the U.S. government. In the United States, the government has traditionally been less involved in the market, so direct government involvement through buyouts, loans, or subsidies was unlikely. The best route that steel firms could hope for assistance was quotas or tariffs. Labor and capital from different locations united to lobby for assistance. Tariffs and quotas are relatively blunt instruments—although they can be targeted to specific firms, most protect the industry as a whole. Ironically, the unions in the United States are generally thought to be weaker than in Europe; through a united front, however, they were more effective at influencing the pattern of government assistance. Later, I argue that the success of U.S. unions in achieving concessions from the government depended more upon the government's choice of policy instrument than upon traditional features of union-government relations. Unions in both adversarial systems (typical of the United Kingdom) and corporatism systems (typical of Belgium and Sweden) failed to prevent government closure plans.

COUNTRY CHOICE

The case studies in this chapter are intended purely to illustrate the plausibility of the causal arguments, particularly in relevance to electoral systems. In the theoretical model, the majoritarian ideal types are two-party majoritarian with strong parties and two-party majoritarian with weak parties. The United Kingdom is used to illustrate the strong-party majoritarian case; the United States, the weak-party majoritarian case.[11] In the weak-party model, features of the agenda-setting process and legislative rules are important determinants of policy outcomes. These specific features of the U.S. political environment are incorporated into the case discussion, as in chapter 3.

Belgium, Sweden, and Germany were chosen to illustrate the strong-party PR case. The PR formulas and the district magnitude of these PR systems differ. All have complex two-tiered districting systems.[12] In these complex districting systems, the final allocation of seats takes place at the upper level on the basis of all the votes.[13] In part, because of these differences in the electoral formula and proportionality, these countries have different numbers of parties. Sweden has one big party and three or four smaller parties; the large party generally dominates coalition politics and often forms a minority government with or without the support of one of the other parties. Germany has two large and one or two small parties; most coalition governments are minimal winning and minimum-connected winning. Belgium has, since the 1970s, had a highly fragmented party system.[14] Governments are usually minimum winning coalitions (Laver and Schofield 1990). Nevertheless, these cases demonstrate that while there are many differences in the details of each PR system—such as the number and size of parties—these differences are not as important as the similarities between countries with proportional representation electoral systems.

TIME PERIOD

The late 1970s and early 1980s time period was chosen for a number of reasons. The need for restructuring in the steel industry was apparent in all six countries by the 1980s. This period was also a time of political upheaval in all the countries analyzed. In most of these countries, right-wing, market-oriented governments entered office, often after long periods of socialist rule (Sweden, Belgium, and the United Kingdom). However, not all market-oriented governments restructured in the same way. In the United Kingdom, a right-wing government pushed to downsize and privatize steel. In Sweden, a center-right government stepped in with subsidies to prop up steel and eventually nationalized most of the steel industry (a marked change from Social Democratic policies of the previous forty years). A right-wing government in Germany pumped huge amounts of taxpayers' money into the steel industry. Pure partisan politics does not explain why some right-wing governments supported steel while others pushed for closures and restructuring. In each case, industry geography and political institutions interact with partisan politics to drive outcomes.

WHAT ABOUT THE ROLE OF OTHER POLITICAL INSTITUTIONS?

Other institutions, aside from the electoral role, exert influence over the role of industry geography on political clout. The federal structure of government can affect how geographical concentration matters—for example, regional concentration might help an industry get state/provincial aid, but dispersion can help if aid is distributed at the federal level. For example, in Germany, about 50 percent of assistance comes through federal/state regional development programs (Weiss 1983). Also, financial bills passed in the Bundestag have to be ratified by the Bundesrat, which houses representatives of the sixteen lander. The Bundesrat needs a two-thirds majority to veto such a bill, but it can delay government proposals. Unfortunately, it is not possible to control for the numerous nation-specific factors that influence policy; institutional features that may alter the predictions are discussed on a case-by-case basis.

Perhaps the most important supply-side variable that is not discussed in the case studies is the role of the bureaucracy. In all of the countries, while industry-specific aid is passed in the legislature, the implementation of these programs is done by the ministerial bureaucracy. Once the program is created, funding is passed more or less automatically in the annual budget. Both government and bureaucratic interests bear upon the distribution of funding. In every case, the process for allocating trade and industrial policy is complex, involving multiple ministerial departments with overlapping jurisdiction.[15] Although bureaucratic interests and structure are an important part of the story and help explain the level of government assistance, the bottom line is that politicians, not bureaucrats, are the key policy-making actors. Whatever the institutional process whereby industrial and trade policy is distributed, if a government wants to save a firm or plant for political reasons, it will find a way to do it. In this chapter, I do not study the process where a particular agency allocates aid to firms. Rather, I focus on the policy outcomes.[16]

In the following case studies, I study the pattern of redistribution among steel plants over time. In the PR cases, I focus on how a change in party government affects the restructuring of the steel industry. The incentives to target plants in one region over another arise from economic and demographic differences that structure party affiliation. Nowhere is this more apparent than in the Belgian case.

BELGIUM

Belgium is a strong-party PR system. As such, we should expect government policy to favor those groups represented by the parties in government. Changes in the composition of party government are likely to change the relative winners and losers, and indeed, this is exactly what we observe following the 1981 political realignment when the previous regionally balanced government was replaced by a coalition government dominated by northern interests.

The restructuring of the Belgian steel industry in the 1980s was a strongly divisive political issue,[17] in part because of the geography of Belgian steel. The older steel plants were located in Wallonia, in the south of the country, while the newer steel plants were located in the north, in Flanders. Since the opening of the Sidmar steel complex in the north in 1961, Wallonia and Flanders had feuded over the regional allocation of government assistance to steel. The bulk of the industry was located in Wallonia, in old, poorly located, basic steel plants. The biggest of these firms was Cockerill Steel of Liege. From 1975 onward Cockerill Steel faced one financial crisis after another.[18] The redundancies, capacity closures, and job layoffs necessary to restructure the steel industry battered the already depressed regions of Wallonia (in 1980, unemployment in Liege was 18 percent).[19]

In the late 1970s and early 1980s, the government grew increasingly involved in the restructuring of the steel industry, first through financial assistance, then through partial ownership of Cockerill. In 1978, the government took a 29 percent share of the company's equity and paid off much of its debt. In 1982, Cockerill Steel of Liege and Hainavlt Sambre of Charleroi merged to form Cockerill-Sambre, thus creating the largest single steel complex in the south. Eighty percent of the newly merged firm was owned by the state. In contrast, the Belgian government owned only a minority share of the Sidmar complex in Flanders. The majority of Sidmar was owned by Arbed, a private firm (Bain 1992; Capron 1986).

The restructuring of steel was particularly divisive because it occurred across existing political and linguistic cleavages. Flanders, in the north, is flemish speaking, while Wallonia, in the south, is french speaking. The political cleavages are such that each region has its own brand of catholic, liberal, and socialist party. In the postwar period, coalition governments in Belgium have been dominated by coalitions of the two largest parties, the Wallonian Socialists (Francophone Socialists) and the Flemish Catholics (Christian People's party). Despite frequent changes in government, both the Flemish Catholics and the Wallonian socialists remained a part of government into the early 1980s. The pattern of redistributive politics in Belgium reflects this. When Belgian steel expanded between 1968 and 1975, the coalition government targeted support to both northern and southern regions of the country. Assistance to a firm in one region of the country was matched by compensation to firms in the other region (Bain 1992). When the Catholic-center-socialist government pushed for restructuring in the early 1980s, government assistance was also balanced toward assisting both northern and southern steel plants. The Wallonian socialists and the Flemish Catholic parties, however, were unable to agree on a subsidy plan for Cockerill-Sambre.[20] In September 1980, Belgium's Minister for Economic Affairs, Mr. Claes, announced a plan to split Cockerill into four separate companies. However, heavy opposition within the cabinet—particularly from the southern socialists—forced Claes to withdraw the proposal. This opposition was hardly surprising, given the socialists' regional base of support. In the 1980s, the Cockerill-Sambre town of Liege, the Wallonian socialists won around 40 percent of the vote. The Flemish Catholics won only a handful of votes. Overall, Wallonian political parties won over 80 percent of the vote in Liege.

The trade union movement in Belgium was also organized along linguistic and regional lines. The Christian Trade Union (231,551 members in 1982) supported the Catholic political parties, while the General Belgium Labor Federation (211,289 in 1980) had strong ties to the socialist parties (Bain 1992). The latter had greater strength in the south, the former in the north. The Belgium Labor Federation and the Wallonian socialists—both of whom drew most of their support from the south—fought hard to ensure that public funds were used to assist the southern Cockerill-Sambre plant.

A change in the multiparty coalition government occurred in December 1981, from a center-socialist to a Catholic-liberal coalition.[21] The Christian People's (CVP), Christian Social (PSC), Flemish Socialist (BSP), and Francophone Socialist (PS) coalition was replaced by the Christian People's (CVP), Christian Social (PSC), Flemish Liberal (PVV), and Francophone Liberal (PLP) coalition. Surprisingly, the Francophone Socialists (PS) were cut out of this Catholic-liberal government (although they did win a majority in the Wallonian regional assembly).

In contrast to its socialist predecessor, the new Catholic-liberal government drew much of its political support from the Flemish region (Bain 1992). The Christian People's party (CVP) had by far the largest seat share (20 percent) in parliament; the next largest were the Flemish Liberals with 13 percent. The CVP-led government pushed for reform of the steel industry: specifically, the restructuring and closure of southern steel plants (Capron 1986). It set limits on the amount of public funding available for restructuring—limiting funding for early pensions, for example, to $155 million—and set an end date of 1985 for public funding (Hudson and Sadler 1989). After this date, the Wallonian regional government would be stand alone in assisting Cockerill-Sambre (Bain 1992).

The two major steel unions, the Christian Union Confederation and the Belgium Labor Federation, representing the Flemish and Wallonians respectively, had previously lobbied together at EU headquarters in Brussels against EU interference in the industry. When the General Belgian Labor Federation reacted against the governments plan with a series of short strikes at steel plants in Wallonia in March and April of 1982, the Christian Union Confederation initially supported the strikes. Yet the common front quickly collapsed once it became clear that most of the closures were to take place in Wallonia rather than Flanders (Capron 1986).[22] By early April, the Christian Union had changed its position, condemning the strike action and putting its full support behind the policies of the Catholic-Liberal government (Bain 1992).

In 1984, the government deepened its restructuring plans. As part of the Gandois plan, it was announced that 7,900 to 9,000 jobs would be lost at Cockerill-Sambre between 1983 and 1985—largely due to the closure of a section mill at Charleroi and a rod mill at Liege (Bain 1992). Arbed, owners of the northern Sidmar plant, did close a strip mill, but in Luxembourg, not Belgium. In the deal struck between the Belgian and Luxembourg governments, the Belgian government compensated Arbed by pouring new investment into Sidmar (Hudson and Sadler 1989).

The Belgian case reveals how party change can lead to a radical redistribution of trade assistance between firms within an industry. In Belgium, a change in government led to the restructuring of the industry; the closing of Wallonian steel plants, and the saving of northern Flemish plants. Economically, it made sense to restructure the industry this way—the older, more inefficient plants were located in Wallonia. However, the previous center-socialist government had been unable to agree on a plan to restructure the industry. The Francophone Socialists—the second biggest party in government—had been able to veto at the cabinet level any plans to downsize Cockerill-Sambre. However, a change in government to a catholic-liberal coalition led to a change in the pattern of government assistance. This coalition drew much of its support from the Flemish north and as such had little interest in aiding southern firms. It initiated a radical program to downsize the Wallonian steel industry. The government was able to reward its regional support base at the expense of workers in the regional base of opposition parties.

WEST GERMANY

As in Belgium, a change in coalition government was the impetus for restructuring the German steel industry. Upon coming to power in 1982, the right-wing coalition government implemented large-scale reductions in capacity yet provided enormous funds to cushion the pain of dislocation. However, unlike the Belgian case, the restructuring occurred across the whole of the steel industry and was not regionally focused. While Germany is also a PR country, it lacked the regional differences in party support so evident in Belgium. Both the major parties received similar support from all the major steel regions and, as such, the government gained little from privileging one district over another.

Germany's steel industry was and still is the biggest and most efficient in Europe. The largest firms in the industry are the privately owned companies of Krupp-Stahl, Thyssen Gruppe, Hoesch Werke AG, Klockner Werke AG, Arbed-Saarstahl, and the state-owned Stahlwerke Peine-Salzgigger. Most of Germany's steel plants are located in the Saarland and along the Rhine, in the Ruhr. In the state of North-Rhine Westphalia which contains the Ruhr region, 40 percent of employment is in steel and mining.[23] Just outside the town of Duisburg in the Ruhr is the largest steel complex in Germany (Thyssen). In East Ruhr, the town of Dortmund is dominated by the Hoesch steel company.

Within Europe, the German state was traditionally the least interventionist, leaving the running of the industry largely to private firms. The government had largely restricted its role to overseeing private mergers between steel firms. In the late 1970s, the socialist government used subsidies and loans to bolster the steel industry in the hard-hit Saarland (Bain 1992). However, the level of subsidies was small compared to those of other European governments at the time. The socialist German government was reluctant to agree to EU quotas on steel production in the late 1970s, blaming the crisis on other European governments for their continued financial support of inefficient steel firms (Tsoukalis and Strauss 1986).

The laissez-faire government strategy changed, however, starting in the early 1980s. A right-wing coalition entered government in 1982 and, despite its market-orientated ideology, began pumping taxpayers' money into steel plants in the Saarland and the Ruhr. The Christian Democrats (CDU)[24] and the Free Democrats (FDP) had stepped into government in September 1982, following a no-confidence vote that expelled the Social Democrats (SPD) and FDP coalition from office. In the period prior to the election, German steel production had fallen from 42 million tons in 1981 to 36 million in 1982. The new coalition government, led by Helmet Kohl, took swift action. A month after entering office, the government extended by twelve months the period that unemployed short-term workers could get federal aid. Two months later, the Kohl government bailed out Arbed-Saarstah in the Saarland, although it chose not to rescue the smaller firm of Korf Steel in January 1983.[25]

At about the same time, the steel industry appointed a commission to report on restructuring the industry. In January 1983, it suggested the creation of two "groups": a Rhine group (Thyssen and Krupp) and a Ruhr group (Hoesch, Klockner, and Peine-Salzgitter).[26] The Kohl government endorsed the plan, promising subsidies and hinting at tariffs on steel imports. These promises were reiterated by the CDU just before the general election, in March 1983. In contrast, the SPD appeared to turn a cold shoulder to steel's plight during its election campaign, concentrating instead on noneconomic issues such as national defense.[27] The CDU/FDP coalition was reelected. Moreover, the CDU increased its policy-making power within the CDU/FDP coalition (there was a significant rise in the number of votes for the CDU and a drop for the FDP). The CDU's promises to support steel seemed to have worked. There was a significant shift in voting patterns in steel regions. For over twenty years, the SPD had won the largest number of votes in the Nordrhein-Westfalen region of the Ruhr. For example, in the previous election the SPD had won 47 percent of the regional vote compared to the CDU's 41.5 percent. However, at the 1983 election, the CDU overtook the SPD and won the largest number of votes in that region (47 percent of the vote compared to the SPDP vote share of 44 percent). While in the steel town of Dusiburg, the SPD still won 58 percent of the vote, the CDU vote grew by 5 percent to 34 percent. Dusiburg already had an unemployment rate of 13 percent, and potential job losses were the major issue concerning steelworkers. The government's extension of state financial help to short-term workers in April 1982 had greatly helped many workers in Duisburg:

> In Duisburg alone, 35,000 of the 55,000 steelworkers are on short time, but . . . they were guaranteed 68% of their lost wages for an extra year. Irmgard Karwatzki, a Christian Democratic legislator who is Duisburg's deputy Mayor, believes that this gesture demonstrated a concern for steelworkers that paid off. "They voted for us because we aroused hopes," said Miss Karwatzki. (*New York Times*, 27 March 1983 "Rhine Rebuff Embitters the Socialists")

Government support to steel increased dramatically after it won the March 1983 election. In June 1983, this government authorized $1.17 billion in government subsidies (half from the state governments to aid restructuring). In September 1983, the CDU government authorized a total of $29.1 billion worth of subsidies to industry, transport, agriculture, and housing.[28] In 1986, steel encountered problems again, largely because of the weak American dollar and

U.S. restrictions on steel imports. The government bailed out steel firms by waiving debt repayment. For example, Arbed-Saarstahl did not have to repay $335 million of the $850 million it owed. The CDU/FDP retained office in January 1987. After winning, the CDU/FDP government announced a further $333 million plan to aid restructuring (Bain 1992).

Restructuring involved heavy job losses. The government used redundancy payments and increased unemployment aid to cushion the adjustment process for workers. The German labor unions resisted the government's plans to shrink the size of the workforce. However, they were largely ineffective at opposing these layoffs or plant closures. The German industrial unions are centralized into confederations. The metalworkers union includes steel, autos, and electrical equipment. Collective bargaining takes place at the national level where the union bargains for all their employees. The metalworkers union is associated politically with the SPD. Although the union opposed the CDU's restructuring plans, it was largely ineffective. It was clear that the gains any one steel firm would achieve from delayed closure would impose costs, or closures, on other steel firms. The union was "immobilized" by parochial concerns of workers (Glissman and Weiss 1980). For example, the CDU/FDP government played off Thyssen workers against Krupp workers with the threat of restructuring plans (Bain 1992).

State governments were more effective at stalling government restructuring plans. They were able to win aid for their regions through budgetary legislation. More generally, state governments usually played an important role in the implementation of financial aid, since state funds were typically matched against federal subsidies. In the upper house, the Bundesrat, states allied to legislate aid for steelmaking regions. In many ways, the politics of the Bundesrat resemble that of the U.S. Senate; the Bundesrat is home to representatives of the 16 lander. Even in the lower house, the Bundestag, North-Rhine Westphalia, the largest lander, was able to put together a coalition to push through a Ruhr-aid Program (Glisman and Weiss 1980).[29] The steel dispute led to regional divisions at the union level and regional coalitions at the legislative level.

As in Belgium, the German steel industry was spatially dispersed but regionally concentrated. However, unlike the Belgian case, there were not extreme regional differences in the pattern of partisan support across regions. Although the SPD received their support from the heart of steel towns and the CDU drew its support from the surrounding environs, the large size of PR districts meant that both parties cared about the fate of steelworkers and the implications for regional recession.[30] However, the SPD made a costly political mistake. The CDU capitalized on the SPD's failure to aid steelworkers, and the SPD paid the price in terms of votes. In contrast, in the U.K. case discussed later, the Labour government announced the closure of a steel plant in the safe Labour district just two months before the 1979 election. Labour lost votes, but managed to hold on to the seat. In majoritarian systems, parties can ignore loyal voters but still win seats. If parties ignore their core supporters in a PR system, as the SPD discovered, they will lose both votes and seats.

Although the CDU were very successful at exploiting the SPD's failure to actively intervene in the steel industry, there were few regional redistributional consequences. This is as we might expect: votes in one region were as good as votes in another region, and the CDU had little reason to privilege the Saarland over the Ruhr, or vice versa. Although in practice the government did not differentiate between regions significantly, the potential to do so left the unions impotent to resist the government's restructuring plan.

SWEDEN

Unlike Germany, Belgium, and the United Kingdom, the Swedish government was not under the same external pressure from the EU to restructure its steel industry. Also, a third of the Swedish steel industry produced specialized steel, which was not as adversely affected by new international competition. However, the rest of Sweden's basic steel industry faced similar problems to that of West European firms: overcapacity and falling demand. Given the small economy, the survival of the Swedish steel industry depended on selling steel exports to world markets. The pressure of international competition forced the Swedish industry to restructure. Unlike the British government, however, who radically restructured then privatized their nationalized steel industry, the Swedish government combined closures and restructuring with a gradual program of nationalizations into the mid 1980s. This type of intervention was a significant change in policy. As in the case of Belgium, government change triggered these developments. Under a long period of social democratic rule, the industry had largely remained under private ownership. In 1976, the change in government from social democratic to a right-liberal coalition heralded a period of increasing government involvement in the industry.

Unlike the cases of Britain and Belgium, the restructuring of Swedish steel did not target some plants over others. In large part, there were no strong partisan differences across regional steel divides. However, as we would expect in a PR system, the government used industrial policy to favor its political supporters over those groups that traditionally supported the opposition. In particular, following the demise of the long-incumbent social democratic government, the new right-wing liberal coalition rewarded its traditional support base, small businesses, by buying out their ownerships in declining and loss-making industries at competitive prices. Without extreme regional differences in partisan support, such as those evident in Belgium, PR systems discourage favoring one region over another. Yet PR governments still use industrial policy to shore up their support base. This desire to reward loyal supporters spurred the radical shift in policy following a major change in government in 1976.

In 1976, the three largest steel producers in Sweden were Granges AB, Stora Kopparbergs Bergslaggs AB, and Norrbottens Jarnverk AB, the latter being a state-owned entity created by the Social Democrats in 1970. Steel production was located at three main sites: Lulea, Oxelosund, and Domnarvet. In 1978, these firms merged into a single company, the Swedish Steel Corporation (SSAB). The Swedish government owned 50 percent, Granges 25 percent, and Stora 25 percent of SSAB.[31] At the time, the government agreed to invest in reconstruction and capital project loans. In 1978, the Swedish parliament agreed to continue funds to support operating expenses in the SSAB but only if it promised not to lay off workers until 1983 (Bain 1992). In 1981, the government bought out Stora's 25 percent share in SSAB and promptly closed the blast furnace at Domnarvet (which had been owned by Stora). The government agreed to give over $800 million to aid restructuring. The cost to SSAB of guaranteeing no job layoffs from 1981 to 1983 was estimated at $64 million (Bain 1992). In 1982, however, the Social Democratic party returned to power. It pushed for greater restructuring of the industry. At the end of 1986, the government purchased Grange's 25 percent share in SSAB. After 1987, the electric steel mill in Domnarvet was closed.

Why the switch to public takeovers? Swedish politics had been characterized by decades of social democratic (SDA) rule. The SDA, however, lost the election in October 1976. A majority coalition was formed between the center party, the liberal party, and the conservative party (FP, CP, and MSP parties, respectively).[32] The leader of the center party (CP), Thorbjörn Fälldin, became prime minister. The FP/CU/MSP coalition collapsed in October 1978, leaving a liberal minority government (FP) with only 39 of the 349 seats in the Riksdag. After the 1979 election, the FP/CP/MUP re-formed a majority government, again led by the center party leader, Fälldin. Throughout these changes, Nils Asling of the center party (CP) remained minister for industry. The center party drew strong support from small businesses. It was notorious for funneling public money to help business mergers and/or buy out capital. This was known as the Asling doctrine. For example, in the same period, Asling bought large sections of the paper and pulp industry because these firms were owned by groups of small forest owners—traditional supporters of the center party.[33]

The unions in Sweden are extremely powerful, but they are not the reason that steel firms were nationalized and jobs protected. Unions in Sweden, like those in Germany, are highly centralized confederations. The metalworkers union is one of the largest members of the Trade Unions Confederation. The unions have strong ties to the socialist SDA (Bergman 2000). The Swedish unions initially put up a united front. Early on, different unions and workers from different plants lobbied hard for government support. However, as in the previous cases, the unions were reduced to inaction because of competition between site closures: would jobs be lost at Lulea or Domnarvet? Which sites would get new investment? In the end, bargaining over restructuring occurred at the local level. As Bain (1992, 106) comments, "Internal union problems developed between the three locations and between the unions at each site. The sites were in competition with each other over where the cutbacks would take place and where new technology would be installed."

In Sweden, a shift in the party composition of the government led to a drastic change in government policy toward the steel industry. Without extreme regional differences in partisan support, such as those evident in Belgium, the Swedish government did not favor one region over another (Bergman 2000). Yet the government still used industrial policy to shore up its support base. The mechanism for restructuring, buying out capital in the industry, reflects the center-right coalition's wish to protect business owners.

UNITED KINGDOM

In contrast to Belgium, Germany, and Sweden, the United Kingdom is a majoritarian system with many single-member electoral districts. Under such a system, the governing party cares about retaining a majority of seats, but overall vote share is relatively unimportant. As hypothesized earlier, the government rewards marginal districts. Since its fate depends upon retaining these key seats, the government is prepared to lose vote share in its safe districts or in opposition strongholds. These predictions are borne out in the British steel industry. For example, we shall see that a Labour government initiated the closure of a steel plant in the heart of a safe Labour constituency shortly before an election. In contrast, Thatcher's market-orientated Conservative government refused to close a loss-making plant in Scotland because doing so threatened marginal Conservative constituencies.

The steel industry in the United Kingdom was nationalized under the British Steel Corporation in 1950, privatized by the Conservatives in 1951, then renationalized by Labour in 1967. The radical turnabouts in steel policy are frequently used as the classic example of the effects of an adversarial system, where switching party governments leads to radical policy swings. The Conservative and Labour responses to the steel crisis in the 1970s and 1980s, however, were much the same—plants were closed under both governments (Dudley and Richardson 1990). Most steel plants were located in strong Labour constituencies; nonetheless, BSC's restructuring plans, involving numerous plant closures and layoffs, were initiated under a Labour government.

Despite its status as a nationalized industry, the British Steel corporation (BSC) had a great deal of autonomy in running the industry. The government's role was limited to oversight of the BSC and a say in how subsidies were used and loans were spent (Dudley and Richardson 1990). Following the crisis that hit British steel in the mid-1970s, successive governments poured billions of dollars into paying off BSC's debt and subsidizing production. Both the Conservative and Labour parties had similar policy responses to the steel crisis in this period. Under a Labour government in 1973, the Steel White Paper forecast the BSC's plans to restructure by closing smaller, older facilities—such as Corby, Consett, Ebbw Vale, and Shotton—and concentrating production in plants at five coastal sites: Ravenscraig, Teeside, Scunthorpe, Llanwern, and Port Talbert. In March 1979, while Labour was still in government, the BSC announced the closure of Corby. It was estimated that 73 percent of people in the town owed their livelihoods to the steelworks.[34] The Conservative government took power in May 1979, and plant closures and job layoffs continued under their tenure in office. For example, the closure of Normanby Park and Scunthorpe were announced in 1980 (Bain 1992). Finally, in 1988, the Conservative government announced plans to privatize what remained of British Steel.

Steelworkers in the United Kingdom are traditionally loyal supporters of the Labour party, and steel towns are typically located in safe Labour districts. Workers in towns such as Shotton, Corby, and Consett organized to protest plant closures. However, their protests fell on deaf ears. The unions were largely ineffective in preventing closures. There were eighteen unions representing steelworkers in the United Kingdom, although the biggest, the Iron and Steel Confederation, had 50 percent of workers (Bain 1992). Negotiations on layoffs and closures were done locally (e.g., the local settlement over the closure of the Clydebank works) (Bain 1992). The BSC and the government used the threat of closures to keep workers divided. For example, steelworkers in Wales refused to support workers at the Ravenscraig plant. If Ravenscraig were to be kept open, it would mean closures at coastal sites in Wales. The BSC and the government also kept the unions fragmented by threatening to close plants where workers were "uncooperative" with management. In 1980, there was a series of short strikes over potential closures;[35] overall, however, the government faced little effective resistance to BSC's plans to restructure the industry. Even the opposition Labour party refrained from criticism. Labour opposition to the closures was muted, in part because it had begun the plan for closures before it lost office (Hudson and Sadler 1989).

The one major anomaly in the government's "market-oriented" plan to restructure the steel industry was its protection of Ravenscraig in Scotland. A continued slump in demand for sheetmetal made it clear that one of the United Kingdom's three wide strip mills should be closed: Port Talbot or Llanwern, both in South Wales or Ravenscraig in North Lanarkshire. Although originally one of the coastal plants BSC had planned to keep open, Ravenscraig was now the most likely target for closure. The Welsh plants were closer to English consumers of steel and Port Talbot had a deep-water harbor that gave it direct access to imported raw materials. In contrast, Ravenscraig had major cost disadvantages; its port was not deep water and was located far from the plant. The collapse of the automobile and shipping industry in Scotland meant there were few Scottish consumers of steel.[36] In 1982, Ravenscraig's loses had grown to over $100 million a year (Bain 1992). In 1982, British Steel's chairman, Ian MacGregor, suggested the closure of the plant to the government. The Thatcher government, however, insisted that the plant be kept open. An all-party House of Commons select committee argued that keeping Ravenscraig open kept the BSC from being competitive internationally. Despite the government's repeated demands that the BSC stop losing money, the government would not back the BSC's decision to close Ravenscraig.[37] Instead, Ravenscraig was given a three-year reprieve. The economic costs of keeping it open were enormous. By 1983, its loses added up to 50 percent of the BSC's weekly deficit (Hudson and Sadler 1989).

Why was Ravenscraig different from Consett, Corby, or Normanby Park? In each case, regional forces joined to lobby against the closure of the steel plant (Hudson, Sadler, and Townsend 1992). The key difference between Corby and Ravenscraig was not the loudness of regional demands but the political geography of the two plants. Corby was located in a safe Labour region in England, while the closure of Ravenscraig would have affected the remaining Conservative districts in the industrial belt of Scotland. Ravenscraig is set outside of Glasgow, in the countryside of North Lanarkshire. The town of Motherwell is industrial and votes Labour; however, the steel plants are dispersed in a twelve-mile radius around Motherwell in the Dumfries and Strathclyde region. Closing the Ravenscraig steelworks would have had devastating effects on the surrounding community, where unemployment was already over 20 percent. Strathclyde Regional Council estimated that about fifteen thousand nonsteel jobs would be lost as a consequence of closing the plant.[38] Overall, the Dumfries and Strathclyde region was represented by eight Conservative and twenty-six Labour MPs. The nearby Conservative district of Ayr would have certainly felt the economic impact of Ravenscraig's closure. In 1979, Conservative George Younger held this seat with a eight thousand-vote majority (a roughly 15 percent vote differential between Younger and his nearest rival). Nonetheless, Ayr was not a regarded as a safe Conservative seat. Indeed, all Conservative seats in the West of Scotland were considered marginal by the party.[39] Younger held the position of secretary of state for Scotland in the Thatcher cabinet and reportedly threatened to resign over the closure of Ravenscraig (Dudley and Richardson 1990).[40] An election was due in the fall of 1982, and the Conservative government was "nervous" about its electoral fate in south-central Scotland (Dudley and Richardson 1990). Had Ravenscraig closed, the Conservatives would have almost certainly lost their few remaining seats in the heavily populated southwest of Scotland: "In the end it will be a political decision," says Mr Jimmy Milne, general secretary of the Scottish Trades Union Congress. "There are not many Tory seats left in Scotland, but there would be even fewer if the Government agreed to close Ravenscraig.(*Financial Times*, 9 July 1985)

The steel town of Corby in Northamptonshire, however, was less lucky in its political geography. Its plants were closed three years earlier. Plans for the plant's closure were initiated under the previous Labour Callaghan government (1976–79). Corby's plant was not in a marginal district, nor was it close to a cluster of marginal districts, nor was its Labour MP on the Callaghan cabinet.[41] Corby, like Motherwell, voted Labour. However, included in its Kettering constituency were 25,000 voters from predominantly rural areas. In October 1974, Labour won a majority of the votes in Kettering. This was not surprising, as Kettering was traditionally a safe Labour seat (Labour won 50 percent of the vote, the Tories 31 percent, and the Liberals 19.2%). The closure of Corby steel works was announced in March 1979, by a Labour government, only two months before the 1979 general election. At that election Labour still managed to hold onto the Kettering seat—although with a much reduced plurality: 45 percent of the vote to Labor and 42 percent to the Conservatives. The closure of the steelworks meant the loss of six thousand jobs in a town of fifty thousand. Approximately 70 percent of the people in the town owed their livelihood to the steelworks (*Hansard Debates*, 13 March 1989). Labour votes were lost, but the Labour candidate still held his seat.[42] Had this been a marginal district to begin with, the seat would probably have turned over to the Conservative party. Of course, had Corby been a marginal district to begin with, it is unlikely that Labour and the BSC would have announced its closure in the first place. Corby's strong support for the Labour government was the source of its downfall.

Unlike the closure of Corby, the closure of Ravenscraig was politically unacceptable to the party in government. Ravenscraig's closure threatened the few Conservative seats remaining in the west of Scotland. The *Financial Times* described the issue of Ravenscraig as "one of the most delicate political and economic issues of the decade."[43] In December 1982, the BSC and the government announced that Ravenscraig would have a three-year reprieve. This paid off. In the May 1983 general election, George Younger kept hold of his Ayr seat. In the country as a whole, the Conservatives won by a landslide (397 seats to Labour's 207).

In the end, however, Ravenscraig did close. In 1985, BSC announced the closure of the cold strip mill at Gartcosh. This was a major blow to the Ravenscraig plant; further processing of Ravenscraig steel would have to be done in England and Wales. The government waited until after the 1987 general election to announce that privatization would lead to the probable closure of Ravenscraig. The hot strip mill closed in 1990 and the final blast furnace was turned off in September 1992.

THE UNITED STATES

In contrast to the earlier cases, the United States is an example of a weak-party system. Both the United States and United Kingdom are majoritarian countries, but in the United States, policy is not dictated by the ruling party elites. Rather, policy is generated through coalition formation in the legislature. The major difference with the parliamentary systems of Europe is that these coalitions are not solely formed on the basis of party but change across issues and across time. While on one bill, two congressional legislators might find themselves in coalition; on the next issue, they may find themselves in opposing camps. Although with respect to industrial policy, many decisions are made at the presidential level, the president still requires congressional support for many of his actions. In the weak-party setting, institutional rules such as agenda-setting power and seniority are influential in determining which coalitions form.[44]

By 1982, it had become clear that the worldwide crisis in steel was not going to miss the U.S. steel industry. As in other countries, the industry faced problems of overcapacity and older, inefficient plants. The major problem in the U.S. case was the increase in import competition from the EU, Japan, and South Korea. The U.S. steel industry was fragmented into a number of private firms; among the largest were U.S. Steel Corporation, Bethlehem Steel, and LTV (Bain 1992). Most steel firms are located in the industrial belt in the Midwest and Northeast: Indiana, Michigan, Ohio, Illinois, and Pennsylvania. Sixty-two percent of all U.S. steel production occurs in these states (McGillivray and Schiller 1998). During this period, many firms did close down because of lack of profitability.[45] Job losses tended to occur in areas with already high unemployment. Restructuring brought some devastating plant closures; for example in Youngstown, the closure of the Youngstown Sheet and Tube corporation led to ten thousand jobs lost between 1977 and 1980—about 10 percent of the towns total population (Bain 1992).

The U.S. government did not play a direct role in the restructuring of U.S. steel firms. Unlike West European countries, the government did not provide subsidies, loans, or redundancy payments against the closure of plants, nor did it contribute to the cost of upgrading plants. Instead the government used voluntary export restraints, quotas, and trade law to assist ailing steel firms. In 1977, a "trigger" price mechanism was put in place to keep world imports from falling below a specified price level (K. Jones 1986). In 1982, a U.S.-EU steel pact was announced. The EU agreed to restrict exports and U.S. steel producers agreed to withdraw charges of dumping and unfair trade practices (Levine 1985). In 1984, President Reagan further protected U.S. steel producers by negotiating a wide-reaching set of voluntary export restrictions with steel producing nations.[46]

In part because the government did not selectively aid some plants over others, workers and capital from different firms and locations lobbied together to oppose imports of cheaper steel. Between 1973 and 1980, the United Steel Workers of America and the U.S. Steel Corporation had a formal agreement to lobby together against imports in return for guaranteed wage increases (Bain 1992). Unlike unions in other countries, the U.S. steel union played an important role the industry's fate. The United Steel Workers of America not only represented steelworkers; it also represented workers in mining iron ore, copper, aluminum, chemical facilities, and rubber industries. This alliance extended Steel's political clout across the U.S. According to one steel union lobbyist:

> Steelmaking is concentrated in the middle of the country, but we are in every congressional district. We have about 650,000 members nationwide. . . The geographical spread of our union . . . gave more support to the steel movement than from just the geographical concentration of just steel workers. We can get our members of other industries (*in our union*) to write their members (*representatives*) in support of our efforts.[47]

The political strength of the steel union therefore spread beyond the small number of states that have large steel producers. Common industrial linkages made coalition formation among these legislators less costly. Congressional legislation on steel assistance was always a credible threat.

In majoritarian systems with weak parties, such as the United States, legislators with agenda-setting power have a great deal of political clout. Steel had strong institutional proponents. In particular, it had a well-placed institutional advocate in Senator John Heinz (Republican-PA). Heinz sat on the important Finance Committee Subcommittee on Trade, an appointment that gave him a powerful institutional position from which he could try to secure trade benefits for the industry.

The steel industry lobbied hard for administered protection to try to counter the surge of imported steel coming from Europe and Japan. However, it also lobbied congressional members to try and pressurize the administration and Commerce Department to act on antidumping cases. In 1984, the steel industry filed a case under section 201 to get the International Trade Commission to rule that imports were causing injury to the U.S. steel industry. Senator Heinz introduced a bill, S.2380, to limit foreign sales to 15 percent of the domestic market (Pressman 1984). The threat that Senator Heinz, a Republican, would add the bill onto any trade legislation coming through the finance committee, and later on the Senate floor, kept the pressure on the administration to address the steel industry's complaints through other mechanisms. In June 1984, the ITC ruled that the steel industry had been injured by foreign imports and recommended quotas and tariffs on imported steel. In September, President Reagan rejected the ITC recommendations, but he did create a system of voluntary export agreements with steel-producing nations to limit the amount of steel imported into the United States to 20 percent of the U.S. market (Meny and Wright 1986). In part, Reagan wanted to undermine Senator Heinz's attempt to attach a more protectionist steel bill to a House trade bill under consideration in the Senate.

However, Presidential Reagan also wanted to curry favor with steelworkers in Pennsylvania, Indiana, and Michigan. In the upcoming 1984 presidential election, steel-producing states, with their large number of electoral votes and party-competitive races, were expected to play an important role.

An important element to the steel industry's sustained political strength, even in the face of declining employment, was the unity between capital and labor. One congressional staff member put it this way, "You look at Steel, (*lobbyist for steel company*) and (*lobbyist for steel company*) never broke ranks with (steel) labor on trade. They have stayed strong. Their employment has plummeted but they are still powerful."[48]

The steel industry used their regional concentration in the industrial Midwest and the geographic dispersion of metalworkers to pressure Congress and the administration into granting them voluntary export restrictions. Plants did close, but the U.S. government did not pick or choose which would survive; the world market did.

In summary, steel's dispersion around populous states meant that a large number of Congressmembers and the president wanted to help the ailing industry. These legislators formed a natural basis for putting together a coalition to protect steel. Unlike the pattern observed in Europe, legislators made no effort to assist some firms at the expense of others. Support for steel required a legislative majority; excluding certain firms only reduced supporters for any bill. Political change had little effect on the political clout of the steel lobby. Congressmembers from the Midwest and presidents looking for reelection needed the support of midwestern voters. Changes in the party composition of Congress or in the presidency did not alter the legislative incentives. Both new and old legislators sought the same kind of protection and brought the same votes to the coalition. However, political change is important in terms of agenda-setting. Without the seniority of Senator Heinz to direct the agenda, the latent support for U.S. steel might never have been realized.

CONCLUSION

While we might haggle over the details, from the 1970s onward the basic outlook for steel in most developed Western economies was the same. There was chronic overcapacity in the steel industry at a time when demand was shifting from bulk steel to specialized products, and competition from the developing world was growing. These economic pressures could not be ignored, and plant closures were inevitable. Yet, while economics dictated that some plants would close, industry geography and the electoral system determined which ones actually closed. In PR systems, the regional location of steel plants was important in determining the distribution of government assistance if strong differences in party support existed across regions. In strong- and weak-party majoritarian systems, what mattered was whether or not the steel plants were located in regions with a high or low concentration of politically important electoral districts. Although the case studies are purely illustrative, they appear to match the predictions in chapter 2. Using evidence from the steel industry, I have demonstrated that policy outcomes are contingent on both industry geography, the electoral rule, and party behavior. The interaction of these three factors affects both the derivation and aggregation of legislators' preferences on trade and industrial policy.

CHAPTER 5

Redistributive Politics and Industry Stock Prices

IN DECEMBER 1981, a Catholic-liberal coalition came to power in Belgium and replaced the previous center-socialist coalition government. As discussed at length in the previous chapter, this political change lead to a major restructuring of the Belgian steel industry. Southern Wallonian steel plants closed, while most northern Flemish plants were spared. This case demonstrates two major themes of this book: the role of industry geography and political institutions in trade and industrial policy and the difficultly of directly measuring government assistance to industries. Testing the argument quantitatively is tricky, both because trade and industrial policy is nontransparent, and because the complex interaction of industry geography and political institutions means that—depending on the real-world circumstances—an industry's geography may be positively correlated, negatively correlated, or completely uncorrelated with political outcomes. However, my argument does have testable implications for differences in the variance of political outcomes between different types of electoral systems. I exploit these testable implications by developing an alternative measure—dispersion between industry stock prices—to test my theory of how political change interacts with political institutions to determine industrial policy. I start by using examples from the steel industry to demonstrate the problems associated with direct measures of industrial assistance. I then derive an alternative dependent variable, a measure of stock-price dispersion between industries. In addition to providing an alternative measure, this dispersion-based dependent variable allows me to test additional implications of the theory.

As well as the familiar aggregate market indicators such as the DOW, NASDAQ, or FTSE100, many stock markets have industrial or sectoral indices. These indices, like the overall market measures, are composed of a weighted average of the stock prices of different firms. In the industrial indices, however, all the firms are from the particular industry. Figure 5.1 graphs monthly changes in the overall general market and the steel indices for Belgium for the early 1980s. It also graphs a measure of political change. I will return later to discuss the construction of this political change measure and for now simply note that the spike on the graph corresponds to the transition from the socialist-center to the catholic-liberal coalition in December 1981. The graphs show the monthly percentage change in the indices rather than the actual indices themselves. Hence, the spike in the steel index in December 1981 means that the steel index rose in value by nearly 20 percent from its value in November 1981. This

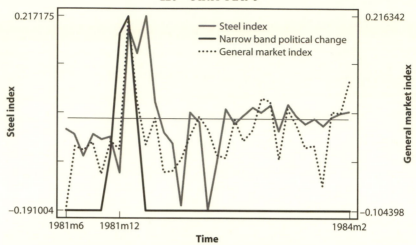

FIGURE 5.1. Price Change and Political Change in Belgium, 1981–1984. Political change with KSM smoother (0.05). In December 1981, the Christian People's party, the Christian Social Party, the Liberty and Progress, and the Francophone Liberal parties formed a new government.

indicates that, on average, investors in the Belgian stock market thought the value of steel industry was 20 percent more at the end of December 1981 than they had thought it was at the beginning of the month.

The purpose of this chapter is to associate changes in industrial indices with political change, with the causal mechanism being that political changes meant that new interests are represented and so policies change accordingly. Since industrial policy privileges some industries at the expense of others, changes in industrial policy alter the relative profitability, and hence the value, of firms. If a government that has tended to ignore the pharmaceutical industry is replaced by one that credibly promises to aid pharmaceuticals, then we should expect pharmaceutical stocks to rise relative to the rest of the market.[1]

My theory implies that the effect of political change on relative stock prices depends upon the moderating effect of the political system. Whether investors bid up the price of pharmaceutical stocks before, after, or at the point of political change depends upon the extent that political change is anticipated and policy change is predictable; both vary across electoral systems. In PR systems, negotiating a compromise among coalition partners can be a lengthy process, and the full extent of policy change is hard to foretell. In majoritarian systems, which are characterized by single-party government, there is less uncertainty about the timing or policy impact of political change. Hence, while it is expected that a change in government will alter the relative value of firms in both PR and majoritarian systems, the temporal impact of political change on stock market prices is expected to be more diffuse in PR systems and more immediate in majoritarian systems.

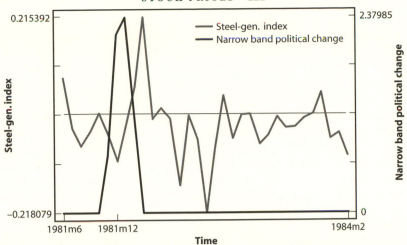

FIGURE 5.2. Differences in Price Change between the General Market and Steel Indices and Political Change in Belgium, 1981–1984. Changes are calulated as monthly percentage change in the price index. Political change with KSM smoother (0.05). See the appendix to chapter 5 for definition. In December 1981, the Christian People's party and the Christian Social party switched coalition partners, forming a new government with the Liberty and Progress and the Francophone Liberal parties. The Flemish and Francophone Scioalist left the governing coalition.

These predictions are tested using general stock indices and industry subindices for fourteen industrialized countries from 1973 to 1996. The evidence shows that political changes affect the relative value of different industries' stock across all political systems. Yet there are important differences. As predicted, the full response of stock prices to political change is dispersed over a longer time period in PR than in majoritarian systems. Further, only in majoritarian systems do economic changes have a significant effect on the dispersion of price changes between various industries. While majoritarian systems are more directly responsive to political and economic change, PR systems overall experience greater variability of price changes. Rather than remain abstract about the goals and methods of this chapter, I return to the Belgian case.

When the Catholic-liberal coalition swept into power in December 1981, the stock market responded favorably. Not only did the steel index jump nearly 20 percent, but so also did the overall market index (see figure 5.1). Why the market expressed more confidence in the catholic-liberal coalition relative to its socialist predecessor is not the topic of this chapter. Instead, I focus on the market's evaluation of steel relative to the rest of the market. Figure 5.2 shows the percentage price change in the steel index minus the percentage price change relative to the overall market index. As can be seen from figure 5.2, controlling for overall market movement, in June 1982, the steel industry loses a few percent relative to the rest of the market. Yet four months earlier, in February 1982, steel outperforms the rest of the market by 20 percent. This jump corresponds with the government's announcement of its restructuring of the steel industry.

Until December 1981, postwar coalition governments in Belgium had been dominated by the two largest parties, the Francophone Socialists and the Flemish Catholics. It was a surprise when the Francophone Socialists were shut out of coalition government.[2] Once in office, the Catholic-liberal government announced its intention to remove the subsidies to the steel industry. Given this announced removal of aid, the market's positive evaluation appears at first counterintuitive. If the government is removing aid and hence reducing the profitability of the industry, we would expect stock prices to fall. Of course, with a detailed knowledge of the Belgian case, this change is both explainable and predictable. It is worth taking a moment to explore the disparity between what we would expect at a first glance and what a detailed examination reveals, since it illustrates the difficulty of systematically measuring the winners and losers of government policy. As I examined in chapter 4, the Belgian government's steel policy had extreme regional implications. The restructuring of the industry meant large job losses for Cockerill-Sambre in Wallonia. In contrast, it secured the future prosperity of the firm Arbed, which had a large plant in the Flemish town of Sidmar. The Belgian steel index is composed primarily of Flemish firms. Hence the graphs in figures 5.1 and 5.2 show only the up side for the steel industry in the North, and not the losses in the South. As can be seen, the announcement of restructuring increased the value of firms listed in the Belgian steel index by about 20 percent relative to the rest of the market. The overall losses for the southern firms are missed. As a general lesson, this suggests that while it is easy to assess the winners and losers in a case-study setting, in large statistical studies assessing winners and losers is extremely hard. For example, had I not known the composition of the Belgian steel index, the evidence would contradict the idea that incoming governments in PR systems shift benefits toward their supporters.

The Belgian case illustrates the critical points behind the analysis in this chapter. Stock markets provide a mechanism through which to measure how government policy privileges one industry relative to another. Individual investors, on a case-by-case basis, estimate the impact of government policy. Markets then aggregate this data. Observing how the market responds, for example, to the imposition of a tariff is a useful alternative method of assessing the value of the protection compared to estimating the effective tariff and elasticity for the protected good. Stock prices capture the perceived costs and benefits of government policy change whatever the policy instrument: be it tax, regulatory, monetary, trade, or industrial policy. Market investors have incentives to include all the idiosyncrasies that relate to the particular industry. However well-intentioned researchers are, they cannot possibly include this detail across a wide range of industries. This breadth is the advantage of using stock market data and explains the recent shift toward examining political events through market data.[3] Unfortunately, as a practical matter it is impossible to assign different indices to groups who support different parties. I have anecdotal evidence that the utility industry and the brewers support the Conservatives in the United Kingdom,[4] and that the textile industry supports the CDU in Germany, but I do not have data on government-industry ties that covers a wide range of industries. Therefore using market indices as a direct measure of governments' attempts to privilege one industry relative to another is not feasible. In response, I measure dispersion between industry indices.

When political change leads to policy change, some industries win and some lose. Although without the detailed knowledge discussed above it often impossible to say which industries will win and which will lose, policy changes shift the relative valuation of firms. When policy change occurs, stock prices diverge. To illustrate, consider the following simple example for a multiparty PR system. Suppose there are three parties: A, B, and C. In addition, for simplicity, suppose that the economy is composed of only three industries: steel, textiles, and farming. Suppose that the steelworkers represent the core supporters of party A. Similarly, suppose the parties B and C typically draw their supporter from textile- and farmworkers, respectively. Suppose parties B and C are from an incumbent multiparty government but that this coalition breaks up, perhaps as the result of an election, and a new coalition government forms between parties A and C.

As discussed in the theory chapter (chapter 2), the new government is likely to shift policies. Since neither of the new incumbents supports textiles, assistance for that industry is likely to decline; in contrast, the inclusion of party A in the government is likely to increase the government's responsiveness to calls for assistance from the steel industry. As such, firms in the steel industry are likely to become more profitable and, hence, valuable, while the value of textile-related industries declines. To make the calculations simple, suppose that the value of assistance is 15 percent. Upon the political change, we should expect textile-related stocks to decline by 15 percent and steel stocks to increase by 15 percent. Although the aggregate market might remain unchanged, on average, prices between industries have dispersed by 10 percent (($|15\%|$ + $|-15\%| + 0\%$)/3). In this particular example, examining dispersion throws away the evidence about which industries were rewarded; however, in general we do not know this information. Yet even when we do not know which sectors or industries would be privileged by the new government, changes in government policy should increase dispersion as some industries win and some industries lose. The dependent variable "price dispersion"[5] measures the extent to which changing industry prices diverge from the market average. It does not measure prices levels but rather the variance of price changes. It is constructed by summing across industrial groups the extent to which the percentage change in price for each industry differs from that of the market average.

The basis of the analysis in this chapter is as follows. Since changes in government policy privilege some industries at the expense of others, dispersion between industry stock prices serves as a proxy by which to measure changes in trade and industrial policy. Since my theory suggests that the electoral system interacts with political changes to generate changes in policy, I test how political change affects changes in the dispersion among industry indices in different political systems. The chapter proceeds as follows. First, I briefly revisit the theory to derive how political change influences the dispersion of stock prices. Second, I discuss my data, and I formally define my measure of dispersion, placing it in the context of alternative measures. A disadvantage of the measure "price dispersion" is that it is an indirect measure of the amount of policy change. This creates several measurement issues, perhaps the most serious of which is the extent to which price dispersion precedes or trails political change. The timing of stock market response and other specification issues are discussed here. Third, I describe the measure of political change and how to incorporate the possibility of dispersion either preceding or trailing political change. Fourth, I present my analyses of monthly stock data for fourteen industrial democracies between 1973 and 1996.

THEORY REVISITED

The electoral system and the strength of parties influence both the policy preferences of parties in government and how these preferences are aggregated. These arguments were laid out in full in chapter 2, so here I reiterate my logic only to the extent necessary to sensibly discuss the issue of market responses. In proportional representation systems, the low cost of party entry means that parties focus their policy objectives on rewarding their core supporters. Since in PR systems it is rare for a single party to obtain a legislative majority, implementing policy requires cooperation between parties. As such, the final policy is likely to contain some aspects of the things that each of the coalition ruling parties want, as well as, perhaps, aspects of policies that potential veto players want. The desires of out-of-government veto players might be especially important for minority coalitions that require the support of nongovernment parties to pass their policies in the legislature. As a result, trade and industrial policy in PR systems represents a compromise of the policy goals of numerous actors. The essential factor for the tests in this chapter is that when the government changes, industrial policy shifts, becoming a compromise of things that the new parties in government want.

Tsebelis (1995, 1999, 2002) argues that veto players in PR systems make it difficult for coalition partners to reach compromise agreements. One implication of his theory is that policy stability characterizes political change in PR systems. Yet such arguments have typically been constructed in the context of ideological issues (Bawn 1999). Parties have relatively fixed ideological positions on a wide range of issues. The mass membership of the party can prevent the parliamentary party, and particularly the leader, from altering the party's ideological stance. This can make it very difficult for party leaders to negotiate a compromise in coalition government. Leaders have far more control over policy issues that are not in the core ideology of the party.[6] Trade and industrial policy is such an issue; it tends not to have an ideological component. While some parties tend to be more protectionist or free-trade-oriented than others, redistributive trade and industrial policy is of a far higher dimensionality than the standard right-left ideological issue. It can also be distributed differentially across voters and across geographically specific electoral districts. As such, it is much easier to reach agreement, and indeed, such policies can even be used as transferable benefits to buy off veto players. Policy will be redistributed toward the industrial supporters of new coalition partners and away from the industrial supporters of old coalition partners. I expect that redistributive industrial policy will change in response to political change in PR systems. However, bargaining delays—such as buying off veto players— diffuses the impact of political change on market prices. Market prices adjust as soon as policy change is anticipated. However, it is difficult for investors to predict when the package of policy changes will be announced and what the exact package of policy compromises will be.

Counter to much of the extant literature, which typically addresses ideological policy issues, this theory suggests that governments in strong-party majoritarian systems want to privilege marginal districts. Majoritarian systems are characterized by two-party competition and majority governments. The party that captures the marginal (party competitive) seats wins the election. Given these incentives, whichever party is in government wants to garner support in marginal districts. As a result, the industrial policy of both parties is targeted toward privileging the same districts. However, this need not imply that political change has no effect on industrial policy. Although parties want to enrich the same districts, they might choose different policy instruments or firms or both through which to do so. Furthermore, elections, typically the only time governments are replaced in majoritarian systems, provide evidence through which parties assess which districts are likely to be the battleground marginals for the next election. Given these factors, policy change is likely to accompany political change, although it is likely to be smaller in magnitude since to a large extent the target districts remain unchanged whichever party is in office. Unlike PR systems where policy change requires negotiation between coalition members as well as any nongovernment veto players, the majority status of most governments in majoritarian systems means that party elites can implement policy with minimal delay. The bargaining difficulties and veto-player arguments prevalent in coalition dynamics are overcome. The arguments in chapter 2 suggest that weak-party majoritarian systems are also likely to shift policy in response to political change.

The theory predicts that in both majoritarian and PR systems, political change will lead to the redistribution of trade and industrial policy. However, in PR systems, bargaining delays and the need to buy off veto players diffuses the temporal impact of political change.

The electoral system also moderates government response to economic change. In majoritarian systems, party elites can implement policy choices without the lengthy interparty negotiations required in PR systems. As such, as economic conditions change, governments in majoritarian systems can more directly and rapidly alter policy. This prompt reaction from the government is rapidly incorporated by the market. Governments in PR systems are less likely to respond decisively to economic shocks: correspondingly, we should expect the market to respond less decisively.

The theory predicts how political and economic change influences shifts in redistributional trade and industrial policies. Unfortunately, my measure of stock-price dispersion does not directly measure policy change, and is instead only a proxy for it. This creates several measurement issues, perhaps the most serious of which is the relationship between policy change and stock-market response. It is to this issue that I next turn.

THE TIMING OF STOCK MARKET REACTIONS

When government policies privilege an industry, then firms in that industry become more profitable. This rise in profitability increases demand for the stock of these firms, which in turn drives their stock price higher. Unfortunately, it is not always certain when such price shifts will occur. Implementation of policies often lags months, even years, behind political change, suggesting that market adjustment should follow political change. However, efficient market theory argues that as soon as a future change in profitability is anticipated, this information is immediately incorporated into the price. Therefore, the timing of the market response to political change depends upon the extent to which political change is anticipated and policy change is predictable.

Public opinion surveys provide markets with information about who is expected to win elections. To this extent, markets should anticipate political change before the election result is announced. It is unlikely, however, that political change is fully anticipated by rational investors and incorporated into prices much in advance of a change in government. Unless political change is known with certainty, there is always a difference between the realized outcome and this anticipation. Sudden scandals, a downturn in the economy, or a policy failure can rapidly change a party's fortunes. In addition, the timing of elections is at the discretion of the incumbent government in many countries in the study

(Smith 1996, 2004). Hence the election date often remains unknown until about a month beforehand. This discretion over the timing of elections reduces the ability of the market to anticipate political change. The situation is further complicated in PR systems, since the formation of governments is less dependent on new elections and since election results can result in numerous possibilities for coalitions. Taken together, these factors suggest that markets are unlikely to preempt political change by more than a few months.

Yet even once political change is known, the full extent of policy change is often still uncertain. As argued above, although all parties in majoritarian systems want to target marginal districts, election results can change parties' perceptions of which districts are marginal. On the whole, I expect the market to respond much more decisively to political change in majoritarian systems, since coalition dynamics and the need to buy off veto players rarely complicate the formation of redistributive policy. In PR systems, not only is political change hard to predict; redistributive policy is determined by bargains. Which package of policies the government chooses to appease the various coalition members and to buy off veto players could vary. Negotiating a compromise among coalition partners can be a lengthy process, and the full extent of policy change is hard to foretell. The full announcement of ministerial positions in PR countries is made after the election date (Schofield and Laver 1985). In majoritarian systems, which are characterized by single-party government, there is less uncertainty about the policy impact of political change. In the PR case, the full extent of political change is often revealed incrementally, in the days and months following the change in party government. Hence the impact of political change on stock market prices is expected to lag behind political change in some cases and precede it in others. The timing of the effect is expected to be more immediate in majoritarian than in PR systems.

Investors are assumed to be fully rational; as such, we might expect them to design diversification strategies to hedge against political risk. While hedging implies that investors can avoid many of the risks, it does not imply that stock prices are immune to political change. One might be tempted to argue that if it rains today, investors will not rush out and buy stocks in umbrellas because it will probably be sunny tomorrow. In the same way, if the left wins tomorrow, we should not expect investors to rush out to buy stocks in industries that support the left, because the right will probably get into office at the next election. Investors might expect that in the long run, 50 percent of the time a left-wing government will be in power, while the other 50 percent of the time the party-in-government will be the right wing. Investors diversify to hedge against this. If this argument holds for all investors, stock prices will not be expected to change with a change in government (even a surprise change). However, even if in the long run investor profits are unaffected by government policy (which is certainly not the case in irreversible policies such as restructuring declining industries), many investors care about profits today more than profits tomorrow. Hence, despite the fact that investors can design diversification strategies to hedge against political risk, we should still expect stock prices to react to a change in government. The following example illustrates this argument.

Suppose a new government forms, but in order to implement certain aspects of its legislative agenda, it needs the support of additional legislators. In the context of veto-player arguments, we might suppose that the government needs to buy off some members of particular groups. To be more concrete, suppose that the new government needs to buy off any one of three legislators (or other groups), and that each of these legislators has three firms or industries that she would like privileged. To keep the example simple, suppose the government needs to give one of the three legislators $9 worth of transfers to gain her support. We might think of this example in terms of a lucrative government procurement to an industry in his or her district. While rational expectations indicate that a transfer of $9 will occur to one of the nine potential recipients, the government could pick any of one of the three legislators and reward any one of the three associated firms/industries.[7] Hence in expectation the valuation of each of these nine firms should increase by $1 in anticipation of the bargaining outcome, and upon the revelation of the legislative bargain, the valuation of the chosen firm should jump up by $8, while those of the other eight firms should fall by $1 to their previous level. No investor need lose money from the revelation of the bargaining outcome, since it is easy to hedge against. Despite rational expectations, price changes lag behind political change as well as precede it.

The advantage of using stock prices as a measure of expected change in government policy is that many industrialized countries have stock markets. However, stock markets differ considerably in their size across the sample of countries. In 1989, Italy had just over two hundred domestic companies listed on its stock exchange, while the UK had over two thousand. Italians still prefer investing in bonds to equities.[8] In Germany and France, industries tend to seek capital from banks rather than from shareholders. Ranked in terms of their market capitalization as percentage of GDP, the biggest stock markets are the United States, the United Kingdom, Belgium, the Netherlands, and Germany. Among the smallest are Italy, Austria, and Denmark.[9] If the secondary market lists only a small proportion of domestic companies, it is unlikely that the stock market will have a large reaction to government change. As such, we should expect that the findings will be strongest in those stock markets with the largest market capitalization. On the other hand, less-developed stock markets tend to be more volatile. Markets with low market capitalization could well exhibit larger sector-specific shifts in prices relative to the average. The empirical analysis includes a control for the size of the stock market in relation to the GDP, although the inclusion or exclusion of this control produces no substantive changes in the results.

Another potential problem with using stock-market data is globalization. Over time, there have been changes in the operation of these stock markets.[10] Before the 1980s, the international flow of capital was severely constrained and most European markets were very small. Stock markets are becoming increasingly global and interconnected, and there is a danger that price shifts are correlated across countries, driven by a few internationally felt shocks. I correct for cross-sectional correlation and control for the overall market volatility in the empirical analysis. More generally, as stock markets grow stronger, more domestic industries are going public and listing on their national exchanges. The number of domestic industries listed on European stock markets has grown considerably since the 1980s. If stock markets list predominantly domestic companies, then stock prices should react to domestic policy changes, whether investors are local or international.

MARKET DATA AND PRICE DISPERSION

Fourteen industrialized countries are grouped into majoritarian and PR: Australia, Canada, France, the United Kingdom, and the United States being majoritarian; Austria, Belgium, Denmark, Germany,[11] Italy, the Netherlands, Norway, Sweden, and Switzerland being PR.[12] Each time series is of similar length, monthly data from 1973 through 1996. The general market indices, composite industry indices and industry subindices are provided by Datastream.[13] The general price index for each country is Datastream's total market index, available for each country from 1973 to 1996. The industry subindices list the weighted average movement in price across firms within each industry category. Datastream's indices are calculated similarly across countries and are scaled to have the same starting values. The number of industry subindices varies by country, and the number of firms in each subindex varies by country.

THE DEPENDENT VARIABLE

Policy change affects stocks prices; some industries become more advantaged and others are hurt. So above and beyond existing market variance, policy changes increase the price dispersion between the industries within a country.

An industry subindex measures a weighted average of stock prices for firms within a specific industry.[14] Redistributive policy is not the only variable that affects the price of industry subindices. Changes in world prices, interest-rate movements, technology shocks, and change in the GDP, for example, all affect industry share prices. These tend, however, to have similar effects on the general index as they do on the industry indices (Campbell, Lo, and MacKinlay 1997).[15] One way of controlling for these effects is to subtract movements in the general stock index from those in the industry index. This also controls for general shifts in the price of stocks—which may be tied to investors' expectations about government competency or ideology rather than redistributive policy.

The following example illustrates the construction of the dependent variable, price dispersion, and how it differs from the more commonly used measurement price level. Suppose that a stock market lists only two industries, A and B. Consider two scenarios. First, suppose that government redistributive policy remains stable. While the market might experience shifts, perhaps in response to economic conditions or confidence in the government, the effects are largely similar for both industries. For instance, both firms might experience a 10 percent growth in their value. Alternatively, government policy might change to favor one industry, perhaps in response to a political change. In this second scenario, one industry experiences a relative gain and the other experiences a relative loss. For example, one might grow by 20 percent, while the other remains constant. The average market movement is the same 10 percent as in the first scenario, but unlike the first case, in which there was zero price dispersion, here the average dispersion in prices from the market average is 10 percent. The dependent variable measures the extent to which prices diverge between industries. It does not measure levels, but rather variance. This second-order statistic—price dispersion—serves as a proxy for redistributional policy change.

I define price dispersion as follows:[16] consider country n, where $\Delta base_t$ is the percentage change in the price of the general market index in month t, and ΔS^t_i is the percentage change in the price for the industry index i in month t. If there are m industry subindices for country n, then the level of dispersion for country n at time t is:

$$Dispersion_{n,t} = \sum_{i=1}^{m} |\Delta S^t_i - \Delta base_t| / m.$$

This measure is similar to others proposed in the literature (Loungani, Rush, and Tave 1990; Lilien 1982; Zagorsky 1994). These studies, based on the United States only, used the squared difference between individual stock prices and the market average, rather than the absolute difference used here. A second difference is that my measure does not weight the industry index by market capitalization. On the latter issue, my reasoning was based on the need to assess relative winners and losers rather than to measure the value of transfers. Using the squared differences as proposed by these alternative measures produces similar results.[17]

Campbell and Lettau (1999) examine differing sources of variance in stock prices. In addition to the industry-level variance that I consider, they also estimate market and firm level volatility. They find strong correlations between all three sources of volatility. Their study examines U.S. markets only. Unfortunately, the data required for their measures is unavailable for all the countries in my study. Their measures of volatility, at all levels, are susceptible to rapid price shocks, such as the one associated with the 1987 market crash. Since markets around the world are highly correlated, this suggests variation in industry price-level dispersion could be driven by a few internationally felt shocks. Fortunately, my measure of dispersion controls for change in the average level of prices and so is less dominated by a few market collapses. However, Campbell and Lettau's results suggest some important control variables. I include a measure of overall market volatility, which I calculate as the squared change in price levels over the previous month (i.e., $[\Delta \text{base index}_t]^2$. I also include a lagged dependent variable, which reduces autocorrelation. The inclusion of these two controls markedly improves the fit of the model, yet their inclusion leaves both the substantive and statistical significance of the political change variables unaltered.

Campbell and Lettau's results also suggest that market, industry, and firm level measures of volatility tend to move in similar patterns and are all susceptible to large shifts in prices. Table 5.2 shows the correlation between dispersion measures across markets. While related, dispersion is much less correlated across markets than are price levels. While this mitigates the problem of the domestic stock market reacting to international changes, it does not eliminate the problem. The larger, more developed markets show greater correlation. For robustness, I perform a series of tests to check that these correlations between markets are not responsible for the results. First, I use a GLS model and allow for contemporaneous correlation across countries in the error structure. Unfortunately, this technique requires completely rectangular data and so necessitates dropping several countries for whom the time series is shorter. Second, since the United States is the largest and most influential market, I examine whether dispersion in the U.S. accounts for the dispersion within other markets. To do so, I include U.S. dispersion as a right-hand-side variable for the other countries. In neither of these robustness tests do the results alter significantly.

MEASURING POLITICAL CHANGE

The theoretically important predictor is change in government. However, operationalizing change in government is a nontrivial task. Majoritarian systems are characterized by large, infrequent government changes. In majoritarian countries, political turnover is usually triggered by elections. In contrast, the coalition governments endemic in PR systems often break up and re-form between elections. As such, PR systems typically have more frequent, incremental changes in government composition. Rather than use a dichotomous measure of government change,[18] I develop a continuous measure: the absolute change in the distribution of parliamentary seats among government parties.[19] The formula for this variable is

$$\sum_{k=1}^{m} \left| (s_{k,t} \times g_{k,t}) - (s_{k,t-1} \times g_{k,t-1}) \right|$$

Where $k = 1, \ldots m$, represents each of the parties holding seats, $S_{k,t}$ is party k's seat share in month t, and $g_{k,t}$ is an indicator variable that takes value one if party k is in government is in month t, and takes value zero otherwise.[20] This variable measures political change whether it occurs as a result of elections or as a result of a change in coalition partners.

A couple of examples illustrate the construction of the political-change variable. In a majoritarian system, suppose that party A is in government with 52 percent of parliamentary seats and an election is held. If subsequently party B takes over the government with 52 percent of the parliamentary seats, the change is calculated as 104 percent. Similarly, in a PR system, suppose that parties A and B are in coalition with 30 percent and 25 percent of the seats, respectively. Following an election, parties A and C form a coalition with 30 percent and 30 percent of the seats. In the variable "political change" this will be measured as 55 percent. If, instead of the first coalition, parties B and C had formed a government with 25 percent and 30 percent of parliamentary seats respectively, this would have registered as 60 percent on the change scale. Obviously, in both PR and in majoritarian systems, parties that win seats but do not join the government do not affect this variable. These examples reveal that there will be differences in the magnitude of variances between the two systems. In majoritarian governments, larger, less-frequent changes in government occur compared to those found in PR systems.

As discussed earlier while political change nominally takes place in a single period, the market reaction sometimes precedes political change and at other times it lags behind. Representing political change as a single spike is inappropriate. Furthermore, from a practical viewpoint, attempting to explain monthly changes in stock price dispersion with a variable that is, on average, only nonzero every few years is unlikely to be successful. Such an approach could only hope to explain the deviation from the average price dispersion in the particular month of the political change. Hence for theoretical and practical reasons, it is necessary to look for the market's reaction in the months around, and not just on, the month of the election.

Perhaps the most straightforward fix is to include numerous lag and lead measures of political change. I include lags and leads of the political-change variable for the six months preceding and following the actual political change. While these lags and leads provide one method to assess the time relation between political change and price dispersion, the large number of variables introduced makes observation of the underlying pattern difficult. For this reason, I

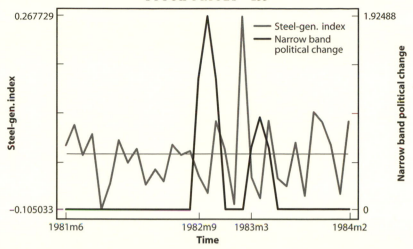

FIGURE 5.3. Differences in Price Change between the General Market and Steel Indices and Narrow-Band Political Change in Germany, 1981–1984. Changes are calcualted as monthly percentage change in the price index. Political change with KSM smoother (0.05). See appendix 5.1 for definition and discussion in text. In September 1982, the Christian Democratic Union/Christian Social Union (CDU) and Free Democrats (FDP) formed a government when the Social Democrats (SPD)/FDP coalition dissolved. Six months later, in March 1983, the CDU/FDP were reelected to government.

simply report the analysis of the lags and leads variables as a final test and instead use a series of smoothers to spread the effect of political change over a number of months. In particular, I use locally weighted scatterplot smoothing (KSM in STATA version 6). The political-change variable is weighted so that the central point gets the largest weight and points farther away—based on the specified bandwidth—receive less. The greater the bandwidth, the greater the smoothing. I chose two bandwidths, 0.05 and 0.15 (narrow and broad). The results are robust to different choices of narrow and broad bandwidths.[21]

The best way to observe the impact of this smoothing is graphically. In figures 5.3 and 5.4, the vertical axis measures the difference between the change in German steel and the change in the German general market index from 1981 to 1984. It also measures the level of political change that occurred in September 1982 and March 1983 in Germany. The Christian Democratic party (CDU) and the Free Democratic party (FDP) took over government in September 1982, when a no-confidence vote expelled the Social Democratic party and its coalition partner, the FDP, from office. Six months later, in March 1983, Kohl called an early election. The CDU/FDP were reelected. Moreover, the CDU had increased its policy-making power within the CDU/FDP coali-

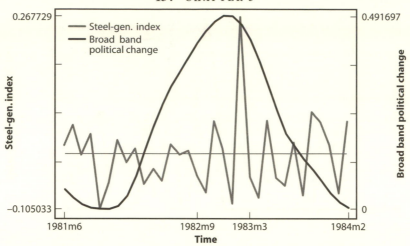

FIGURE 5.4. Difference in Price Change between the General Market and Steel Indices and Broad-Band Political Change in Germany, 1981–1984. Changes are calculated as monthy prcentage change in the price index. Political change with KSM smoother (bandwidth 0.15). In September 1982, the Christian Democratic Union/Christian Social Union (CDU) and Free Demcrats (FDP) formed a government. The Social Democrats (SDP) left office. Six months later, in March 1983, the CDU/FDP were reelected to government.

tion (there was a significant rise in votes for the CDU, but a drop in votes for the FDP). Despite the CDU's right-wing ideology, regional incentives caused them to target industrial policy toward the steel industry, as was discussed in chapter 4. We should expect such political changes to influence steel stock prices. However, the question remains as to when this should occur. The value of the steel index fell heavily in 1981 and continued to fall until the government coalition changed in 1982. Steel stocks strongly outpaced the general market index after the 1982 shift in government, but before the 1983 election, solidifying the CDU vote. Figure 5.3 shows the political-change variable with narrow-bandwidth smoothing. In contrast, figure 5.4 shows the political-change variable with broad-bandwidth smoothing.

As argued previously, bargaining difficulties within coalitions in PR systems diffuse the impact of political change. The new German government did not immediately formulate or implement its restructuring plan for the steel industry. If the political-change variable has a narrow bandwidth, as shown in figure 5.3, the market's reaction to government restructuring in the steel industry is missed. However, when political change has a broader bandwidth, the impact of Germany's steel restructuring plan is captured under the political-change variable (see figure 5.4).

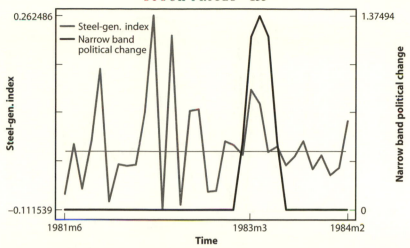

FIGURE 5.5. Difference in Price Change between the General Market and Steel Indices and Narrow-Band Political Change in Australia, 1981–1984. Changes are calculated as monthly percentage change in the price index. Political change with KSM smoother (bandwidth 0.05). See appendix 5.1 for definition and discussion in text. In March 1983, the Labour Party took over from the Liberal/National Country government.

Figures 5.5 and 5.6 show how steel prices reacted to a switch in government in a majoritarian system. In March 1983, the left-wing Labour party entered office in Australia. At the time, the steel industry was concentrated in several important marginal districts in Australia (McGillivray and Smith 1997). We should expect that steel prices rose in the expectation that the Labour government would redistribute in favor of the steel industry. There was a small shift in the steel index. It increased 1 percent above the general market index in the month prior to the election of the Labour government. In the Australian case, the narrow bandwidth on political change (fig. 5.5) captures the reaction of the market. The broader bandwidth (fig. 5.6) obscures the effect. The results from the quantitative empirical analysis back the German and Australian examples; narrower bandwidth captures the stock market reaction to political change better in majoritarian systems, and broader bandwidth better captures the effect of political change in PR systems.

MODEL SPECIFICATION

The pooled data for the fourteen countries is comprised of approximately 3,400 country-month observations. There are a number of methodological problems linked to cross-sectional, time-series analysis (Beck 2001; Beck and Katz

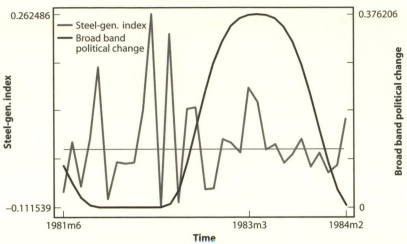

FIGURE 5.6. Price change between the General Market and Steel Indices and Broad-Band Political Change in Australia, 1981–1984. Changes are calculated as monthly percentage change in the price index. Political change with KSM smoother (bandwidth 0.15). See appendix 5.1 for definition and discussion in text. In March 1983, the Labour Party took over from the Liberal/National Country government.

1995; Green, Kim, and Yoon 2001). In response, methodologists have proposed numerous techniques, such as fixed-effect panel models, random-effect models, and GLS techniques. Although tests exist to determine which techniques are appropriate, as a practical matter which model is the most appropriate is often hard to discern. For example, the Hausman test distinguishes between fixed- and random-effect models based upon whether the assumption of zero correlation between the country-specific intercepts and the covariates can be justified. My data typically rejects the null hypothesis, suggesting random effects are inappropriate. Yet this is not true for every specification. While these issues of appropriate technique are important, I am spared the problem of hanging my results on the choice of technique. Both the substantive and statistical significant of my results are robust to the analysis used.[22] Given the robustness of the results, I report only a limited number of model specifications in table 5.1. The results for a sample of alternative model specifications are available in appendix 5.1, as is the list of the variable means, the standard deviations, and the definitions.

In general the results in table 5.1 support the predicted pattern. I start by considering the effect of political change. In model 1, I do not distinguish between electoral systems, and I treat political change as a single unsmoothed data point ("political change"). The positive and significant coefficient indi-

TABLE 5.1
Alternative Generalized Least Squares and Fixed Effects Analyses of the Effects of Political
and Economic Change on the Level of Price Dispersion in Industry Subindices
in Fourteen Countries, 1973–1996

Variables	Model 1 GLS	Model 2 GLS	Model 3 Fixed Effects	Model 4 GLS
Political change (unsmoothed)	.024* (.011)	—	—	—
Political change in majoritarian systems (narrow bandwidth, .05)	—	.124* (.066)	.132 (.088)	.144* (.072)
Political change in majoritarian systems (broad bandwidth, .15)	—	−.025 (.143)	−.114 (.198)	−.136 (.163)
Political change in PR systems (narrow bandwidth .05)	—	−.045 (.064)	−.040 (.072)	−.046 (.064)
Political change in PR systems (broad bandwidth, .15)	—	.484*** (.122)	.483** (.140)	.433** (.121)
PR dummy	—	.096** (.032)	—	.036 (.041)
Interest rate	.005* (.002)	—	—	—
Interest rate majoritarian	—	.010** (.002)	.008* (.003)	.006* (.003)
Interest rate × PR	—	.002 (.002)	.004 (.003)	−.003 (.002)
Inflation rate	.003 (.002)	—	—	—
Inflation × majoritarian	—	.007* (.003)	.008* (.004)	.006* (.003)
Inflation × PR	—	.000 (.003)	.006 (.004)	.003 (.002)
Election in this or the last 3 months	.011 (.020)	—	—	—

(continued on following page)

TABLE 5.1
(continued from previous page)

Variables	Model 1 GLS	Model 2 GLS	Model3 Fixed Effects	Model 4 GLS
Election in this or the next 3 months	−.001 (.019)	—	—	—
Ideological change	.047 (.071)	−.037 (.087)	−.062 (.096)	−.056 (.090)
Ideology of government	−.018** (.004)	−.018** (.004)	−.026** (.005)	−.020** (.004)
Number of parties in government	−.005 (.005)	−.008 (.005)	−.001 (.009)	−.013* (.006)
Regional autonomy (federalism)	.026* (.013)	.026* (.013)	—	.024* (.013)
Presidentialism	−.027* (.014)	−.039** (.014)	—	−.026 (.016)
Lagged dependent variable	.344** (.014)	.335** (.014)	.285** (.015)	.319** (.015)
Market volatility	18.445** (.695)	18.584** (.694)	19.587** (.741)	17.014** (.736)
Market capitalization/GDP	−.017 (.020)	.018 (.046)	.026 (.041)	−.034 (.026)
Price dispersion in the United States	—	—	—	.169** (.020)
Constant	1.25** (.040)	1.18** (.046)	1.30** (.050)	.978** (.062)
Number of observations	3,409	3,409	3,409	3,061
Number of groups	13	13	13	12

Note: Standard errors in parentheses. Method of analysis: GLS and Fixed Effects. Estimates obtained using xtreg and xtgls procedures in STATA, version 6.0. *R* squared for the fixed effects analysis in model 3: within 0.32, between 0.50, overall 0.31.

The time series are variable length.

**p < .01; **p < .05. One-tailed test.

cates that if political change occurs within a given month, that price dispersion increases between industry subindices across all political systems. In the remaining models, I distinguish between electoral systems and differentiate between narrow-band and broad-band political change. To do so, I use a narrow measure of political change interacted with indicator variables for both PR and majoritarian systems. I also have similar broad measures of political change for both systems. These measures are shown in models 2 through 4 and described in appendix 5.1.

As predicted, the effect of political change is more immediate in majoritarian systems than in PR systems. In majoritarian systems, the narrow measure of political change has a statistically significant coefficient of around 0.12, with the broader measure being smaller in magnitude and statistically insignificant. This accounts for about 3 percent of the variance in the dispersion measure. In contrast, broad, rather than narrow, measures of political change account for dispersion of stock prices in PR systems. The estimated causal effect on the broad political change measure for PR systems in model 2 is 0.48, which accounts for about 10 percent of the variance in the dispersion measure. Although it appears that the effect of political change on redistributive policy is stronger in PR systems, this is hard to gauge. The nature of political change is very different in PR or majoritarian systems—the latter are characterized by large, infrequent changes, the former by incremental, frequent changes—so it is difficult to judge what a unit of political change means in a PR or a majoritarian system. In addition, because of differing components of industry subindices, the construction of the dependent variable is not constant across markets. The key result is that political change increases the level of price dispersion in both PR and majoritarian systems, and this pattern of broad political change mattering in PR and narrow political change mattering in majoritarian systems is a consistent theme throughout all analyses.[23] This implies that political change leads to redistribution in both types of electoral system; however, the timing of the stock markets' reaction varies across the two types of electoral system.

Before moving on to consider economic factors, I pause to examine alternative political variables. For example, one might argue that it is not political change per se that matters, but rather, for example, elections or the change in the ideological position of the government. Model 1 includes two dummy variables for the presence of an election.[24] The first is an indicator for whether an election has occurred within this or any of the previous three months. The second indicates the presence of an election in this or any of the three following months. The election variable controls directly for cases where elections took place without a change in incumbent. In neither model 1, nor in the other models that are run, did the presence of either election variable significantly influence the level of price dispersion, once political change is controlled for. It appears that elections are influential only to the extent that they lead to political change.

The results above support the argument that political change leads to changes in redistributional policy. Yet perhaps it is not change in party government but change in government ideology that is important. Although earlier I speculated that parties are not wedded to redistributional issues to the same extent that they are to ideological issues, this question deserves testing. I construct a measure of government ideology and change in government ideology using the *European Journal of Political Research*'s five-point ideological scale. I use party seat shares as weights and calculate the average government ideology. In addition, I create a measure of ideological change using an analogous construction to that of political change (formula below). This variable was then smoothed in the same manner as the narrow measure of political change.

$$ideological\ change = \sum_{k=1}^{m} \left| \left(ID_{k,t} \times s_{k,t} \times g_{k,t} \right) - \left(ID_{k,t-1} \times s_{k,t-1} \times g_{k,t-1} \right) \right|.$$

let $k = 1, \ldots m$, where m is number of parties holding seats.
let $S_{k,t}$ be the seat share for party k in month t;
let $g_{k,t} = 1$ if party k is in government in month t;
let $g_{k,t} = 0$ if party k is not in government in month t;
let $ID_{k,t} =$ the ideology of the government coalition (RANK).

Once political change is controlled for, shifts in the ideological composition of the government have no significant effect. As a further check, I created an analogous change variable based on party positions on trade issues, using data from the Comparative Manifesto Project (Issues P406 and P407).[25] This variable, not reported, has no significant impact on price dispersion. Yet, while change in the ideological composition of the government has little impact on price dispersion, the overall left-right ideological stance of the government does ("government ideology"). Scholars such as Cameron (1978) and Alvarez, Garrett, and Lange (1991) suggest that in different settings, left or right ideological parties generate larger shifts in policy upon taking office. The negative coefficient on government ideology suggests that moving from the extreme left to the extreme right reduces dispersion by about 0.068. Since the standard deviation of the dispersion measure is 0.44, this is equivalent to approximately 15 percent of one standard deviation. One possible explanation for this difference is that, on average, left-wing governments are more interventionist, which exaggerates the impact of any policy changes.

There are four other political variables: PR, regional autonomy, presidentialism, and the effective number of parties.[26] The first three of these are dummy variables indicating whether the system is PR, has features of regional autonomy such as federalism, and whether it is presidential. The analyses suggest that PR and regional autonomy increase dispersion, while presidentialism and the number of parties reduce dispersion. Although PR systems average about 1.5 more governing parties than majoritarian systems, the net effect of the PR and the number of party variables indicates that on average PR countries have one-tenth of a standard deviation more dispersion than majoritarian systems. Unfortunately, there is no time-series variation for the three dummies and only limited time-series variation for the "number of parties" variable; hence, we cannot place too much credence in these results, since they can be discounted as simply country-level effects.

Political change increases price dispersion in both PR and majoritarian systems, with the effect being more immediate in majoritarian systems and more diffuse in PR systems. The theory also suggests that the electoral rule influences how governments respond to economic conditions, with majoritarian government predicted to respond more directly to changes in economic conditions than PR governments. I next move to the question of response to economic conditions.[27] Model 1 includes variables for the interest rate (measured as the discount rate) and the inflation rate.[28] Both of these variables influence price dispersion with the larger and more significant factor belonging to the interest-rate variable. In the remaining models, the interest and inflation-rate variables are interacted with indicator variables for political systems. The impact of these variables differs drastically across politically systems. Although the effects are small in magnitude, an increase in the interest or inflation rate produces a statistically significant increase in price dispersion in majoritarian systems, but the impact of these variables is insignificant in PR systems. I also tested for the effect of the growth rate and the unemployment rate on the amount of price dispersion. In neither type of system did these variables significantly affect price dispersion. This is probably due in part to measuring these variables on a far coarser scale than the other variables. For example, the GDP data is available only at the quarterly level.

Throughout the analyses, I utilized the control variables "market volatility" and the "lagged dependent variable." These variables were strongly significant, yet their inclusion or exclusion leaves the effect of the remaining variables relatively unchanged. The control variable "market capitalization" was statistically insignificant; excluding this variable does not alter the findings. Although not reported here, removing the very undercapitalized markets (less than 40 percent of GDP in 1989) strengthens the results.[29] Earlier in the chapter I discussed how the number of domestic firms listed on European stock markets has risen sharply since the 1980s. Restricting the time domain of the full sample to the post–1980 period also strengthens, but does not substantively change, the results.

Linkages between equity markets must also be accounted for. Table 5.2 shows the correlation in the dispersion measure across countries. Even though the relationship is much weaker than the correlation between price levels, dispersion is highly correlated, particularly among the highly capitalized markets.

Hence, there is a risk that the less-capitalized markets are responding to political change in the United States rather than to domestic political factors. For example, on 6 November 1996, the sharp rise in trading on the Canadian market was attributed to a "breathed sigh of relief . . . (that there were) no surprises in the U.S. election."[30] As a control for this effect, model 5 includes U.S. price dispersion as a independent variable. The coefficient of 0.17 indicates that around 17 percent of price dispersion in other markets is driven by dispersion within the U.S. Despite this large effect, the impact of the other regressors remains largely unchanged.[31]

For ease of interpretation and presentation, I smoothed the political change variable over the months surrounding political change. While the analyses reported above suggest that a narrow measure of political change best captures price dispersion in majoritarian systems and that a broad measure of political change is most appropriate in PR systems, we should be concerned that these results are an artefact of the construction of the smoother. To investigate this possibility, I replace the smoothed measure of political change with a series of lags and leads on the political change. In particular, I generate both lead and lag political change for six months and interact these with the political system. This analysis is reported in table 5.3. To shorten notation, let MPC_{t-1} represent political change in the previous month multiplied by a dummy for majoritarian system and let $PRPC_{t+1}$ represent political change in the following month multiplied by a dummy for PR system.

I then perform joint hypothesis tests to determine whether the overall effect of political change over a series of lags and leads can be considered nonzero. In support of earlier results, I reject the null hypothesis that in majoritarian systems, political change in the current month, the previous month, and the next month all have zero effect on price dispersion.[32] In contrast, in PR systems, the probability of these three variables all simultaneously being zero cannot be rejected at the 5 percent level, although only just.[33] In common with the earlier results, these tests support the prediction that political change has a more significant effect in majoritarian than in PR systems. If political change is considered over a longer period, the reverse effect is visible. For instance, the joint hypothesis test that all six lags, six leads, and immediate political change coefficients are all simultaneously zero is rejected only in PR systems.[34] Like the earlier results, these tests support the prediction that political change has a more immediate effect in majoritarian than in PR systems.

Overall, the findings suggest that political change affects the level of redistribution in both majoritarian and PR countries. In both cases, political change positively and significantly affects the level of price dispersion among industry indices. However, there are temporal differences between PR and majoritarian systems. The impact of political change on price dispersion is relatively immediate in majoritarian systems. In contrast, in PR systems, the effect of political

TABLE 5.2

The Correlation in the Price Dispersion Measure between Different Stock Markets

	Australia	Austria	Belgium	Canada	Denmark	France	Germany	Ireland	Italy	Japan	Netherlands	Norway	Sweden	Switzerland	U.K.	U.S.
Australia	1.00															
Austria	-0.14	1.00														
Belgium	0.34	-0.03	1.00													
Canada	0.50	-0.12	0.35	1.00												
Denmark	0.11	-0.02	0.13	0.23	1.00											
France	0.37	-0.04	0.40	0.45	0.14	1.00										
Germany	0.13	0.25	0.23	0.28	0.17	0.25	1.00									
Ireland	0.22	0.07	0.35	0.35	0.12	0.33	0.28	1.00								
Italy	0.15	-0.06	0.17	0.14	0.07	0.28	0.16	0.05	1.00							
Japan	0.22	0.06	0.19	0.17	0.19	0.23	0.21	0.26	0.06	1.00						
Netherlands	0.27	0.00	0.37	0.34	0.31	0.35	0.39	0.30	0.30	0.25	1.00					
Norway	0.36	0.00	0.36	0.24	0.19	0.30	0.08	0.12	0.24	0.12	0.20	1.00				
Sweden	0.08	-0.04	0.07	0.14	0.07	0.20	0.13	0.21	0.21	0.08	0.18	0.07	1.00			
Switzerland	0.03	0.13	0.15	0.27	0.14	0.22	0.33	0.30	0.08	0.09	0.26	-0.04	0.24	1.00		
U.K.	0.34	-0.09	0.39	0.49	0.16	0.32	0.30	0.51	0.21	0.16	0.46	0.16	0.16	0.27	1.00	
U.S.	0.41	-0.08	0.41	0.59	0.26	0.38	0.29	0.45	0.14	0.15	0.40	0.17	0.20	0.33	0.55	1.00

TABLE 5.3

Generalized Least Squares Analysis of the Effects of Political and Economic Change on the Level of Price Dispersion Using Leads and Lags for Political Change

Variable	Estimate	Standard Error	
A. Majoritarian system			
Political change			
t+6	0.002	0.015	Joint hypothesis test
t+5	0.007	0.015	χ^2 (13) = 19.56
t+4	−0.037	0.016	Pr. = 0.107
t+3	−0.008	0.016	
t+2	0.027*	0.016	
t+1	0.005	0.016	Joint hypothesis test
t	0.031*	0.016	χ^2 (3) = 9.47
t-1	0.039**	0.016	Pr. = 0.024
t-2	−0.016	0.015	
t-3	0.004	0.015	
t-4	−0.008	0.015	
t-5	0.005	0.014	
t-6	0.002	0.014	
B. PR system			
Political change			
t+6	0.009	0.014	Joint hypothesis test
t+5	0.011	0.014	χ^2 (13) = 24.94
t+4	−0.004	0.015	Pr. = 0.023
t+3	0.009	0.015	
t+2	0.030*	0.015	
t+1	−0.028	0.015	Joint hypothesis test
t	0.027*	0.015	χ^2 (3) = 7.62
t-1	−0.011	0.014	Pr. = 0.0547
t-2	0.017	0.014	
t-3	0.008	0.014	
t-4	0.003	0.014	
t-5	0.045**	0.014	
t-6	0.008	0.014	

(continued on following page)

change takes longer to filter through and its diffuse effects are felt over a longer time period. As predicted, majoritarian systems are more responsive to economic change. Changes in inflation and interest rates affect price dispersion only in majoritarian systems. Prices on stock markets in PR countries are not similarly affected.

TABLE 5.3

(continued from previous page)

Variable	Estimate	Standard Error
C. Control variables		
PR (dummy)	0.087**	0.031
Interest rate	0.007**	0.002
Interest rate × PR	−0.003	0.002
Inflation rate	0.009**	0.003
Inflation rate × PR	0.002	0.003
Election within past 3 months	0.008	0.023
Election within future 3 months	0.011	0.023
Ideological change	−0.034	0.087
Number of parties in government	−0.002	0.005
Regional autonomy	0.030*	0.013
Presidentialism	−0.044**	0.014
Market volatility	18.160**	0.695
Lagged dependent variable	0.370**	0.014
Market capitalization	0.031	0.023
Constant	1.067**	0.043
Number of countries	13	
Number of observations	3,382	
First-order autocorrelation	−0.072	

Notes: The null hypothesis for the joint hypothesis test is that all coefficients are zero. Dependent Variable: Price Dispersion.

**$p < 0.01$, *$p < 0.05$. One-tailed tests.

CONCLUSION

In this chapter, I used monthly stock price data from fourteen industrialized countries between 1973 and 1996 to assess the impact of political change on the dispersion of industry share prices and how the political system shaped this interaction. The use of stock data to investigate political events is a relatively recent technique.[35] While this means that many properties of such data are poorly understood, stock data provides a potential source for effectively measuring the impact of government policies. Of course, given the relative infancy of this mode of study, there is much to learn, and the hope that better estimators and measures will be uncovered. While the results need to be assessed in this light, the current findings appear robust, suggesting the theoretically predicted relation between political change and industry share prices.

From a broader methodological perspective, this analysis is important because it generates new measures and addresses a different dependent variable. Most extant studies of the distribution of trade protection and industrial assistance have focused on direct measures of who are the relative winners and losers from government policy, such as tariffs or subsidies. Unfortunately, as I have illustrated throughout this book, the wide variety of policy instruments available to government means such measures often fail to capture the distributive impact of trade and industrial policy. In addition, testing is difficult because the link between industry characteristics and policy outcomes is complex; for example, depending on the political context, geographic concentration can have either a positive or a negative impact on an industry's political clout. Creating predictions about alternative dependent variables is important because it enables us to distinguish between theories. It is common for several theories to share a common prediction. If tests are only performed on this common hypothesis, then while we can become more confident in this set of theories, we cannot distinguish between them.

The tests in this chapter rely on price dispersion between industry subindices being at least in part driven by changes to government trade and industrial policy. Given this assumption, I show that political change is an important determination of trade and industrial policy in both PR and majoritarian systems. As parties shift in and out of government, trade and industrial policy are redistributed to favor different industrial groups. Such changes in policy increase the cross-sectional dispersion in stock prices, with newly advantaged industries seeing their stock increase, while the price of those losing favorable policy declines. The temporal impact of political change differs across institutions, with the impact of political change more immediate in majoritarian systems and the effect longer run and more diffuse in PR systems. Majoritarian systems are also more responsive to economic shocks, while changes in economic conditions have few discernable effects on the dispersion of prices in PR countries. PR systems, however, experience overall higher levels of price dispersion.

TABLE 5.A1

Additional Generalized Least Squares Analyses of the Effects of Political and Economic Change on the Level of Price Dispersion in Industry Subindices in Thirteen Countries, 1973–1996

Variables	*Model 1* *GLS Dichotomous Dependent Variable*	*Model 2* *GLS Squared Dependent Variable*	*Model 3* *GLS Robustness Check on Bandwidth*	*Model 4* *GLS Reduced Sample Size*
Political change in majoritarian systems (.05 bandwidth)	2.396* (1.252)	.149** (.061)	—	.179* (.072)
Political change in majoritarian systems (.15 bandwidth)	−2.050 (2.195)	−.016 (.133)	—	−.083 (.147)
Political change in PR systems (.05 bandwidth)	−.642 (.878)	−.030 (.057)	—	.047 (.083)
Political change in PR systems (.15 bandwidth)	4.109** (1.477)	.437** (.108)	—	.417* (.167)
Political change in majoritarian systems (.01 bandwidth)	—	—	.185* (.097)	—
Political change in majoritarian systems (.08 bandwidth)	—	—	.128 (.077)	—
Political change in PR systems (.01 bandwidth)	—	—	.059 (.093)	—
Political change in PR systems (.08 bandwidth)	—	—	.183* (.069)	—
PR dummy	.092* (.050)	.047 (.030)	.155** (.033)	.079* (.038)
Interest rate × majoritarian	.008** (.002)	.011** (.002)	.010 (.002)	.010** (.003)
Interest rate × PR	.000 (.002)	.003 (.002)	.003 (.002)	.006 (.003)

(continued on following page)

TABLE A5.1

(continued from previous page)

Variables	Model 1 *GLS Dichotomous Dependent Variable*	Model 2 *GLS Squared Dependent Variable*	Model 3 *GLS Robustness Check on Bandwidth*	Model 4 *GLS Reduced Sample Size*
Inflation × majoritarian	.002	.005*	.005*	.007*
	(.003)	(.003)	(.003)	(.003)
Inflation × PR	.001	.000	.001	.001
	(.003)	(.002)	(.002)	(.004)
Ideological change	−.018	−.047	−.061	−.135
	(.067)	(.076)	(.096)	(.114)
Ideology of government	−.018**	−.020**	−.019**	−.023**
	(.004)	(.003)	(.004)	(.005)
Number of parties in government	−.003**	−.001	−.006	−.015*
	(.005)	(.005)	(.005)	(.007)
Regional autonomy (federalism)	.019	.019	.025*	−.002
	(.013)	(.012)	(.013)	(.016)
Presidentialism	−.024*	−.038**	.034*	−.014
	(.014)	(.013)	(.014)	(.018)
Lagged dependent variable	.335**	.231**	.339**	.286**
	(.014)	(.012)	(.014)	(.018)
Market volatility	18.525**	13.327**	18.546**	15.351**
	(.693)	(.584)	(.695)	(.794)
Market capitalization/GDP	.028	.025	.016	−.012
	(.023)	(.021)	(.023)	(.026)
Constant	1.095*	.048	1.161**	1.340**
	(.054)	(.041)	(.046)	(.057)
Number of observations	3,409	3,409	3,409	2,262
Number of groups	13	13	13	9

Notes: Standard errors in parentheses. Method of analysis: GLS and Fixed Effects. Estimates obtained using xtreg and xtgls procedures in STATA, version 6.0. The time series are of variable length.

** $p < .01$, * $p < .05$. One-tailed test.

TABLE 5A.2
Variable Means and Variances

Variables	Mean	Standard Deviation	Construction
Dependent variable: price change dispersion among industry subindexes	2.001	.443	$^{a}\sum_{i=1}^{m}\left\lvert\Delta S_i^t - \Delta base_t\right\rvert/m$
Squared dependent variable	.619	.351	$^{a}\sum_{i=1}^{m}(\Delta S_i^t - \Delta base_t)^2/m$
Political change (unsmoothed)	.088	.530	$^{b}\sum_{k=1}^{m}\left\lvert(s_{k,t} \times g_{k,t}) - (s_{k,t-1} \times g_{k,t-1})\right\rvert$
Political change in majoritarian systems (.05 bandwidth)	.028	.098	Interaction of political change and majoritarian dummy variable (KSM smoother, bandwidth 0.05)
Political change in PR systems (.05 bandwidth)	.059	.129	Interaction of political change and PR dummy variable (KSM smoother, bandwidth 0.05)
Political change in majoritarian systems (.15 bandwidth)	.028	.059	Interaction of political change and majoritarian dummy variable (KSM smoother, bandwidth 0.15)
Political change in PR systems (.15 bandwidth)	.059	.078	Interaction of political change and PR dummy variable (KSM smoother, bandwidth 0.15)
Political change in majoritarian systems (.01 bandwidth)	.031	.063	Interaction of political change and majoritarian dummy variable (KSM smoother, bandwidth 0.01)
Political change in PR systems (.01 bandwidth)	0.58	.077	Interaction of political change and PR dummy variable (KSM smoother, bandwidth 0.01)
Political change in majoritarian systems (.08 bandwidth)	.028	.077	Interaction of political change and majoritarian dummy variable (KSM smoother, bandwidth 0.08)
Political change in PR systems (.08 bandwidth)	.059	.100	Interaction of political change and PR dummy variable (KSM smoother, bandwidth 0.08)
Dichotomous political change	.032	.174	1 if $\sum_{i=1}^{m}\left\lvert\Delta S_i^t - \Delta base_t\right\rvert/m > 0$, 0 otherwise.

(*continued on following page*)

TABLE 5A.2
(continued from previous page)

Variables	Mean	Standard Deviation	Construction
Dichotomous political change in majoritarian systems (.05 bandwidth)	.011	.017	Interaction of dichotomous political change and majoritarian dummy variable (KSM smoother, bandwidth 0.05)
Dichotomous political change in PR systems (.05 bandwidth)	.032	.013	Interaction of dichotomous political change and majoritarian dummy variable (KSM smoother, bandwidth 0.05)
Dichotomous political change in majoritarian systems (.15 bandwidth)	.011	.016	Interaction of dichotomous political change and majoritarian dummy variable (KSM smoother, bandwidth 0.15)
Dichotomous political change in PR systems (.15 bandwidth)	.032	.009	Interaction of dichotomous political change and majoritarian dummy variable (KSM smoother, bandwidth 0.15)
PR dummy	.659	.438	PR systems = 1, Majoritarian Systems = 0.
Interest rate	5.98	4.42	$100 \times \mid (\text{interest rate}_t - \text{interest rate}_{t-1}) / \text{interest rate}_{t-1} \mid$
Interest × majoritarian	2.513	4.395	Interaction of interest rate and majoritarian dummy
Interest × PR	3.473	4.203	Interaction of Interest rate and PR dummy
Inflation rate	7.513	3.382	$100 \times \mid (\text{interest rate}_t - \text{interest rate}_{t-1}) / \text{interest rate}_{t-1} \mid$
Inflation × majoritarian	2.802	4.356	Interaction of inflation rate and majoritarian dummy
Inflation × PR	4.712	4.344	Interaction of inflation rate and PR dummy
Election in this or the previous 3 months	.094	.029	Election month $(n - 3)$
Election in this or the next 3 months	.094	.092	Election month $(n + 3)$
Change in ideology	.027	.087	Absolute change in the ideology of the government. See EJPR coding: $$^{b} \sum_{k=1}^{m} \left\mid \left(ID_{k,t} \times s_{k,t} \times g_{k,t} \right) - \left(ID_{k,t-1} \times s_{k,t-1} \times g_{k,t-1} \right) \right\mid$$

(continued on following page)

TABLE 5A.2

(continued from previous page)

Variables	Mean	Standard Deviation	Construction
Government ideology	2.484	1.628	Average government ideology (using EJPR coding and party seat shares as weights).
Number of parties in government	2.222	1.372	Number of parties in government. See EJPR coding
Regional autonomy (Federalism)	.477	.499	1 if unitary, 0 if federal. See EJPR coding
Presidentialism	.582	.493	0 if parliamentary, 1 if presidential. See EJPR coding
Lagged dependent variable	1.980	.414	Lagged dependent variable
Market capitalization/GDP	.438	.437	Stock market capitalization as percentage of GDP (both in dollars)
Market volatility	.003	.008	$(\Delta \text{base}_t)^2$
Price dispersion in U.S.	2.00	.326	$^a \sum_{i=1}^{m} \left| \Delta S_i^t - \Delta \text{base}_t \right| / m$ (U.S.)

[a] For $i = 1, \ldots m$, where i is an industry index, for $n = 1 \ldots 14$ countries, ΔS_i^t is the percentage change in the price for the industry index i in month t, and Δbase_t is the % change in the price of the general market index in month t.

[b] For $k = 1, \ldots m$, where m is number of parties holding seats, let $S_{k,t}$ be the seat share for party k in month t, let $g_{k,t} = 1$ if party k is in government in month t, let $g_{k,t} = 0$ if party k is not in government in month t.

CHAPTER 6

A Theory and Direction for Future Research

OVER THE LAST fifty years, our understanding of political economy has developed radically. In part, our leaps forward are attributable to improved data. The standardization of national accounts and the growth of intergovernmental organizations mean that systematic records of many aspects of nations' economic, political, and social life can be readily compared. Unfortunately with respect to trade policy, it is precisely because government financial records are widely available that governments try to hide evidence of trade assistance. Signatories of the World Trade Organization agreement on subsides and countervailing measures are supposed to notify the WTO Subsidies Committee about subsidies to industry. Until recently, the United States admitted to only forty-nine, relatively small subsidy programs. The EU counterclaimed that there were at least twenty-four large federal programs and over four hundred state subsidy programs in the United States.[1] However, trade and industrial policy in the EU are hardly transparent. Across Europe, tax exemptions and research and development grants are an increasingly popular form of industry assistance. It is even harder to track taxes not collected than to track subsidies that have been handed out.

In the nineteenth century, although records were less systematized, the measurement of trade policy was on the whole much easier. Ships landed, cargos disembarked, and the duty was paid on the spot. Although navigation laws and prohibitions on goods existed (see McGillivray et al. 2001), the process was generally transparent. This is not the case today. Having reached consensus that protection is economically inefficient, developed countries working through such organizations as GATT and WTO have virtually eliminated tariffs. In the postwar period, tariff barriers on manufactured goods have dropped from averages of 40 percent to 4 percent. Unfortunately, agreeing that protection is inefficient overall does not mitigate the political incentives to privilege one group at the expense of another. Increasingly, nontariff barriers (NTBs) are substituted for tariffs.[2] Laird and Yeats (1990) argue NTBs increased between 1966 and 1986 by 37 percent.

One solution to this measurement problem is to study the decision-making process that generates protectionist policy, rather than study the policy outcome itself; but this approach has its own set of drawbacks. Politicians can always find an economic rationale for political decisions. In episode 11 of the BBC's 1976 adaptation of Robert Graves's novel of political intrigue in ancient

Rome, "*I, Claudius*," the Emperor Claudius has ordered his freedmen assistants to investigate the cost of building a safe winter harbor.

NARCISSUS: It will cost ten million, more.

PALLAS: Well the more expensive it is, the less likely it is that it will ever be built.

NARCISSUS: What are you suggesting, that we exaggerate the cost?

PALLAS: O my dear Narcissus, you have money in corn. I have money in corn. Lots of people have money in corn. The more corn that can be landed in winter, the lower the price will be. That worries me.

NARCISSUS: That could be construed as a very selfish point of view.

PALLAS: Are you saying there is less selfishness in wanting the price of corn to be low rather than high?

NARCISSUS: Well there are more people who want it to be low.

PALLAS: Does that not add up to more selfishness rather than less.

NARCISSUS But that is sheer sophistry. One can not argue with you.

PALLAS: Well let's get the engineering report and I'm sure the cost will take care of philosophical considerations.

As the above quote shows, detecting distortions from free trade is extremely hard. While this example is drawn from fiction, it appears such a believable event because it conforms to our common sense that policies under taken for one stated goal are often really for another. In this Roman example, you would only suspect a protectionist policy if you knew the details of both the market for corn and the costs of harbor construction.

The topic of this book has been twofold. First, how do political systems and industry geography interact to determine which industrial groups governments privilege? Second, given the lack of transparency in trade and industrial policy, what tests can be constructed to assess how governments distribute assistance across groups of voters? These two categories might be referred to as theory and evidence. Here, after a brief exposition of the argument, I consider the value of the theory and consider what it implies for further research.

THE ARGUMENT

The theory predicts the pattern of trade assistance as a function of the interaction of industry geography and the electoral rule. Others have looked at this problem (Busch and Reinhardt 2000; Caves 1976; Pincus 1975; Rogowski 1997, 1998; Rogowski et al. 1999; Rogowski and Kayser 2002). The innovation I propose is that the influence of industry geography and the electoral rule on trade policy depends upon two steps. First, industry geography and the electoral system induce the preferences of legislators. Second, the electoral rule and party strength determines which of the preferences are implemented. Among others, Pincus (1975), Caves (1976), and Busch and Reinhardt (1999) look at the first stage in this process and conclude that highly geographically concentrated industries are politically powerful whatever the political system type. Rogowski (1987) and Magee, Brock, and Young (1989) examine the interaction of political geography and the electoral rule at the first stage, concluding that politicians in PR systems are more isolated from cries for protection than politicians in majoritarian systems. I argue that there is no general, unambiguous relationship between either industry geography and political power or electoral system and level of protection. In both cases, the relationship is contingent upon the second step, how legislators' induced preferences are aggregated into policy outcomes. This depends on the electoral rule and features of party competition.

I compare the pattern of trade distribution across three types of political systems: strong-party majoritarian, weak-party majoritarian, and strong-party proportional representation. In strong-party majoritarian, I argue that parties target the redistributive policies of trade and industry toward rewarding those in marginal districts (districts where the vote between rival parties is close). Hence, I predict that industries distributed in such districts receive greater assistance than industries located in safe seats. In strong-party PR systems, we might expect parties to want to win as many seats as possible since more seats might give them more power within the coalition government. However, the possibility of new parties siphoning off their base of support forces incumbent parties to pay attention to their core supporters. Each party in the governing coalition wants to target redistributive rewards towards their core supporters. Hence, the government's trade and industrial policy is a compromise of what each governing party wants. This compromise generates a trade policy, which is in flux, dropping policies targeted toward the supporters of parties that leave office and incorporating policies directed toward supporters of parties entering government. In weak-party majoritarian systems, trade and industrial policy is made by a majority coalition of individual legislators. Specific institutional features such as which legislators have agenda control and seniority strongly influence which legislators receive protection or assistance for industries in their constituency. Beyond these specific features, industries spread over numerous electoral districts provide the basis for a natural coalition among legislators. It is these industries that receive greater levels of assistance.

I argue there is no general relationship between industry geography and political influence across political systems. Depending on the type of political system, the effect of industry size is conditional on electoral spread and location or party-industry affiliations. The effect of geographic concentration on industry political clout appears ambiguous until we account for the interactive effect of political institutions. In PR systems, the incentives to target one region over another arise from economic and demographic differences that structure party affiliation. In contrast, in majoritarian systems, electoral jurisdictions are everything. Strong parties compete only in those regions where the underlying economics and demographics make the area politically important.

Throughout this book the empirical tests support the theory. Yet despite this evidence some might be tempted to argue, but so what? It is still the same industries that win in every country. Indeed even though the statistical analyses of tariffs in chapter 3 support the political arguments, they still found that declining and import-competing industries receive the most protection. In general across industrialized countries, it is the labor-intensive, low-wage, fixed-asset, low-value-added, import-competing industries that receive the highest levels of trade assistance (Cassing, McKeown, and Ochs 1986; Esty and Caves 1983; Munger, and Roberts 1994; Marvel and Ray 1983; Riezman and Wilson 1992). For example, textiles win high import protection across all industrialized countries (Deardorff and Stern 1983; Garrett and Lange 1996; Reizman and Wilson 1992). It is therefore tempting to dismiss the arguments made here as peripheral and of second order in terms of explaining protection. Yet such claims would be wrong. While it is true that the textile industry is protected throughout the OECD—through extensive quotas and higher-than-average tariffs on textile products[3]—nonetheless, there is still tremendous variation in the extent to which it is assisted.[4] In the first part of this chapter I use the arguments set forth in this book to explain the pattern of goverment assistance to the textile industry in Australia, Belgium, the United Kingdom, Germany, and the United States. I use this analysis for two purposes. First, I debunk the idea that the same industries win everywhere. Politics matters. Second, the theory presented in this book predicts and accounts for the pattern of textiles protection across industrialized countries. Elucidating the pattern of assistance serves as a useful vehicle to reiterate the main points of the theory.

THE TEXTILE INDUSTRY

Textiles (both with natural and synthetic fibers) is a large industry throughout the OECD. For example, in the early 1980s the UK had more than 300,000 textile workers, and Germany had more than 500,000. It is a heterogeneous mix of small, medium, and large-sized companies that make a wide variety of products.[5] The older textile firms are industrially decentralized, but in recent years the trend has been toward industrial concentration. Textile firms tend to be spatially dispersed within a country but are often regionally clustered.

Naively we might state that the textile industry gets protected because it is simply too big not to protect. The textile industry has had the privileged position of being protected by a comprehensive set of quotas, negotiated by the EU, Australia, and the United States with all major suppliers (the Multi-Fiber Arrangement, MFA). Table 6.1 shows the number of imports that NTBs affect and the number of items involved. The multi-fiber agreement is slowly being

TABLE 6.1
Nontariff Barriers to Textile Products, 1983

	Textiles, NTB, Coverage Ratio	Manufacturing, NTB, Coverage Ratio	Textiles, NTB, Frequency Ratio	Manufacturing, NTB, Frequency Ratio
Australia	55.6	23.6	25.9	17.9
Austria	0	2.4	1.8	0.9
Belgium and Luxembourg	47.4	33.6	32.7	8.9
France	73.9	27.4	56.0	21.9
W. Germany	18.5	53.5	43.9	11.1
Italy	48.6	9.3	38.4	8.4
Netherlands	35.5	17.8	41.9	10.2
United Kingdom	42.1	14.8	59.8	12.3
United States	37.7	17.1	30.8	6.9
European Union	52.6	18.7	45.2	12.0

Source: Nogues, Olechowski, and Winters 1986; Tables 1C and 1F.
Note: The coverage ratio represents the amount of trade flow that NTBs affect.
The frequency ratio indicates the number of items involved.

phased out, and this lowered protection has already hurt the industry in many European countries. For instance, since 1990 about half of Spain's textiles worker have lost their jobs.[6] Nonetheless, for a long time, cutting jobs in textiles was politically unacceptable for most countries.

Although there are numerous country studies, it is hard to evaluate exactly how much aid textiles received.[7] In addition to the MFA, governments helped with other types of aid. The Belgians gave a lot of restructuring aid under their textile plan, although the EU subsequently decided that much of this aid was an illegal barrier to trade.[8] In 1996, the French gave aid to the textile industry in the form of reduced social security payments conditional on the industry not laying off workers. This tax exception cost the government around $800 million in lost revenue.[9] Yet within Europe, Italy is arguably the most protectionist textile nation.[10] It is clear that all developed countries helped restructuring within the textile industry. Nonetheless, there is interesting variation in extent to which governments responded to cries for help.

In Australia, the textile industry is largely regionally concentrated in Victoria, although it also has a significant presence in New South Wales (Capling and Galligan 1992). A decline in the textile industry would devastate many communities in these regions. Fortunately for textiles, Victoria has a higher number of marginal seats than any other state. More than a third of Victoria's seats are marginal (5 percent or less difference in vote thresholds).[11] Both Australian and U.K. textile firms tend to be located semirural, semiindustrial districts that are characteristically party competitive. Winning the key marginal districts of Bendigo, Ballarat, McMillan, and McEwan has been key to every postwar Australian government. Despite the desire of governments since the late 1970s to remove textile tariffs, none have had the political will to do so (Bell 1993; Capling and Galligan 1992).

The United Kingdom's textile industry is also located in a region where approximately a third of the districts are marginal.[12] While in the UK, cutlery had only a few districts that were marginal (discussed in chapter 1), textiles hit the jackpot. Cable and Rebelo (1980, 51) comment "there is also a direct political link with protection to the extent that Lancashire and West Yorkshire, the main centers of textile production, have a considerable concentration of politically marginal constituencies." Not all large industries are as lucky in their geography. The steel industry in the United Kingdom is largely located in safe Labour seats. As we saw in chapter 4, this was one of the reason for its radical restructuring and downsizing.

In the United Kingdom and Australia, both majoritarian systems, legislators from marginal districts secure the highest levels of assistance for the firms in their district. In PR systems, there are no marginal districts. Seats are divided up proportionately on the basis of votes, and parties are more inclined to target rewards toward traditional supporters. Hence, the extent to which an industry receives assistance depends upon whether the party it supports is in government. German textiles illustrates this nicely.

Within the EU, since the 1970s, the Germans have probably been the least supportive of the textile industry. This decline in assistance followed the Social Democrats' (SPD) 1969 election victory. The textile industry is a traditional supporter of the Christian Democratic party (CDU), which governed for much of the postwar period prior to the 1970s. Germany's textile firms are largely located in the three states of Bavaria, North Rhine-Westphalia, and Baden-Wurttemberg (Underhill 1988). The CDU remains the dominant party for textile workers in these regions. When in government, the CDU delayed liberalization of textiles. For instance, following the formation of the CDU/SPD grand coalition in 1967, SPD ministers proposed expanding the quota ceiling on textiles for Eastern bloc countries. The CDU refused to acquiesce to its coalition partner's demands and the SPD was forced to back down "for the time being" (Firman 1990, 163). Textiles also received considerable support from the Bundesrat, the German upper house, through its strong regional presence in three of the largest states.

Following their election victory in 1969, the SPD formed a coalition with the Free Democrats (FPD) and, no longer constrained by their CDU coalition, the SPD set about liberalizing textiles (Essar and Fach 1989). In the 1970s, Germany was the only major European country not to impose Multi-Fibre Arrangement textile import quotas on developing countries.[13] In addition to removing assistance, the government also revalued the currency (by 9.3 percent in 1969), which further hurt textiles by making imports appear even cheaper. The change in government policy and the consequent irreversible restructuring of the German textile industry shifted Germany's position within the EU. While previously it had been the laggard, the now competitive German industry sought to liberalize textiles, against the vigorous objections of the British. When the CDU came back into power in the 1980s the now-competitive textile industry sought a more open, competitive European market. Textile assistance remained relatively low (see table 6.1).

The case of Belgian textiles exhibits many similar features as the German case. Despite the industry's spread throughout the country, there is a concentration of mills in the northern region of Flanders. Belgium is a PR system. Until 1982, governing party coalitions included a variety of northen- and southern-based parties. There were both northern and southern based parties who drew support from textile workers, and so throughout the entire postwar period there has been continual support for textiles. In 1981, the government instigated a five-year program to "restructure" textiles. The program cost $358 million in financial assistance, about $80 million in technical and commercial aid, and about $30 million for offsetting the social effects of change in the industry.[14] Before this change was fully implemented, there was a radical change in government (the details of which were discussed in chapter 4). After 1982, the government was composed almost exclusively of northern parties. The government continued to assist the restructuring of the textile industry, but anecdotal evidence suggests that it redirected funds toward firms in Flanders. For example, in 1982, the Belgian government gave a first installment of $9 million to Beaulieu, a mass producer of cheap carpets, to expand the bankrupt northern carpetmaker Fabelta Zwijnaarde.[15] The European Commission ruled this an illegal subsidy in 1984 and ordered Beaulieu to repay the aid, which it never fully did.[16] As in the German case, governing parties in PR systems targeted rewards to their supporters. In Belgium, the extreme regional differences in party affiliation determine how regional concentration and location mattered.

In the United States, the textile industry is predominately in the two southern states of North and South Carolina. Sixty percent of all U.S. textile employment is in these two states. Textiles account for about 7 percent of their states' workforce.[17] Not surprisingly, politicians from these states are strongly supportive of the textile industry. However, the intense support of politicians from two states is not sufficient to form a legislative majority. Alone, textile had little hope of attaining protection. Yet textiles achieved widespread congressional support through an alliance with the apparel industry, which is heavily concentrated in the Mid-Atlantic states. McGillivray and Schiller (1998) detail how the textile and apparel industries exploited their joint strength to place three major textiles bills before Congress between 1985 and 1990.[18] Although none of these bills was enacted, textiles' legislative influence secured strong presidential support for a quota agreement.[19] Although the textile-apparel coalition was very successful in the 1970s,[20] by the mid-1980s, its influence waned as the apparel industry's position shifted from protecting domestic jobs to bringing in cheap imports. Without the broad reach of its coalition, the individual industries have been unable to acquire the protection they want. The textile industry also faced tough opposition in Congress from another large, dispersed industry—agriculture. Agriculture feared that if textiles were protected, foreign retaliation would be directed against farming interests.[21]

The textile industry has been further hurt by the loss of senior congressional leaders. For instance, when Ed Jenkins left the House of Representatives, textiles lost a keen supporter who was a member of the influential Ways and Means committee. Textile's political clout has diminished. In the weak-party majoritarian case, the textile industry managed to leverage its limited regional spread by allying with the apparel industry (McGillivray and Schiller 1998). This textile and apparel coalition was both regionally concentrated and electorally dispersed. This type of industry geography maximizes political clout in a weak-party majoritarian system.[22]

The analysis of textiles show that not only is there considerable variation across nations, there can be considerable temporal variation, as the German case illustrated. Furthermore, the textile industry illustrates that governments use the policy instruments at their disposal to redistribute between their favored firms (such as Flanders in the Belgian case). Even though textile is a proverbial winner, the extent of its success (cross-nationally, temporally, and internally between plants) depends upon the interaction of industry goegraphy and the political system. The empirical work in this book has explored cross-national differences in industry tariff rates (chapter 3), temporal changes in industry stock market prices (chapter 5) and cross-national differences in how governments distribute assistance within an industry (chapter 4). Taken together, the empirical findings support the anecdotal evidence in the textile case; both industry geography and the electoral system affect how governments distribute trade and industrial policy.

REDISTRIBUTION: A THEORY AND DIRECTION
FOR FUTURE RESEARCH

Although my focus is one of trade and industrial policy, the theory's predictions are about which groups of voters governments target with benefits. Trade protection is one way to privilege one group relative to another, but it is by no means the only way. Indeed, a major component of this book has been devoted to devising tests that account for the numerous policy instruments a government might use to achieve its political goals. Whether or not an industry is a suitable candidate to provide these rewards depends on its geography: its size, spread, and location. Other redistributive policies could be used to substitute for trade policies in constructing bargains or targeting specific districts. For example, a government could build a dam in a marginal district rather than prop up a declining industry. I specify the industry geography where trade protection would be the best form of redistribution to the group of voters that the government seeks to benefit. In the United Kingdom, if an industry is geographically concentrated in a region rich with marginal districts, then using subsidies to save thousands of jobs targets benefits more effectively than building a dam. However, a comprehensive understanding of trade policy must recognize that trade and industrial policies are just one weapon in a government's armory. To date we have done little to explain when trade protection is the preferred policy instrument.

ENDOGENOUS CHOICE OF POLICY INSTRUMENT

Throughout the exposition of this book, I implicitly assume that the choice of policy instrument to target industries is exogenous. For instance, when considering the restructuring of the steel industry in chapter 4, I explained the U.S. policy choice given that the U.S. government used tariffs; I did not consider why the U.S. government chose to use tariffs in the first place. Similarly, I explained why the U.K. government closed plants in the North of England and Wales while saving the hugely inefficient Ravenscraig complex in Scotland. I did not however examine why the U.K. government chose targeted closure and subsidized restructuring aid over higher tariffs or quotas. In some cases governments are constrained in their choice of policy instrument: EU nations can not impose unilateral tariffs, and until recently they predominately relied on subsidies to assist industry. However, even within these constrained, circumstances governments have considerable leeway in their choice of policy instruments.

Although I refer to trade and industrial policy throughout the paper, regulatory policy, tax policy, exchange-rate policy, and monetary policy can also have a significant redistributive impact. The question is, why use subsidies instead of regulation, or research and development instead of low-interest loans? Many of the extant arguments focus on the transparency of the policy instrument (Falvey and Loyde 1991; Kaempfer et al. 1988; Magee, Brock, and Young 1989). Staiger and Tabellini (1987) and Rodrik (1986) argue that governments commit to tariffs as a way of restraining themselves from providing excess protection. However, another possibility is that governments choose policy instruments that allow them to most effectively privilege those groups they care about.[23]

Many forms of assistance are distributionally blunt: tariffs, antidumping duties, and quotas apply evenly across an industry.[24] Other forms of assistance allow governments to distribute benefits among factors, within industries, and between regions. Subsidies can be tied to number of workers (favoring labor-intensive plants) or tied to debt levels (favoring plants that have made a heavy capital investment). Redundancy payments can be used to target workers of a certain age or skill. Low-interest loans can be targeted to revitalize regional economies. Environmental regulations can also have huge differential impact on firms depending upon their location.

Whether the government will chose a distributionally blunt or targetable policy instrument depends on which is best to help a specific group or district. While governments will use the best instrument to achieve political ends, and so governments are likely to use different instruments under different circumstances, there might be some general trends. Weak-party majoritarian systems are likely to use the geographically blunt types of protection because it is necessary to form a legislative coalition based on geographical jurisdictions. Tariffs, quotas, and Voluntary Export Restrictions reward all members of the industry, which ensure the support of all legislators in the industrial coalition. Strong majoritarian governments typically prefer targetable policy instruments because these enable them to target specific electorates and specific regions. Suppose an industry is dispersed over both safe and marginal districts. Using quotas would mean protecting both safe and marginal districts, whereas the government can use research and development grants to target only those firms in marginal seats. PR governments will use a mix of blunt and targetable policy measures. Targetable policy instruments can be used to benefit specific groups of voters, which is useful if the industry vote is split between parties. However, bargaining among the coalition partners might lead them to choose blunt policy instruments. In chapter 4, there is suggestive evidence that these hypotheses are borne out in the data—the United States prefers to use tariffs and quotas to aid steel. Mansfield and Busch (1993) find that PR systems typically have more nontariff barriers than do majoritarian systems. The effect of political institutions on policy instrument choice has not been explored in the literature and is worthy of future research.[25]

Just as the choice of policy instrument has not received much attention in the literature, neither have the implications of this choice for how preferences are aggregated. Where governments use tariffs or quotas (geographically blunt instruments), workers and capital from different firms and locations unite as a sector to lobby government (United States in the steel case). Where governments use subsidies or loans (instruments that could target specific firms and/ or regions), the political division is regional. Workers and capital in one plant lobby against closure for their plant, and no other. In the latter case, governments can divide the industry's lobbying efforts by playing off one plant against another (Belgium, Germany, United Kingdom, and Sweden in the steel case). Blunt policy instruments create sectoral divisions; geographically targetable policy instruments create regional intraplant divisions. These arguments stand in contrast to the standard argument about coalition formation among industries. For instance, Rogowski's Stolper-Samuelson argument predicts the political division along factor lines (Labor vs. Capital), and Magee's Three Simple tests examines whether political division fall along sectoral or industry lines (Magee 1973; Rogowski 1987).

BRINGING IN THE INTERNATIONAL VARIABLES

Trade is an interaction between nations. Yet to date I have said practically nothing about international negotiations and agreement on trade. Through such organizations as GATT, WTO, and numerous regional trade organizations, nations have agreed to do away with many tariffs, as well as other forms of protection. There is a large literature that deals with trade theory entirely from the international perspective.[26] Given the importance of international considerations, a comprehensive understanding of trade policy requires the reintroduction of the international dimension. Thus far I have completely ignored this issue. I now argue that a bottom-up approach is essential for understanding international negotiations and agreements.[27]

International agreements constrain governments' choice of trade policy. Having entered GATT, WTO, or the EU, nations give up some sovereignty. While from the standpoint of microeconomics, trade liberalization is unambiguously good, from the standpoint of politicians, no longer being able to privilege a politically important group is problematic. The domestic political incentives described here shape bargaining positions for international agreements. Governments that regard privileging a group as politically essential will not easily acquiesce to demands that interfere with such redistribution. The discussion of the textile industry illustrated this clearly. Prior to 1969, the German CDU based government fought hard to exempt textiles from tariff cuts. Following the ascension of the SPD government, who drew little support from textiles, the German government reversed its position and pushed for liberalization. In contrast, the British government still fights vehemently on behalf of textiles. The domestic interaction of industry geography and the political system shapes preferences on trade and industrial policy. International agreements represent these domestic positions.

Of course an explanation for the domestic origins of nations' trade preference is not the whole story of international agreements. Just as domestic institutions affect how legislators' induced preferences aggregate into policy, so the structure of international negotiations, international institutions, and power relations influence the aggregation of nations' trade preferences. Just as I have argued that we cannot ignore the domestic aggregation step, we cannot ignore the international aggregation step. In this context my thesis should be seen as a progressive step. By first understanding the origins of domestic trade preferences, I hope subsequently to explain their aggregation through negotiations. The opposite tack would be to explore international negotiations first in a top-down approach. Yet, I believe such an approach is wrong-headed, since it provides no concept of the motivation and incentives of the bargainers.

International negotiators need to be mindful of whether groups abroad who are hurt by protection can receive the necessary political patronage to obtain retaliation. Politicians must consider the political costs such retaliation creates. Foreign governments can potentially exploit this situation by targeting retaliation against industries politically important to the domestic government. In part because of their regional geography, farmers are a powerful political group in France. In 1992, during the GATT Uruguay trade Round; the United States demanded that the European Union reduce agricultural subsidies and price supports. French farmers who opposed any such changes demanded that the European Union maintain its subsidies. Agricultural exceptions from trade agreements date back to the formation of the GATT, when paradoxically it was U.S. farmers who pushed for their exclusion (Goldstein 1989). Initially the French government adopted the farmers' position, refusing to agree to the cuts in subsidies demanded by the United States. In retaliation, the U.S. government placed import restrictions on French white wine, a move popular with California and other wine-producing states. Politically, the U.S. move was a clever one, since it harmed French wine producers, who were, by and large, in the same politically important districts as farmers. Since failing to agree to subsidy reductions now harmed the politically important districts, the French government relented. In another, more recent case, U.S. President Bush imposed tariffs, of up to 30 percent on a wide array of steel imports. In large part, this was done to win votes in the heavily populated, party-competitive industrial Midwest. Within weeks, the EU responded to Bush's steel tariffs (2002) with trade sanctions on a diverse array of items, including steel products, protective goggles, pinball machines, and motorcycles. Many of these were deliberately chosen to hurt export industries in those industrial midwestern states so politically important to Bush.[28] Trade is an international issue. But at the heart of the conflict between European states and the United States lies domestic political concerns. While the international component of trade imposes additional constraints, the underlying drive behind trade and industrial policy is the desire to privilege one domestic group relative to another. Industry geography and its interaction with the electoral system determine which groups politicians want to privilege. The electoral system determines which politicians can enact their desired policies. While international threats impose additional constraints on which groups can be privileged, the incentive and ability of governments to protect industrial groups is determined domestically by the interaction of industry geography and the electoral system.

Notes

Chapter 1
Redistributive Politics

1. *Financial Times*, 2 December 1983; "Belgium Ordered to Stop Assisting Fiber Producer." On the fight within the EU over toy quotas see the *South China Morning Post*, 8 June 1994, "UK Fights China Toy Quota." On German subsidies to Mecklenburger Metallguss, see *Sunday Telegraph*, 14 April 2002, "Chris Brooker's Notebook"; Also Helsingin Sanomat, "New Strategy Proposal Recommends Significant Increase in Maritime Subsidies." 12 December 2002. On U.S. tariffs see the *New York Times*, 26 November 2002, "U.S. to Seek to Abolish Many Tariffs."

2. Bernhard and Leblang 1999; Clark 2003; Cox 1990; Cox and McCubbins 1986; Dixit and Londregan 1996, 1998; Hallerberg 2002; Golder 2002; Laver and Schofield 1990; Lijphart 1994; Powell 1982, 2000; Rogowski 1987; Roubini and Sachs 1989; Schofield 1998, 2003.

3. See, for example, Mansfield and Busch 1995; Magee, Brock, and Young 1989; Milner 1983; Caves 1976.

4. For excellent reviews of the empirical work on trade, see Anderson and Baldwin 1987 and Rodrik 1995.

5. The industry has been in decline since the 1890s in the United Kingdom, the early 1900s in Germany, and the 1950s in the United States (White 1997).

6. In part as well, this loss of market was due to changes in consumers' tastes, which have moved away from formal dining. The demand for inexpensive cutlery was largely filled by cheap cutlery imports from Japan, South Korea, and China. *Financial Times*, 3 November 1988, "Marketing and Advertising: Unpalatable Facts Put on the Table." See also the *New York Times*, 15 April 1989, "Sheffield Knife Maker Beats the Odds"; and the *Independent*, 15 March 1994. "Sheffield's Sharpest Practice."

7. These figures are approximations. See Cable 1983; Glismann and Weiss 1980, Weiss 1983; USITC 1978, 1985.

8. This legislation originated in the National Security Act of 1947 and the Defense Production Act of 1950.

9. See, for example, Anderson and Baldwin 1987; Balassa 1971; Busch and Mansfield 1999; Conybeare 1993; Gawande and Krishna 2002; Goldberg and Maggi 1999; Gawande and Bandhopadhayay 2000; Goldberg and Maggi1999; Guisinger 2002; Magee, Brock, and Young 1989; Mansfield and Busch 1995; McGillivray 1997; Reidel 1977; Rogowski 1997, 1998; Rogowski, Kayser, and Kotin 1999; and Trefler 1993.

10. Factor mobility is assumed to be low; in other words, changes in relative prices do not lead to the immediate redeployment of factors (Jones 1971). There is a long-standing debate in the trade literature about the mobility of factors and actors trade preferences. In the political science literature, see Alt and Gilligan 1994; Alt et al. 1996; Hiscox 2001; Rogowski 1987; Scheve and Slaughter 2001.

11. In the longer term, capital and labor will shift into the protected industry and the rents from protection to both capital and labor will be diluted.

12. Mayer 1984; Mayer and Riezman 1987; Grossman and Helpman 1994.

13. There are, however, consumer groups that lobby against trade restrictions: U.K. Consumer Association. French Union Federale des Consommateurs. *Guardian*, 30 September 1985, "Motoring: Consumers Fight Price Controls: State Controls and Subsidies in Europe."

14. Higher domestic costs for inputs can also drive manufacturing to other countries where the inputs are lower priced.

15. The *New York Times*, 6 March, 2002, "Steel Tariffs Weaken Bush's Global Hand."

16. Foreign governments can also select retaliatory tariffs to exploit political vulnerabilities. The EU responded to President Bush's steel tariffs (2002) with trade sanctions on a diverse array of items, including steel products, protective goggles, pinball machines, and motorcycles. Many of these were deliberately chosen to damage export industries in states politically important to President Bush (*Economist*, 9 March 2002, "George Bush, Protectionist").

17. Examples of groups opposed to trade restrictions include the American Association of Exporters and Importers (textile and clothing) and the American Institute for Imported Steel.

18. See Dixit 1985. There is a large literature on the impact of free-trade on growth. Most scholars argue the relationship is positive: Barro (1997); Edwards (1992); Krueger (1998). Although, see Grossman and Helpman (1991) and Rodriguez and Rodrik (2000).

19. For excellent reviews of the endogenous trade policy literature, see Cadot, de Melo, and Olarreaga 1997; Hillman 1989; Gwande and Krishna 2001; Nelson 1988; Magee, Brock, and Young 1989; Marks and McArthur 1990; Riezman and Wilson 1992; Rodrik 1995.

20. Caves (1976), Pincus (1975), Becker (1983), Busch and Reinhardt (1999), Hillman (1989).

21. Loosely translated "the miller keeps a knife in his tights." *The Encyclopedia Britannia* (1911) S.V. "cutlery." Robert the Cutler was recorded as a knife maker in Sheffield in 1297.

22. The effective tariff is the tariff rate on domestic industry value added. It is calculated from the nominal rates; however, it accounts for the effect of input tariffs on domestic industry value added. Effective tariffs are typically higher than nominal tariffs although highly correlated. (Lavergne 1981).

23. This decline was exacerbated by increased competition from Germany, whose cutlery industry is located in the town of Solingen (North Rhine-Westphalia). By the 1900s both the U.K. and German cutlery industries were under pressure from cheap U.S. cutlery, which was mainly produced in Connecticut (New Britain and Bridgeport) and New York (Walden) (White 1997).

24. Protection for the cutlery industry goes as far back as to Chamberlain's Tariff Committee of 1904. The discussion of the cutlery case is purely intended to illustrate different concepts and ideas used in the books. I focus on a narrow slice of time in the late 1970s and early 1980s.

25. For example, see Hillman 1991; Marvel and Ray 1983; Esty and Caves 1983; Riezman and Wilson 1992; Cassing, McKeown, and Ochs 1986; Grier, Munger, and Roberts 1994; Mayer 1984; and Trefler 1993.

26. The Stolper-Samuelson theorem claims that under certain assumptions, international trade lowers the real wage of the scarce factors of production (Caves, Frankel, and Jones 1990). Unskilled labor is a scarce factor of production in industrialized countries; hence; it is more likely to demand protection. Holding demand constant, it is also more likely to receive aid, because these workers will suffer a large fall in income (Magee 1973).

27. Cheaper foreign imports are not the only reason for cutlery's decline. The industry has also been accused of a lack of initiative and mediocre marketing. *Financial Times*, 3 November 1988; "Marketing and Advertising: Unpalatable Facts Put on the Table."

28. There are different arguments; see Brainard and Verdier 1997; Hillman 1989; Staiger and Tabellini 1987.

29. See Johnman and Murphy 2002.

30. Concentration measures from monopoly theory in economics are typically used to construct this variable. The Herfindahl index (Boyes and Melvin 1994) takes the market share of each firm in the industry, squares them, and adds them together (where market share is typically measured as the dollar value of domestic shipments). An alternative measure of the effective number of firms, or the four-firm concentration ratio uses the market share of the four largest firms (Pincus 1975). Table 1.1, from Cable 1983, simply uses the percentage share of output from the five largest firms.

31. Although see Pecorino 1996. One caveat is that industrially concentrated industries are more likely to be export oriented—they benefit from economies of scale and so should lobby for open markets, not industry protection (Murphy, Schliefer, and Vishny 1993).

32. *Financial Times*, 3 November 1988, "Marketing and Advertising: Unpalatable Facts Put on the Table."

33. Among others, see Busch and Reinhardt 1999; Caves 1976; Fordham and McKeown 2001; Hansen 1990; Lavergne 1981; McGillivray 1997; Pincus 1975; Rogowski 1997, 1998; Rogowski, Kayser, and Kotin 1999; Schonhardt-Bailey 1991; Snyder 1989.

34. Among the many cutlery firms located in Sheffield in the 1980s were Viner's, Elkington Cutlery, Arkwright's, Joseph Marples, Clarkson's, Camelot Silverware, Sterling Cutlers, and United Cutlers. HMSO 1984: Hayter 1985.

35. Although not all economists agree on the economic impact of geographic concentration; see Appold 1995.

36. One argument is that innovation stalled because the unions halted mechanization (White 1997).

37. *Financial Times*; 11 June 1985, "Cutlery Companies Reap the Rewards of Cautious Policies."

38. Electoral concentration is usually measured by how concentrated an industry is across electoral districts (in the U.S. states). Are industry workers (or plants) located in six districts or sixty districts? Conceptually, we can measure this as a variant of the Herfindahl index using data on industry production output or industry employment, by electoral district. (Conybeare 1984; McGillivray 1995, 1997).

39. See, for example, the various country studies in Anderson and Baldwin 1987.

40. One way to capture the interactive impact of size is to interact measures of electoral concentration with the size of the industry. Another possibility is a variant of

the Herfindahl index, which measures how concentrated the industry is as a proportion of other industries within electoral districts (McGillivray 1997).

41. Although Busch and Reinhardt (1999) find these industries are politically powerful in the United States.

42. Sheffield Training and Enterprise Council, Census of Employment.

43. McGillivray 1995; McGillivray and Smith 1997.

44. Sheffield is where *The Full Monty* was filmed.

45. Heeley was a Conservative seat in 1966 and 1970. In 1970, Labour won 46 percent of the vote, the Conservatives 47 percent, and the Liberals 7 percent. The seat was turned over to Labour in February 1974, when Labour won 48 percent, the Conservatives 35 percent, and the Liberals 17 percent. Butler and King 1966; Butler and Pinto-Duschinsky 1971; Butler and Kavanagh 1980.

46. *Daily Telegraph*; 6 October 1989, "Poll Tax Anger May Cost Tories Marginal Seats."

47. *Financial Times*, 8 September 1989, "Sheffield 7: Cutting Edge Is Still Keen."

48. The definition for strong and weak parties is discussed in chapter 2.

49. For the election of the 603 Members of Parliament (2002), 299 Members of Parliament are elected with a relative majority in the constituencies, 304 according to Land party lists. Voters may cast their first vote for the election in the constituency and their second vote for the election of a party. The second vote determines the disbribution of seats among parties and which party members fill these seats after the first vote seat winners are accounted for. If a party wins more district seats than allocated by the proportional representation vote, the surplus seats are kept by the party. Parties that win at least 5 percent of the second vote or win seats in at least three districts are entered into the overall allocation of seats. The German system is highly proportionate and encourages strategic voting (Bawn 2000). Legislative behavior is also affected by the hybrid electoral system. There is evidence that Bundestag members from district seats care more about redistributive policies than list members do (Stratman and Baur 2002).

50. In 1979, the German cutlery industry had 22.1 percent of world exports; the U.K. cutlery industry, 8.6 percent; and the U.S. cutlery industry only 6.8 percent (Hayter 1985).

51. For example, in 1980, in Solingen-Remscheid, the SPD won 46.7 percent of the vote; the CDU, 37.3 percent, and the FDP 8.9 percent. Many thanks to Kathleen Bawn for generously providing German election data.

52. *Economist*, 18 September 1999, "Gerhard Schroder, Embattled Chancellor."

53. The seven big producers in scissors and shears are located in Massachusetts, Connecticut, South Carolina, and Ohio. The knife industry is largely located in Oregon and New York State (USITC 1985).

54. *Foreign Relations of the United States*, vol. 8, *International Monetary and Trade Policy*. (Washington, D.C.: Department of State), 964–68. Memorandum from the Special Representative for Trade Negotiations (Roth) to President Johnson. 9 October 1967.

55. *Business Week*, July 23 1984. "What's Forcing a Trade Agency into the Political Limelight"; or Presidential Memorandum for the Special Trade Representative concerning Certain Stainless Steel Table Flatware," vol. 43, Federal Regulation 29259, 7 July 1978.

56. Thanks to Iain McLean for this and other less amusing but very smart comments.

57. In Rogowski and Kayser, farmers are also consumers and producers. They can contribute both money and votes.

58. Of course, if industry geography changes, this will also affect the predictions. I do not consider this here, but see Rogowski 1986.

59. *BBC News*. 5 February 1999, "Rover Closure Could Devastate Economy."

60. *Economist*. 16 November 1985; "Middle Aged Manufacturers."

61. *Financial Times*. 9 February 1987, "Rover Funding Deal Likely Soon"; *Financial Times*, 2 January 1987, "Austin Rover seeks 400 M Pounds Cash Boost"; and *Economist*. 16 November 1985, "Middle Aged Manufacturers."

62. *Financial Times*, 11 February 1986, "Motor Industry's Influence Muted."

63. *Daily Telegraph*, 14 November 1998, "Motoring: Forgetting but Never Forgiving Backfire"; *Financial Times*, 23 December 1986, "A New Plan, an Old Problem: The Rover Group"; *Economist*, 8 February 1986, "Now, a Banana Skin with Wheels On."

64. *Financial Times*, 11 February 1986, "Motor Industry's Influence Muted."

65. Although it still held off until after the 1987 election. *Economist*, 11 October 1986, "Pumping Subsidies."

66. Although protection for footwear peaked during the period 1977–81, when the United States had extensive quotas on shoe imports from developing nations. McGillivray and Schiller 1998; Schiller 1999.

67. Quoted in McGillivray and Schiller 1998.

68. The *Los Angeles Times*, 3 April 2002, "Retailers Urge U.S. to Cut Tariffs."

69. Rae 1965, 1995; Cox 1990, 1997.

70. *Economist,* 15 November 1980, "Tory Takeovers."

71. Rogowski and Kayser (2002) imply that PR systems are more protectionist than majoritarian systems. This argument is discussed in an earlier section of this chapter.

72. The problem with using trade flows to measure the level of protection is that many factors other than government policy affect the amount of trade a country engages in.

73. Grilli 1980; see also *Economist*, 8 August 1992; "Aid Addicts"; *Economist*, 23 May 1981, "Facing the Facts: An Economic Survey, A New Crisis."

74. The *Sunday Telegraph*, 20 February 1994, Europe's Subsidy Shambles."

75. Subsidies are illegal under EU rules unless authorized by the commission for restructuring. Despite this, table 1.2 reveals they are widespread among EU member countries. Increasingly the EU commission is stamping down on the use of illegal subsidies. The EU now publishes the "State Aid Scoreboard" to "further increase transparency and to raise awareness for the need of state aid control." (EU Commission 2001). Before 1991, the commission investigated illegal subsidies after the fact. Nowadays, member governments must notify the EU commission in advance to get preapproval for subsidies. For example,the commission has brought legal action against Belgium over illegal subsidies to carpet makers. *Sunday Telegraph*, 20 February 1994, "Europes Subsidy Shambles."

76. Although many of these countries are members of the EU, a trade customs union, their tariff levels and NTBs still differ. The EU has a unified tariff scheme; however, under the EU's general scheme of preferences (GSP), imports labeled sensitive or semi-sensitive can have variable rates of duty; these duties often vary by country of origin and destination (see Cable and Rebelo 1980; Gillson 1999). Although carpets are a

"sensitive" product under the GSP, only Belgium actually levies tariffs. In the 1980s only about 20 percent of French trade was affected by the Common External Tariff (Bobe 1983). This is the reason tariff averages for EU countries vary across member states. Before 1994, when a unified system of quotas was adopted, there were over six thousand national quotas imposed by various member states of the EU (Gillson 1999).

77. Mansfield and Busch (1995) found PR countries were more likely to use NTBs. See Trefler 1993 on using NTB's to measure trade protection.

78. The system of national quotas among EU member countries was dismantled in 1994 and replaced with a unified import quota system. In large part, the unified system was initiated because with the free movement of products within Europe, the separate quota systems did not work very effectively. For example, Japanese cutlery facing high quotas in the United Kingdom, could enter via Spain and then through the free-movement of goods within the EU, make its way into U.K. stores. See McGillivray et al. 2001 for a discussion of how a free-trade area with no rules of origin erodes states external tariff barriers.

79. For excellent discussions see Duchene and Sheperd 1987; and Meny and Wright 1986.

80. *Newsweek*, 29 November 1982, "On the Brink of a Trade War?"

81. Informa Publishing Group, IPC, 1 April 1989, "New Resolve to Control State Aids."

82. *Financial Times*, 11 November 1988, "A Key Contribution to New Thinking."

83. See Guisinger's (2002) analysis of tariffs and import duties as tools to measure protection.

84. Cable and Rebelo 1980; Mansfield and Busch 1995; Busch and Reinhardt 1999.

85. As an example, British cutlery does not export much to other EU countries, but this is probably not due to bureaucratic harassment or regulatory differences; rather, knife blades are typically 1.5 inches longer in Europe than in Britain. People like them better that way. *Financial Times*, 8 September 1989, "Sheffield 7: Cutting Edge Is Still Keen."

86. See earlier discussion in section "Geographic Concentration."

87. Although see excellent work on the politics of financial markets by Brander 1991; Gilligan and Krehbiel 1988; Herron 2000; Herron et al. 1999; Freeman, Hayes, and Stix 2000; Hayes, Stix, and Freeman 2000; Goodhart 2001; Roberts 1990; Sobel 1999.

88. *Economist*, 13 May 1995, "Peugeot Citroen: Clawing Its Way to the Top?"

89. *Economist*, 22 November 1997, "The Addicts in Europe."

90. See also Campbell, Lo, and MacKinlay 1997; Shiller 2000; Grossman and Levinson 1989; Lenway, Rehbein, and Starks 1986; Hartigan, Perry, and Kamma 1986; Schnietz and Oxley 1999. For research on how politics affects and is affected by financial markets, see Freeman, Hayes and Stix 2000, Hayes, Stix, and Freeman 2000; Herron 2000; Herron et al. 1999; Goodhart 2001; Brander 1991; Roberts 1990; Gilligan and Krehbiel 1989.

91. In the field of financial economics, event analysis is the methodology commonly used to study how firm-specific events impact stock prices (Brown and Warner 1980, 1985).

92. For the precise formula and a detailed discussion, see chapter 5.

Chapter 2
Who Are the Decision Makers and What Motivates Them?

1. There are many types of PR formula: e.g., D'Hondt, Hare, Modified Sainte Lague, etc. Similarly, there are different types of majoritarian rules: e.g., first-past-the-post, majority rule with runoffs, single transferable votes, alternative votes, limited vote, etc.

2. Although see Lijphart's (1990) critique of Rae (1971).

3. Fairer in terms of the ideology/party of the legislator, not in terms of accountability (Powell 2000).

4. Although small parties can gain representation, particularly if their support is concentrated regionally.

5. Again, cross-combinations of these properties exist. Minority governments and multiparty governments exist in multiparty majoritarian systems. Multiparty PR systems can have single-party minority governments. Some of these cross-combinations are discussed in the appendix.

6. The nature of the government bargaining process also has important policy implications. Cabinet instability and short-lived governments characterize many PR systems. Under PR in Italy, small parties bargained continually over the breakup and formation of coalitions (Mershon 2002). Grilli, Masciandoro, and Tabellini (1991) argue that in PR systems, governments anticipate that they will not be in office for long and so engage in inflationary policies and rent-seeking behavior. However, in some PR systems, centrist parties form a part of successive government coalitions; for example, the Christian Democrats in Italy. In other words, despite frequent cabinet breakups, some parties remain in power for long periods of time. Scholars argue that this creates relatively stable policy outcomes (Laver and Schofield 1990). Yet, even when a change in party government occurs, policies are believed to change less under PR multipartism, either because of compromises induced at the legislative stage or because of difficulties reaching compromises among ideologically different veto players (Laver and Budge 1992; Tsebelis 1995, 1999, 2002). It is commonly argued that multiparty government leads to policy stability in PR systems because it is difficult to change the status quo (Roubini and Sachs 1989; Rustow 1950).

By contrast, in majoritarian systems, a shift in government is widely believed to lead to radical policy changes (Hibbs 1977; Rustow 1950; Sugden 1984; Epstein 1994). One explanation is that majoritarian governments are not beset by the same bargaining difficulties that hinder PR governments. Majoritarian systems tend to be characterized by majority single-party governments. The strong party in majority government does not have to negotiate with other parties because parties in the legislature cannot prevent policy change (Tsebelis 1995, 1999, 2002). On balance, it may not be possible to say which electoral system has less policy change. In majoritarian systems that are fewer veto players to prevent policy change; however, the parties have incentives to adopt similar policy positions. In PR systems parties adopt divergent, extreme policy positions, in large part because they anticipate having to compromise on policy when in government.

7. See Bawn, Cox, and Rosenbluth 1999 for an excellent discussion of how to measure electoral cohesiveness and party strength in a comparative framework.

8. See also Mitchell 1999.

9. See Brady, Cooper, and Hurley 1979; Rohde 1991; Cox and McCubbins 1993.

10. Although this is an increasingly controversial statement. See, Aldrich 1995; Cox and McCubbins 1993; Rhode 1991.

11. The strength of parties is partly a function of the electoral rule but only partly because there are examples of strong-party majoritarian systems and weak-party PR systems. I choose to treat the level of party discipline as an exogenous factor.

12. Laver and Schofield (1990), in their discussion of coalition formation, provide a detailed summary of different approaches to parties. See also Muller and Strom 1999.

13. I assume ideology is fixed; however, there is a large literature on how the distribution of ideological preferences among voters affects the ideological positions of parties. This literature implies that parties alter their ideological positions over time to get votes (Roemer 2001).

14. What voters really care about is their well-being, which will be a function of income and prices. However, for simplicity, this is referred to as income.

15. Parties with high party discipline are conceived of as unitary actors. However, parties are often internally divided. See Strom 1990b for insights into how power struggles within parties affect government formation. In contrast in weak party systems, voters choose individual candidates rather than a party label, and legislative decisions are made by coalitions of individual legislators rather than by parties.

16. I ignore optimal tariff arguments for now. An alternative hypothesis that is consistent is that redistributive trade assistance is in addition to optimal tariffs.

17. For a discussion of factor mobility see Mussa 1982; Grossman 1983; Hiscox 2001, and Alt et al. 1996.

18. One could argue that incumbents are constrained from supplying protection to the one industry in their constituency because of the political risks involved with imposing costs on some of their constituents to help others. For simplicity, I assume that all the constituents of an electoral district are employed or have capital in the district's single industry.

19. See Robertson 1976.

20. One rejoinder to this argument is that if voters are sophisticated, shouldn't we expect the price of marginal and safe districts to converge? Sophisticated voters in safe districts would sell themselves to the opposition at exactly the price that voters in marginal districts demand. Or marginal districts would raise the price they demand to whatever price a politician would have to pay to get a safe seat to switch. However, for the voters in a safe district to switch their votes to make their district appear marginal requires an impossibly difficult coordination problem. Even if voters attempted to coordinate, doing so would reveal to the government that their district is safe even if the vote outcome makes the district look more marginal. It is cost effective to target voters in marginal seats.

21. Seats are typically allocated according to the proportion of votes in each district. Although in the Netherlands and Israel, the whole country comprises a single electoral district, these are rare exceptions. However, a common feature is that leftover votes not allocated at the district level are aggregated and assigned to seats at the national level. The effect of this second-tier allocation is to bring seat allocations close to vote allocations.

22. Laver and Schofield (1990) provide an excellent discussion.

23. The vote threshold is lower than 5 percent in many PR countries.

24. Although not always. Some countries have noncompensatory upper tiers—for example, Malta.

25. From 1971 to 2000, Denmark had 175 legislative seats, in total, 17 districts with a total of 135 seats, and an upper tier with 40 seats.

26. Among others, see Ferejohn 1974; Hibbing and Theiss-Morse 1995; and Stein and Bickers 1995.

27. For a formal discussion, see McGillivray and Smith 1997 and Snyder 1989.

28. See also Snyder 1990.

29. Thanks to Tim Power, Barry Ames, and John Carey for ideas on redistributive politics in Brazil.

30. See discussion in chapter 1.

31. Senator Danforth (R-MO) was Chair of the Finance Subcommittee on Trade from 1981 to 1986. Senator Mitchell (D-ME) was a member of the Finance Committee and then became Senate majority leader, from 1989 to 1994.

32. In most countries outside of the United States, the state pays a large proportion of election expenses. The United Kingdom is unusual within Europe in that the state does not contribute to party campaign expenses. However, election timing is endogenous and the election campaign period is short, hence money is not key in determining outcomes. The *Economist*, 26 June 1996, "Only in Britain." See Smith's (1996, 2006) work on endogenous election timing.

33. Obviously, the above discussion illustrates the problem of considering stylized examples rather than working with real cases. There are many factors that modify the model's predictions. Yet, had I started with an empirical study of the industrial composition of each district, the simple political incentive would have been disguised. For this reason, I believe that the most productive avenue to explore is theorizing from a simple structure, and then, once the basic political incentives are understood, asking how real world features complicate the picture.

34. *Sydney Morning Herald*, 8 Decemaber 2000, "Grassroots Democracy in Danger of Turning into a Dust Bowl."

35. Australia exhibits a fascinating array of different electoral rules, but the dominant rule in lower-house elections is the single transferable vote.

36. Specifically, any candidate with more than 12.5 percent of the vote.

37. Although there is controversy about this. See Tsebelis 1997, chap. 7, p. 191; and Golder 2003.

38. Optimal tariffs are not an option.

Chapter 3
Party Strength as a Determinant of Industry Tariffs

1. There are notable exceptions. See Anderson and Baldwin 1981; Mansfield and Busch 1993; Finger, Hall, and Nelson 1982; Rogowski 1987; Milner 1983; Lohman and O'Halloran 1994.

2. This chapter draws heavily from McGillivray 1997.

3. Note that in 1982, the Department of Industry, Trade, and Commerce (ITC) was merged with the Department of External Affairs. The Privy Council Office is also involved in those matters that come to the Cabinet's attention. Other departments and agencies share responsibilities on specific matters. Hine (1985) argues that most trade

and tariff issues are dealt with by the bureaucracy in these bodies, the majority of whom favor free trade. However, he adds that trade officials within the ITC are constrained when the industry involved is politically sensitive.

4. For example, the United States threatened to impose tariffs on Canadian automobiles, and the United States and Canada negotiated the Auto Pact of 1965 (free trade in vehicles, parts, etc.).

5. Each state automatically gets one representative; however, additional representatives depend on population size.

6. See, Bawn, Cox, and Rosenbluth 1999; Aldrich 1995; Cox and McCubbins 1993; and Gilligan and Krehbiel 1989, 1990.

7. The *Washington Post*, 5 May 2002, "Is This Any Way to Build a Trade Policy?"

8. In particular, the states of Ohio and Pennsylvania. *Economist*, 13 May 2002, "What Happened to Free Trade?"

9. *Economist*, 5 January 1980, "American Farming."

10. Note, however, that the president can trade concessions to buy votes. Members of his own party may be more receptive to pressure (Baldwin 1985), as might representatives from marginal electorates. These representatives will be the most easily bought off.

11. One would expect that where trade is important to a congressmember's constituency interests, she will attempt to get committee assignments where they can influence trade policy (Denzau and Munger 1986). Hansen (1990) finds that industries that are located in the districts of powerful or influential congressmen are more likely to be granted protection from the International Trade Commission (ITC). We might suspect, then, that industries located in the districts of Ways and Means Committee members receive more favorable levels of protection than other industries. However, it is also plausible that Ways and Means Committee members are cautious about legislating to protect industries concentrated in their districts. Such an action could be seen as an abuse of power. The Ways and Means Committee is supposed to guard against excessively particularized legislation. However, committee members can aid decentralized industries that are situated in their districts without appearing to abuse their position, given that industry is located in a large number of electoral districts. Also, unlike ITC decisions, trade bills need to be passed by a majority of the legislators in the house.

12. Pressure groups appear to respond strategically to this. Schattschneider (1935) comments on the regional and state-level organization of industry pressure groups in the United States.

13. Generally, there are many problems matching industry data to the tariff and employment figures (see U.S. Census Bureau "U.S. Commodity Exports as Related to Output, 1966 and 1965," p. 124). In Canada, the 1971 census is used to obtain geographical information on employment by electoral district. This data was provided by *Statistics Canada* and lists industry employment by a three-digit Canadian SIC code by electoral district. I assume that industry employment is constant from 1970 to 1971 (1970 being the year tariff rates are available). Wilkinson and Norrie's 103 industry commodity categories are matched to the 1971 Canadian standard industrial classification using *Statistics Canada*'s (1972) numeric index. Around 130 industrial categories are matched across the electoral district employment data and the nominal and effective tariff data. In the United States, data on employment by county are provided in the 1977 *Census of Manufacturers* from the U.S. Census Bureau. Unfortunately, U.S., con-

fidentiality requirements mean that firms are categorized by employment size intervals, rather than employment size. To calculate employment by industry and by electoral district, the midpoint in the interval is used. Information on "employment" and "number of establishments" is aggregated from the county to the electoral district level. In most states, counties aggregate neatly into electoral districts; in some cases, however, single counties contained multiple electoral districts. Approximations were made using the assumptions that all counties are internally homogenous with respect to industrial geography. I assume that the geographical distribution of industry employment is constant from 1977 until 1979. In the United States, the industry tariff data used are based on the 1963 version of the MUSIC classification scheme, an SIC-based import code. The industry employment data are SIC 1972 code. I have transformed the data so that the coding on dependent and independent variables "match." The concordance is provided in Lavergne 1981. This matches the MUSIC item to a weighted sum of 1963 SIC items. This creates around four hundred categories.

14. Effective rates are available for Canada and the United States. Which set of rates should be used is controversial (Baldwin 1985; Chen 1974). Effective and nominal rates are highly correlated and the findings were similar using both types of measurement (see McGillivray 1995). The tariff levels used to test the U.S. model are calculated at the four-digit industry level by Lavergne (1981; 1983). He uses an average, weighted by a country's own imports to summarize the commodities into four-digit standard industrial classifications (SIC), which yields around 400 industry categories. Wilkinson and Norrie (1975) calculate the tariff levels used to test the Canadian model. They use a similar averaging scheme to create over 100 industry categories that roughly correspond to the three-digit Canadian Standard Industrial Classification (CSIC). Note: the effective and nominal rates of protection for automobiles in the Wilkinson and Norrie data is replaced by the tariff rate calculated by Connidis (1983). Connidis argues that Wilkinson and Norrie did not average the tariff in the automobile industry appropriately, given the U.S.-Canadian AutoPact of 1965. However, the empirical tests are also run using the original Wilkinson and Norrie calculations for automobiles. The results are the same (McGillivray 1995).

15. Diagnostic tests revealed mild heteroskedasticity. White's method is used to correct the coefficient standard errors.

16. In the text, a variable that is described as significant has a statistical significance level of at least 5 percent in a one-tailed test.

17. Data on unemployment by county for the United States is available from the 1980 census of population. Unemployment by county is aggregated from the county to the electoral-district level. The variable unemployment is the ratio of unemployed in the electoral district to the total workforce. In Canada, unemployment is the ratio of total employment to total population (the results are the same if I used total employment or total population minus total employment). I make the assumption that internally all electoral districts are homogeneous with respect to the retired, under-eighteen and homemaker proportion of the Canadian population.

18. This multiplicity of measures is because "marginality" is a key theoretical variable in the strong-party majoritarian model. In Canada, elections at the district level are sometimes characterized by multiparty, rather than two-party, competition. With three or more parties, the theory suggests that the government still targets those seats that are most likely to be important in determining whether it maintains a legislative

majority. Instead of taking the vote differential between the two largest parties, I take the vote differential between the Liberals and the vote for the party with the highest vote that is not the Liberal party. If the Liberals won a district seat, this variable measures how many votes they won that seat by. If they did not win, this variable measures the number of votes they needed to take the seat. As discussed in the text, another variable was created to measure "underlying marginality." In this case district marginality $= -|$ %vote for Liberal party$_j - 9\% - $ %biggest vote for rival party$_j |$. The results were similar regardless of which measure of marginality is used (see McGillivray 1995).

19. Indeed, in the 1963 and 1965 parliaments, the Liberals formed the government, but they were four and two seats short of a majority, respectively.

20. To test robustness, I also tested the 1976 Congress. The results were similar.

21. This still leaves the question, why do more populated states get higher levels of protection in Canada? Perhaps, this imbalance is because different parties have regional strongholds in different states. The Liberal party was in power for most of this period, and it has a strong hold in the more populated States. Canadian politics also tends to revolve around the two larger states of Ontario and Quebec. Thanks to a reviewer for this point.

22. Diagnostic tests revealed no evidence of heteroskedasticity.

23. An alternative measure was also employed—industry employment in each district as a share of manufacturing employment in that districts. The findings are similar whichever measure of district concentration is used (see McGillivray 1995).

24. Lavergne (1981) attempts to assess the level of tariff protection for industry in the United States in the 1970s. See also Reidel 1977; Heilleiner 1977; Wilkinson and Norrie 1975.

25. Rogowski et al. (1999) and Rogowski and Kayser (2002) use price differences across countries to get around the transparency problem and identify which industries were most heavily assisted.

Chapter 4
Restructuring and Redistribution in the Steel Industry

1. *Financial Times*, 22 November 1982; "Manufacturing Future Rests on the Fate of Ravenscraig."

2. See Baden-Fuller 1989 and Sadler 1984 on the influence of economic variables (firm effects) and other political variables on plant closure.

3. "Germany" refers to the Federal Republic of Germany.

4. As described in the *Economist*, 11 December 1982; "Putting Dinosaurs to Sleep."

5. *Washington Post*, 3 January 1980, "100,000 Steelworkers Begin Walkout in Britain: New Walkout by British Steelworkers Threatens Further Harm to Economy."

6. *Economist*, 11 December 1982, "Putting Dinosaurs to Sleep."

7. The case studies draw extensively from such studies; for example, Meny and Wright 1986; Bain 1992; Hudson and Sadler 1989; Dudley and Richardson 1990; K. Jones 1986; Duchene and Shepherd 1987; Scheuerman 1986; Daley 1986; Tsoukalis and Strauss (1986); Esser and Vath 1986; Capron 1986; Bell 1993; Esser and Fach 1989; Levin 1985; Wilkes and Wright 1987.

8. In part, this is because steel wages tend to be higher than those of other industries competing for the same labor pool Esser and Vath 1986.

9. The *New York Times*, 27 March 1983, "Rhine Rebutt Embitters the Socialists." In 1982, the rate of unemployment was around 20 percent in steel regions in the United Kingdom, France, and Southern Belgium. Across EU states, the average rate of unemployment was closer to 10 percent (Meny and Wright 1986).

10. From 1977 to 1980, the EU had informal controls on steel output. Formal production quotas were abolished in 1988. The EU also provided aid to retrain and create new jobs. *Financial Times*, 24 June 1988, "Europe's Steel Rejoins the Free World."

11. See discussion of the low level of party cohesion in the United States in chapter 3. Also Cox and McCubbins 1993; Laver and Shepsle 1994.

12. In the lower tiers, Belgium used the Hare rule (until 1987), and in the upper it uses D'Hondt (until 1987), with district magnitudes of 7 (30 districts) and 23 (9 districts) respectively. Sweden uses Modified Sainte Lague in both its tiers, with district magnitudes of 11 (28 districts) and 39 (1 district) respectively.

13. Germany is a "mixed" electoral system. Half of Parliament is elected from single-member districts with plurality rule, the other half using d'Hondt and the list vote. However, the overall allocation of seats in the Bundestag is decided by the nationwide vote. In terms of proportionality, the list vote is the decisive vote, and as such Germany is defined as PR.

14. By 1981, fourteen parties were represented in parliament. See de Winter, Timmermans, and Dumsat 2000 for an excellent description of the Belgian party system.

15. In the United Kingdom, many decisions on trade policy are the direct responsibility of the Department of Trade. It works with the Department of Industry, which tends to be sympathetic to domestic pressures for assistance. But the Department of Trade represents both exporters and import-competing industry, and so is less sympathetic due to the possibility of retaliatory measures. The Department of Employment sometimes weighs in, and the Department of Treasury is involved if subsidies are the chosen policy instrument. Germany also has a complex system of assistance to industry—in part because of its federal structure, it has a hierarchical system of trade assistance based on federal/state/local subsidies (Weiss 1983).

16. Another reason for focusing on the policy outcomes is that the process to distribute aid is not transparent. In the United Kingdom, decision-making is done behind closed doors—tripartite discussions between bureaucrats, industry, and unions that are veiled in secrecy.

17. For an excellent survey, see Capron 1986.

18. *Economist*, 27 September 1980, "Belgian Steel: Tough Break."

19. *Economist*, 7 November 1981. "Belgium: Fudge for King and Country."

20. *Economist*, 7 November, 1981 "Belgium; Fudge for King and Country"; *Economist*, 27 September 1980, "Belgian Steel: Tough Break."

21. The center-socialist government resigned, in part, because of the north-south dispute over aid to steel. *Associated Press*, 27 September 1981; "General Elections Scheduled in Belgium."

22. *Economist*, 20 March 1982; "Belgium: You're Hurting."

23. *Economist*, 10 April 1982, "The Ruhr and Basque Regions." Steel is an even bigger proportion of the workforce in the Saarland (Esser and Vath 1986).

24. I refer to only the CDU; however, the CDU and Christian Social Union of Bavaria (CSU) have a long-standing political partnership.

25. *Economist*, 20 November 1982, "Steel Closures: Scotched?"

26. *Economist*, 29 January 1983, "West Germany's Steel Is Split between Rhine and Ruhr." This merger never occurred, in part because of problems dealing with the Klockner firm. *Economist*, 11 June 1983, "West German Steel: Clash over Klockner."

27. *New York Times*, 27 March 1983, "Rhine Rebuff Embitters the Socialists."

28. *Financial Times*, 7 September 1983, "Bonn Defends Plans for Increased State Aid."

29. *Economist*, 29 January 1983, "West Germany's Steel Is Split between Rhine and Ruhr."

30. At the local level, all steel communities had SPD mayors (Esser and Vath 1986).

31. The *Economist*, 15 November 1980, "Tory Takeovers."

32. In 1976, seat percentages of the parties in government were CP, 24.6 percent; FP, 11.2 percent and MUP, 15.8 percent. SDA remained out of government but won 43.6 percent seats in 1976.

33. *Economist*, 15 November 1980, "Tory Takovers."

34. Hansard Debates, 13 March 1989.

35. *Washington Post*, 3 January 1980, "100,000 Steelworkers Begin Walkout in Britain: New Walkout by British Steelworkers Threatens Further Harm to Economy."

36. *Independent*, 12 January 1992, "Is There Life after Ravenscraig? As Steel Closure Spells the End of Scottish Heavy Industry, Michael Fathers Finds Jobs Are More Important than Symbols."

37. See Meny and Wright 1987; Richardson and Dudley 1986; Richardson 1988.

38. *Economist*, 20 November 1982, "Steel closures: Scotched?"

39. Younger's margin of victory in the Ayr district narrowed to 182 votes in 1992 after the plant was finally closed (less than 1 percent vote differential between the two largest parties).

40. *Economist*, 20 November 1982, "Steel Closures: Scotched?"

41. Although in 1976, fourteen ministers in the Labour government were in steel constituencies where closures were threatened (Hudson and Sadler 1989).

42. After redistricting in 1983, the seat of Corby became a marginal Tory seat.

43. *Financial Times*, 22 November 1982, "Manufacturing Future Rests on the Fate of Ravenscraig."

44. This section of the chapter draws heavily from McGillivray and Schiller 1998; and Schiller 1999. See Schiller 2000 for an analysis of the U.S. Steel case, 1994–2000.

45. For list of plant closures from 1978 to 1982, see Scheuerman 1986.

46. *Economist*, 4 July 1981. "Free Trade Is a Two-Way Street."

47. Originally quoted in McGillivray and Schiller 1998.

48. Quoted in McGillivray and Schiller 1998.

Chapter 5
Redistributive Politics and Industry Stock Prices

1. For example, see The *Montreal Gazette*, 7 November 1996; "U.S. Election Heats Stocks." Pharmaceutical stocks fell amid fears of a politically unfavorable outcome in congressional elections.

2. *Economist*, 7 November 1981; "Belgium: Fudge for King and Country."

3. Among others see Brander 1991; Gilligan and Krehbiel 1988; Herron 2000; Heron et al. 1999; Quinn and Jacobson 1989; and Roberts 1990.

4. See the *Financial Times* Election Share Index; 6 April 1992, "Stock Price Index Moves against Victory for Major."

5. For the precise formula and a detailed discussion, see the empirical section of this chapter.

6. See Boix 1998; Strom 1990a; and Muller and Strom 1999 on the motivations of parties.

7. Bargaining theory suggests it is optimal for the government to randomize over the legislator (see Baron and Ferejohn 1989). If the government always relied on one legislator, then the reservation value of this legislator would rise and the alternative supporters could be bought off more cheaply.

8. There are a number of reasons for these differences, including historical legacy and the legal structure of property rights in the economic market.

9. *Economist*, 30 August 1997, "Comic Opera: Italy's Stock Exchange."

10. *Economist*, 25 October 1997, "Survey of Fund Management."

11. Note: Germany is a "mixed" electoral system. Half of Parliament is elected from single-member districts, the other half from the list vote. However the overall allocation of seats in the Bundestag is decided by these list votes. Given the number of district seats, each party is awarded additional list seats as is needed until the total number of seats is proportional to the number of votes that party received. In other words, in Germany, maximizing votes and seats are equivalent.

12. There are many differences in the details of each electoral system in the fourteen time series. However, these differences are not as important as the similarities between countries within each type of political system. Few of the countries perfectly fit the stylized model of a two-party majoritarian system with single-party government or a multiparty PR system with multiparty government. Austria has had periods of two-party competition. Germany, with its two large parties and small third party, also displays features of two-partyism. The theory predicts, however, that parties in a two-party PR system behave differently than do parties in a two-party majoritarian system. Germany and Austria remain in the group of PR systems. All the majoritarian countries have experienced multiparty competition at some time or another. Nonetheless, party competition in each of the majoritarian countries is dominated by two large parties, or two large "teams" of parties. France is the only majoritarian system with multiparty competition and multiparty government. However, two teams of left and right parties form in the general assembly; one of these teams forms the government. The parties in government are a "team" rather than a "coalition" because they are typically bound by preelection pacts.

13. Datastream Corporation 1999, Data on Stock Market capitalization was provided by Global Financial Data.

14. For example, Datastream constructs the following industry subindices: Aerospace and Defense, Automobiles, Banks, Beverages, Brews-Pubs-Restaurants, Chemicals, Construction and Building Material, Distributors, Electricity, Electronic Equipment, Engineering and Machinery, Food and Retail Drugs, Food Production, Forestry, Gas Distribution, Health, Information and Technical Hardware, Insurance, Investment Companies, Life Assurance, Leisure, Media, Mining, Oil and Gas, Packaging and For-

estry, Personal and Household Goods, Pharmaceuticals, Real Estate, General Retail, Speciality Finance, Software and Computer Services, Steel, Support Services, Telecom, Household and Textiles, Tobacco, Transportation, and Water.

15. Of course, not all industries respond in exactly the same way to these exogenous shocks; some tend to move less than the general market index, some more (Campbell, Lo, and MacKinlay 1997).

16. Note that changes in prices are used instead of levels because of potential scaling problems (markets have risen sharply in value since 1973, so large price changes in earlier periods would be obscured if levels rather than changes were used). Technically, this variable should be labeled price-change dispersion; however, the term is rather unwieldy, hence, the simpler label price dispersion.

17. These results are available in appendix 5.1.

18. The models were also tested using a dichotomous measure of political change that takes the value of 1 when the composition of the party government changes. See appendix 5.1. The findings are similar.

19. An alternative measure could be developed using cabinet portfolios, but as Blais, Blake, and Dion (1993) argue, "as cabinet seats tend to be directly proportional to parliamentary seats in coalition governments, taking parliamentary seats will give results not much different from those based on cabinet seats." There are still drawbacks to using this measure. Does a party's percentage of seats represent its relative policy influence? In other words, this measure does not consider the pivotalness of parties. While this would be desirable, it is extremely difficult to identify which parties are pivotal. Although power indices designed to do so exist, there is no consensus on their usefulness, and so they have not been used in the analysis.

20. Political data from the *European Journal of Political Research*, special annual data issues beginning with vol. 24 (1993); also Mackie and Rose 1983.

21. For example, a narrow band of 0.01 and broad band of 0.08. The results using these bandwidths bear out the predictions as well and are available in appendix 5.1.

22. Although not for all specifications, Hausman tests typically reject the null hypothesis of independence between regressors and country-specific intercepts. This suggests that fixed-effects are more appropriate than random-effects models. Fortunately, both fixed- and random-effects models are similar to the GLS analyses reported. The GLS modeled was estimated using STATA's xtgls, specifying heteroskedastic panels and first order autocorrelation. Given the large number of time periods for each nation (around 275), Beck and Katz's (1995) critique of feasible GLS and suggestion to use panel-corrected standard errors instead can be ignored. Without the inclusion of the lagged dependent variable, first-order autocorrelation between residuals is typically around 0.3. With the inclusion of the lagged dependent variable, first order autocorrelation is between 0 and −0.06 for most model specifications. The magnitudes and significance of the regression coefficients are remarkably insensitive to whether or not the lagged dependent variable is included. Similarly, although the inclusion of market volatility drastically improves the fit of the model, its inclusion or exclusion has only small effects on other regression coefficients.

23. Using a dichotomous measure of political change and a squared version of the dependent variable produces similar results. See appendix 5.1.

24. In addition to the prospects for political change, political business cycle theorists (for example, Nordhaus 1975) anticipate governments alter their behavior prior to elections to enhance their prospects for reelection.

25. Budge, Robertson, and Hearl 1987.

26. These variables are taken directly from EJPR coding from 1973 onward. The variable descriptions, means, and standard deviations are summarized in appendix 5.1.

27. Economic data is gathered on a quarterly basis for GDP and a monthly basis for inflation, interest rates, and unemployment. The data is from a variety of sources. See the IMF 's "International Financial Statistics," CD-ROM (1999); and the OECD's "Quarterly and Monthly Labor Force Statistics" (various years).

28. Monthly data on inflation rates was not available for Switzerland. However, in regressions not involving inflation, the inclusion of Switzerland did not alter the results.

29. The excluded countries are Austria, Denmark, Italy, and Norway. Those results are available in appendix 5.1.

30. The *Montreal Gazette*, 7 November 1996, "U.S. Election Heats Stocks."

31. As an additional test, I allowed for cross-sectional correlation between units. Since this test requires strictly balanced panels, it required a reduced time dimension. As such, I do not report the results; however, the analysis is consistent with those reported.

32. The null hypothesis is that the coefficients on MPC_{t-1}, MPC_t, and MPC_{t+1} are all simultaneously zero. The test statistic is $\chi^2(3 \text{ d.o.f.}) = 9.47$. The probability of observing this under the null is only 0.024, thus rejecting the null hypothesis.

33. $\chi^2(3 \text{ d.o.f.}) = 7.62$ (Pr. = 0.055)

34. The null hypothesis is that the coefficients on $MPC_{t-6}, \ldots, MPC_t, \ldots, MPC_{t+6}$ are all simultaneously zero. The test statistic is $\chi^2(13 \text{ d.o.f.}) = 19.56$. The probability of observing this under the null is 0.107. The corresponding test for PR systems has $\chi^2(13 \text{ d.o.f.}) = 24.94$ (Pr. = 0.024).

35. Among others, see Gilligan and Krehbiel 1989; Herron 2000; Heron et al. 1999; Goodhart 2001; Hays, Stix, and Freeman 2000; Brander 1991; Roberts 1990; and Alesina et al. 1992.

Chapter 6
A Theory and Direction for Future Research

1. Sectoral and Trade Barriers Database 1998, 2001, http//mkaccdb.eu.int. In 1998, the United States updated its list of subsidy programs. The EU still claims there are still unreported subsidy programs in sensitive industry sectors, and subsidies at the subfederal level are largely ignored. Data on EU subsidy programs is compiled by the EU Commission in the annual publication "State Aid Scoreboard."

2. Between 1985 and 1995, Garrett (1998) found a strong negative correlation between tariffs and NTBs in OECD countries (quoted in Guisinger 2002). However, other evidence suggests that NTBs and Tariffs are positively correlated (see Rodrik 1995).

3. Beginning in 1974, and extended several times until 1995, bilateral quotas on textiles and clothing between industrial and developing countries have been organized through the MultiFiber Arrangment (MFA). In 1995, this was replaced by the WTO

Agreement on Textiles and Clothing, which is expected to be phased out by 2005. The average textile tariff is 17 percent in the United States and 12 percent in the EU.

4. EU Market Access Sectoral Report 1989; http://mkaccdb.eu.int.

5. The size and industrial concentration of the textile industry does vary across countries. The U.K. industry in 1981 had 299,000 workers and 5,105 firms. The German textile industry had 522,000 workers but only 2,587 firms. In 1982, the United States had 897,000 workers and 13,257 firms. Figures from The World Bank Trade and Production Database, 1976–1999; companion paper, by A. Nicita and M. Olarrenga 2001.

6. http://www.eiro.eurofound.ie/1997/03/InBrief/EU9703111N.html. Tina Weber, "Commission Rejects French Textile Plan," by ECOTEC, March 28, 1997.

7. See Chadar, David, and Feigend 1987; Firman 1990; Shepard, Duchene, and Saunders 1983; Underhill 1998; Wilks and Wright 1987.

8. *Financial Times*, 15 February 1984, "EEC Stops Belgian Textile Aid"; *Financial Times*, 2 December 1983, "Belgium Ordered to Stop Assisting Fibre Producers."

9. European Information Services, *European Report*, 6 October 1999, "State Aid: France Loses Textiles Case in European Court."

10. *Economist*, 6 June 1981, "European Fibres"; also *Economist*, 23 May 1981. "Italy: Survey."

11. "Australian Broadcasting Company News," 6 October 2001. "Welcome to the Country's Most Marginal Seats." Australian Broadcast Company, 1998 Election News. ABC election analyst Antony Green (www. abc. net. au /election98/ news/ issues / issvic.htm).

12. In West Yorkshire, in 1983, in 8 out of 23 seats the vote difference between the two top parties was less than 5 percent of the total vote (true of 7 seats in 1987, 6 seats in 1992). Lancashire's figures are not as impressive: in 1983, 3 of 16 seats were marginal. However, by comparison, in 1983, in South Yorkshire only 2 of 15 districts were marginal, in North Yorkshire, only 1 of 17 districts were marginal.

13. *Financial Times*, 16 November 1992, "Buccaneering Capitalism in a Not So Free Market."

14. *Financial Times*, 15 February 1984, "EEC Stops Belgian Textile Aid."

15. *Financial Times*, 2 December 1983, "Belgium Ordered to Stop Assisting Fibre Producers."

16. *Sunday Telegraph*, 20 February 1994, "Europe's Subsidy Shambles"; *Financial Times*, 2 December 1983, "Belgium Ordered to Stop Assisting Fibre Producers." The Belgian government gave misleading assurances that the aid was recovered. The commission took the Belgian government to the European court of justice. House of Common's Hansard Debates for 10 July 1989. *Financial Times*, 11 August 1983, "Belgium to Fight Textile Aid Curb."

17. U.S. Census of Manufacturers 1989.

18. Schiller 1999. See Baldwin 1985; Cline 1990; and Destler and Odell 1987 for excellent studies of textile protection.

19. These bills were vetoed by Presidents Reagan and Bush.

20. In chapter 1, I discuss footwear's role in this coalition.

21. The 1985–68 textile bill failed in Congress. To prevent this happening again, the "Daschle amendment" was attached to the 1987 bill. This promised that if foreign nations increased their imports of U.S. agricultural products, they would be allowed to increase their textile imports. This didn't convince the agricultural lobby to vote in the

bill's favor (with the exception of corn growers). See McGillivray and Schiller 1998; Schiller 1999.

22. See McGillivray and Schiller 1998.

23. For political economic explanations, see Rodrik 1986; Hillman and Ursprung 1988; Feenstra and Lewis 1991; Mayer and Riezman 1987.

24. Admittedly governments can still use different commodity tariffs to differentiate between firms producing somewhat different products within that industry. In general, however, the benefits from tariffs fall evenly across an industry.

25. Another possibility is that whether the government uses subsidies or tariffs depends on the type of union structure. Unions that are organized by sector demand direct protection—tariffs or quotas or industry subsidies—because they want to keep workers. However, unions that are large and overarching are interested in the total number of jobs, and not with preserving a particular industry. Such unions might be more inclined to fight for better redundancy and retraining packages. Thanks to Carles Boix for this point.

26. See discussion in Martin and Simmons 2001.

27. See Grossman and Helpman 1995; Levy 1997; Pahre 2001, 2002; Marvel and Ray 1983.

28. *Economist*, "The World This Week: Business" 20–26 April 2002; *Economist*. 9 March, 2002. "George Bush, Protectionist."

References

Aldrich, J. H. 1995. *Why Parties? The Origin and Transformation of Political Parties in America*. Chicago: University of Chicago Press.

Alesina, A., G. D. Cohen, and N. Roubini. 1992. "Macroeconomic Policy and Elections in OECD Democracies." *Economics and Politics* 4:1–30.

Alt, J., F. Carsen, P. Heum, and K. Johansen. 1996. "Asset Specificity and the Political Behavior of Firms: Lobbying for Subsidies in Norway." *International Organization* 53:93–116.

Alt, J., J. Frieden, M. Gilligan, D. Rodrik, and R. Rogowski. 1996. "The Political Economy of International Trade: Enduring Puzzles and an Agenda for Inquiry." *Comparative Political Studies* 29:689–717.

Alt, J., and M. Gilligan. 1994. "The Political Economy of Trading States: Factor Specificity, Collective Action, and Domestic Political Institutions." *Journal of Political Philosophy* 2:165–92.

Alvarez, M., G. Garrett, and P. Lange. 1991. "Government Partisanship Labor Organization and Macroeconomic Performance." *American Political Science Review* 85:539–56.

Ames, B. 1993. "The Reverse Coattails Effect: Local Party Organization in the 1989 Brazilian Presidential Election." *American Political Science Review* 88:41–72.

———. 2001. *The Deadlock of Democracy in Brazil*. Ann Arbor: University of Michigan Press.

Amorim, Neto O., and G. W. Cox. 1997. "Electoral Institutions: Cleavage Structures and the Number of Parties." *American Journal of Political Science* 41:149–74.

Anderson, K., and R. Baldwin. 1987. "The Political Market for Protection in Industrialized Countries." In *Protection, Cooperation, Integration, and Development*. Edited by A. M. El-Agraa. London: Macmillan Press.

Appold, S. J. 1995. "Agglomeration, Interorganizational Networks, and Competitive Performance in the U.S. Metalworking Sector." *Economic Geography* 71:27–54.

Austen-Smith, D. 1991. "Rational Consumers and Irrational Voters: A Review Essay on Black Hole Tariffs and Endogenous Policy Theory by MBY." *Politics and Economics* 3:73–92.

Austen-Smith, D., and J. Banks. 1988. "Elections, Coalitions, and Legislative Outcomes." *American Political Science Review* 82:405–22.

———. 1991. "Monotonicity in Electoral Systems." *American Political Science Review* 85:531–37.

Baden-Fuller, C.W.F. 1989. "Exit from Declining Industries and the Case of Steel Castings."*Economic Journal* 99:949–61.

Baghwati, J., and R. Feenstra. 1982. "Tariff Seeking and the Efficient Tariff." In *Import Competition and Response*, edited by J. Bahgwati. Chicago: University of Chicago Press.

Bailey, S., ed. 1979. *Political Parties and the Party System in Britain*. Westport, Conn.: Hyperion Press.

Bain, Trevor. 1992. *Banking the Furnace: Restructuring of the Steel Industry in Eight Countries*. Kalamazoo: W. E. Upjohn Institute for Employment Research.

Balassa, B. 1971. *The Structure of Protection in Developing Countries*. Baltimore: Johns Hopkins University Press.

Baldwin, R. 1985. *The Political Economy of U.S. Import Policy*. Cambridge: MIT Press.

———. 1989. "The Case against Infant-Industry Tariff Protection." *Journal of Political Economy* 77:295–305.

Baron, D. P. 1993. "Government Formation and Endogenous Parties." *American Political Science Review* 87:34–47.

Baron, D. P., and D. Diermeier. 2001. "Elections, Governments, and Parliaments in Proportional Representation Systems." *Quarterly Journal of Economics* 116:933–67.

Baron, D. P. and J. A. Ferejohn. 1989. "Bargaining in Legislatures." *American Political Science Review* 83:1181–1206.

Barro, R. J. 1997. *Determinants of Economic Growth: A Cross-Country Empirical Study*. Cambridge: MIT Press.

Barro, R. J., and L. J. Lee. 1994. *Data Set for a Panel of 138 Countries*. Cambridge: Harvard University, January.

Bawn, K. 1999. "Money and Majorities in the Federal Republic of Germany: Evidence for a Veto Player's Model of Government Spending." *American Journal of Political Science* 43: 707–36.

———. 2000. "Voter Responses to Electoral Complexity: Ticket Splitting, Rational Voters, and Representation in the Federal Republic of Germany." *British Journal of Political Science* 29:487–505.

Bawn, K., G. Cox, and F. Rosenbluth. 1999. "Measuring the Ties that Bind: Electoral Cohesiveness in Four Democracies." In *Elections in Japan, Korea, and Taiwan under the Single Non-Transferable Vote: The Comprehensive Study of an Embedded Institution*, edited by B. Groffman, S. Lee, E. Winckler, and B. Woodall. Ann Arbor: University of Michigan Press.

Beck, N. 2001. "Time-Series Cross-Section Data: What Have We Learned in the Past Few Years?" *Annual Review of Political Science* 4:271–93.

Beck, N., and J. Katz. 1995. "What to Do (and Not to Do) with Time-Series Cross-Sectional Data in Comparative Politics." *American Political Science Review* 89:634–47.

Becker, G. 1983. "A Theory of Competition among Pressure Groups for Political Influence." *Quarterly Journal of Economics* 98:371–400.

Bell, S. 1993. *Australian Manufacturing and the State*. Cambridge: Cambridge University Press.

Benoit, K. 2000. "Which Electoral System Is the Most Proportional? A New Look with New Evidence." *Political Analysis* 8:381–88.

Bergman, T. 2000. "Sweden: When Minority Cabinets Are the Rule and Majority Cabinets the Exception." In *Coalition Governments in Western Europe*, edited by W.C. Muller and K. Strom. New York: Oxford University Press.

Bernhard, W., and D. Leblang. 1999. "Democratic Institutions and Exchange Rate Commitments." *International Organization* 53:71–97.

Beynon, H., R. Hudson, and D. Sadler. 1991. *A Tale of Two Industries: The Contraction of Coal and Steel in the North East of England.* Milton Keynes: Open University Press.

Black, D. 1948. "On the Rationale of Group Decision Making." *Journal of Political Economy* 56.

Blais, A., D. Blake, and S. Dion. 1993. "Do Parties Make a Difference? Parties and the Size of Government in Liberal Democracies." *American Journal of Political Science* 37:40–62.

Bobe, Bernard. 1983. "Public Assistance to Industries and Trade Policy in France." World Bank Staff Working Papers no 570. Washington, D.C.

Boch, R. 1997. "The Rise and Decline of Flexible Production: The Cutlery Industry of Solingen since the Eighteenth Century." In *Worlds of Possibility: Flexibility and Mass Production in Western Industrialization*, edited by C. F. Sabel and J. Zeitlin. Cambridge: Cambridge University Press.

Boix, C. 1998. *Political Parties, Growth, and Equality.* Ann Arbor: University of Michigan Press.

Bowler, S., D. M. Farrell, and I. McAllister. 1996. "Constituency Campaigning in Parliamentary Systems with Preferential Voting: Is There a Paradox?" *Electoral Studies* 15:461–76.

Box-Steffensmeir, J., et al. 1997 "The Strategic Timing of Position Taking in Congress: A Study of the North American Free Trade Agreement." *American Political Science Review* 91:324–38.

Boyes, W., and M. Melvin. 1994. *Macroeconomics.* Boston: Houghton Mifflin.

Brady, D. W., J. Cooper, and P. Hurley. 1979. "The Decline of Party in the U.S. House of Representatives, 1877–1968." *Legislative Studies Quarterly* 4:381–407.

Brainard, S. L., and T. Verdier. 1997. "The Political Economy of Declining Industries: Senescent Industry Collapse Revisited." *Journal of International Economics* 42:221–37.

Brander, J. A. 1991. "Election Polls, Free Trade, and the Stock Market: Evidence from the 1988 Canadian General Election." *Canadian Journal of Economics* 24:827–43.

Brown, S., and J. B. Warner. 1980. "Measuring Security Price Performance." *Journal of Financial Economics* 8:205–58.

———. 1985. Using Daily Stock Returns: The Case of Event Studies." *Journal of Financial Economics* 14:3–31.

Budge, I., and M. Laver. 1993. "The Policy Basis of Government Coalitions." *British Journal of Political Science* 23:499–519.

Budge, I., D. Robertson, and D. Hearl, eds. 1987. *Ideology, Strategy, and Party Change: Spatial Analysis of Post-War Election Programs in Nineteen Democracies.* Cambridge: Cambridge University Press.

Busch, M. L. and E. Reinhardt. 1999. "Industrial Location and Protection: The Political and Economic Geography of U.S. Non-tariff Barriers." *American Journal of Political Science* 43:1028–50.

———. 2000. "Industrial Location and Trade Politics in Europe." Working Paper.

Butler, D. 1975. *The British General Election of October 1974.* London: Macmillan Press.

Butler, D., and D. Kavanagh. 1974. *The British General Election of February 1974.* London: Macmillan Press.

———. 1980. *The British General Election of February 1979.* London: Macmillan Press.

Butler, D., and A. King. 1966. *The British General Election of 1966.* London: Macmillan Press.

Butler, D., and M. Pinto-Duschinsky. 1971. *The British General Election of 1970.* London: Macmillan Press.

Cable, V. 1983. "Economics and the Politics of Protection: Some Case Studies of Industries." World Bank Staff Working Paper no. 569. Washington, D.C.

Cable, V., and I. Rebelo. 1980. "Britain's Pattern of Specialization in Manufactured Goods with Developing Countries and Trade Protection." World Bank Staff Working Paper no. 425. Washington, D.C.

Cadot, O., J. de Melo, and M. Olarreaga. 1997. "Lobbying and the Structure of Protection." CEPR Discussion paper no. 1574. London: Center for Economic Policy Research.

Cameron, D. 1978. "The Expansion of the Public Economy: A Comparative Analysis." *American Political Science Review* 72:1243–61.

Campbell, J., and M. Lettau. 1999. "Dispersion and Volatility in Stock Returns: An Empirical Investigation." National Bureau of Economic Research, working paper no. 7144.

Campbell, J. Y., A. W. Lo, and A. C. MacKinlay, *The Econometrics of Financial Markets.* Princeton: Princeton University Press, 1997.

Capling, A., and B. Galligan. 1992. *Beyond the Protective State: The Political Economy of Australia's Manufacturing Industrial Policy.* Cambridge: Cambridge University Press.

Capron, M. 1986. "The State, the Regions, and Industrial Redevelopment: The Challenge of the Belgian Steel Crisis." In *The Politics of Steel: Western Europe and the Steel Industry,* edited by Y. Meny and V. Wright. Berlin: Walter de Gruyter and Co.

Cassing, J., T. J. McKeown, and J. Ochs. 1986. "The Political Economy of the Tariff Cycle." *American Political Science Review* 80:843–62.

Caves, R. E. 1976. "Economic Models of Political Choice: Canada's Tariff Structure." *Canadian Journal of Economics* 9:279–300.

Caves, R. E., J. A. Frankel, and R. W. Jones. 1990. *World Trade and Payments.* New York: HarperCollins.

Chadar, F., W. David, and C. Feigend. 1987. *U.S. Industrial Competitiveness.* Lexington, Ky.: Lexington Books.

Chen, J. H. 1974. "U.S. Concessions in the Kennedy Round and Short-Run Labor Adjustment Costs." *Journal of International Economics* 4:323–40.

Chwe, M. 2001. *Rational Ritual, Culture, Communication, and Common Knowledge.* Princeton: Princeton University Press.

Clark, W. R. 2003. *Capitalism, Not Globalism: Capital Mobility, Central Bank Independence, and the Political Control of the Economy.* Ann Arbor: University of Michigan Press.

Cline, W. R. 1990. *The Future of World Trade in Textiles and Apparel.* Washington, D.C.: Institute for International Economics.

Connidis, L. A. 1983. "The Effective Rate of Protection for Motor Vehicle Manufacturing in Canada." *Canadian Journal of Economics* 1:98–104.

Conrnes, R., and T. Sandler. 1996. *The Theory of Externalities, Public Goods, and Club Goods*. Cambridge: Cambridge University Press.

Conybeare, J.A.C. 1984. "Politicians and Protection: Tariffs and Elections in Australia." *Public Choice* 43:203–09.

———. 1991. "Voting for Protection: An Electoral Model of Tariff Policy." *International Organization* 45:56–81.

———. 1993. "Tariff Protection in Developed and Developing Countries." *International Organization* 37:441–65.

Cox, G. W. 1987. *The Efficient Secret*. Cambridge: Cambridge University Press.

———. 1990. "Centripetal and Centrifugal Incentives in Electoral Systems." *American Journal of Political Science* 33:903–35.

———. 1997. *Making Votes Count: Strategic Coordination in the World's Electoral Systems*. New York: Cambridge University Press.

Cox, G. W., and M. D. McCubbins. 1986. "Electoral Politics as a Redistributive Game." *Journal of Politics* 48:370–89.

———. 1993. *Legislative Leviathan: Party Government in the House*. Berkeley and Los Angeles.: University of California Press.

Deardorff, A. V., and R. M. Stern.1983. "Economic Effects of the Tokyo Round." *Southern Economic Journal* 49:605–24.

Denzau, A., and M. Munger. 1986. "Legislators and Interest Groups: How Unorganized Interests Get Represented." *American Political Science Review* 80:89–106.

Destler, I. M., and J. S. Odell. 1987. *Anti-Protection: Changing Forces in United States Trade Politics*. Washington, D.C.: Institute for International Economics.

de Swaan, A. 1973. *Coalition Theories and Cabinet Formation*. San Francisco: Jossey-Bass.

de Winter, L., A. Timmermans, and P. Dumont. 2000. "Belgium: On Government Agreements, Evangelists, Followers, and Heretics." In *Coalition Governments in Western Europe*, edited by W. C. Mullcr and K. Strom. New York: Oxford University Press.

Diermeier, D., and T. Fedderson. 1998. "Cohesion in Legislatures: The Vote of Confidence Procedure." *American Political Science Review* 92:611–21.

Diermeier, D., and A. Merlo. 2001. "An Empirical Investigation of Coalitional Bargaining Procedures." Unpublished manuscript.

Dixit, A. 1985. "Tax Policy in Open Economies." In *Handbook of Public Economics*, vol. 1, edited by A. Auerbach and M. Feldstein. New York: Elsevier Science Publishing Co.

Dixit, A., and J. Londregan. 1996. "The Determinants of Success of Special Interests in Redistributive Politics." *Journal of Politics* 58: 1132–55.

———. 1998. "Ideology, Tactics, and Efficiency in Redistributive Politics." *Quarterly Journal of Economics* 113:497–29.

Downs, A. 1957. *An Economic Theory of Democracy*. New York: Harper and Row.

Duchene, F., and G. Shepherd. 1987. *Managing Industrial Change in Western Europe*. New York: Frances Pinter.

Dudley, G. F., and J. J. Richardson. 1990. *Politics and Steel in Britain, 1967–1988*. Dartmouth, England: Ashgate Publishing.

Dutt, P., and M. Devashish. 2002. "Political Ideology and Endogenous Trade Policy: An Empirical Investigation." Paper presented at the Leitner Political Economy Working Series, Yale University.

Duverger, M. 1954. *Political Parties: Their Organization and Activity in the Modern State*. London: Methuen.

Edwards, S. 1992. "Trade Orientation, Distortions, and Growth in Developing Countries." *Journal of Development Economics* 39:31–57.

Epstein, L. D. 1994. "Changing Perceptions of the British System." *Political Science Quarterly* 109:483–98.

Epstein, D., and S. O'Halloran. 1996. "Divided Government and the Design of Administrative Procedures: A Formal Model and Empirical Test." *Journal of Politics* 58:393–417.

Esser, J., and W. Fach. 1989. "Crisis Management: The Steel Industry." In *Industry and Politics in West Germany: Toward the Third Republic*, edited by P. Katzenstein. Ithaca: Cornell University Press.

Esser, J., and W. Vath. 1986. "Overcoming the Steel Crisis in the Federal Republic of Germany, 1975–1983." In *The Politics of Steel: Western Europe and the Steel Industry*, edited by Y. Meny and V. Wright. Berlin: Walter de Gruyter and Co.

Esty, D., and R. Caves. 1983. "Market Structure and Political Influence: New Data on Political Expenditure, Activity, and Success." *Economic Inquiry* 21:198–205.

EU Commission. 2001. *State Aid Scoreboard*. 2nd ed. Brussels: Commission of the European Communities.

European Journal of Political Research. 1993–97. Annual Data Issue.

Falvey, R. E., and P. Lloyde. 1991. "Uncertainty and the Choice of Protective Instrument." *Oxford Economic Papers* (July): 463–78.

Feenstra, R., and T. Lewis. 1991. "Negotiate Trade Restrictions with Political Pressure." *Quarterly Journal of Economics* 106: 1287–1307.

Ferejohn, J. 1974. *Pork Barrel Politics: Rivers and Harbors Legislation, 1947–1968*. Stanford, Calif.: Stanford University Press.

Finger, J. M., H. K. Hall, and D. Nelson. 1982. "The Political Economy of Administered Protection." *American Economic Review* 72:452–66.

Firman, R. 1990. *Patchwork Protectionism*. Ithaca: Cornell University Press.

Ford, R., and W. Suyker. 1990. "Industrial Subsidies in the OECD Countries." OECD Department of Economics and Statistics, Working Papers no. 76.

Fordham, B., and T. McKeown. 2001. "Selection and Influence, Interest Groups, and Congressional Voting on Trade Policy." Manuscript.

Francis, W. L., L. W. Kenny, R. B. Morton, and A. B. Schmidt. 1994. "Retrospective Voting and Political Mobility." *American Journal of Political Science* 38:999–1024.

Franks, C.E.S. 1987. *The Parliament of Canada*. Toronto: University of Toronto Press.

Freeman, J. R., J. Hayes, and H. Stix. 2000. "Democracy and Markets: The Case of Exchange Rates." *American Journal of Political Science* 44:440–68. Freeman, R. B., and J. L. Medoff. 1979. "New Estimates of Private Sector Unionism in the United States." *Industrial and Labor Relations Review* 32:143–74.

Gallagher. M., M. Laver, and P. Mair. 1992. *Representative Government in Western Europe*. New York: McGraw-Hill.

Garrett, G. 1998. "Global Markets and National Policies: Collision Course or Virtuous Circle?" *International Organization* 52:787–825.

Garrett, G., and P. Lange. 1996. "Internationalization, Institutions, and Politial Change." In *Internationalization and Domestic Politics*, edited by R. O. Keohane and H. Milner. Cambridge: Cambridge University Press.

Gawande, K., and U. Bandhopadhayay. 2000. "Is Protection for Sale? A Test of the Grossman-Helpman Theory of Endogenous Protection." *Review of Economics and Statistics* 80:128–40.

Gawande, K., and P. Krishna. 2001. "The Political Economy of Trade Policy: Empirical Approaches." In *Handbook of International Trade*, edited by J. Harrigan. New York: Basil Blackwell.

Gilligan, T. W., and K. Krehbiel. 1988. "Complex Rules and Congressional Outcomes: An Event Study of Energy Tax Legislation." *Journal of Politics* 50:625–654.

———. 1989. "Asymmetric Information and Legislative Rules with a Heterogeneous Committee." *American Journal of Political Science* 33:459–490.

———. 1990. "Organization of Informative Committees by a Rational Legislature." *American Journal of Political Science* 34:531–64.

Gillson, Ian. 1999. "Industry Characteristics of Sensitive Products in the EU's Generalized System of Preferences." University of Nottingham, July.

Glismann, H. H., and F. D. Weiss. 1980. "On the Political Economy of Protection in Germany." World Bank Staff Working Paper no. 427. Washington, D.C.

Godeck, P. 1985. "Industry Structure and Redistribution through Trade Restrictions." *Journal of Law and Economics* 28:687–703.

Goldberg, P., and G. Maggi. 1999. "Protection for Sale: An Empirical Investigation." *American Economic Review* 89:1135–55.

Golder, M., and W. Clark. 2003. "The Sociological and Institutional Determinants of the Number of Parties in an Electoral System: An Improved Empirical Analysis." Paper presented at the Midwest Political Science Association Annual Meeting.

Golder, S. N. 2003. "Pre-electoral Coalition Formation: the Case of France." Manuscript.

Goldstein, J. 1989. "The Impact of Ideas on the Origin of Trade Policy: The Origins of U.S. Agricultural and Manufacturing Policies." *International Organization* 43:31–72.

Goodhart, L. 2001. "Coalition Governments and Political Business Cycles." Harvard University, mimeo.

Green, D. P., S. Y. Kim, and D. Yoon. 2001. "Dirty Pool." *International Organization* 55:441–68.

Grier, K. B., M. C. Munger, and B. E. Roberts. 1994. "The Determinants of Industry Political Activity, 1978–1986." *American Political Science Review* 88:911–26.

Grilli, E. 1980. "Italian Commercial Policies in the 1970s." World Bank Staff Working Paper no. 428. Washington, D.C.

Grilli, E., and M. la Noce. 1983. "The Political Economy of Protection in Italy: Some Empirical Evidence." World Bank Staff Working Paper no 567. Washington, D.C.

Grilli, V., D. Masciandaro, and G. Tabellini. 1991, "Political and Mon-etary Institutions and Public Financial Policies in the Industrial Coun-tries," *Economic Policy* 6:341–92.

Grofman, B., and A. Lijphart, eds. 1984. *Choosing an Electoral System: Issues and Alternatives*. New York: Praeger.

Grossman, G. M. 1983. "Partially Mobile Capital: A General Approach to Two-Sector Trade Theory." *Journal of International Economics* 15:1–17.

Grossman, G., and E. Helpman. 1991. *Innovation and Growth in the Global Economy*. Cambridge: MIT Press.

———. 1994. "Protection for Sale." *American Economic Review* 84:833–50.

———. 1995. "Trade Wars and Trade Talks." *Journal of Political Economy*. 103:675–708.

Grossman, G. M., and J. A. Levinson. 1989. "Import Competition and the Stock Market Return to Capital." *American Economic Review* 79:1065–87.

Guisinger, A. 2002. "Trade Protection and Liberalization: Is there a Role for Diffusion?" Manuscript.

Gwande, K., and P. Krishna. 2002. "Political Economy of U.S. Trade Policy: The Empirical Evidence." Forthcoming in *Handbook of International Economics*, edited by James Harrigan. Oxford: Basil Blackwell.

Hallerberg, 2002. "The Treaty of Maastricht and the Making of Budgets in Europe, 1980–2002." Unpublished ms.

Hansen, W. 1990. "The International Trade Commission and the Politics of Protectionism." *American Political Science Review* 84:21–46.

Harrigel, G. 2000. *Industrial Constructions: The Sources of German Industrial Power*. Cambridge: Cambridge University Press.

Hartigan, J. C., P. R. Perry, and K. Kamma. 1986. "The Value of Administered Protection: A Capital Market Approach." *Review of Economics and Statistics* 68:610–17.

Hays, J., H. Stix, and J. R. Freeman. 2000. "The Electoral Information Hypothesis Revisited." Manuscripts.

Hayter, R. 1985. "The Restructuring of Traditional Industries in Time of Recession." *Royal Dutch Geographical Society*. 76:106–20.

Helleiner, G. K. 1977. "The Political Economy of Canada's Tariff Structure: An Alternative Model." *Canadian Journal of Economics* 4:318–26.

Herron, M. 2000. "Estimating the Economic Impact of Political Party Competition in the 1992 British Election." American Journal of Political Science 44:326–37.

Herron, M. C., J. Lavin, D. Cram, and Jay Silver. 1999. "Measurement of Political Effects in the Stock Market: A Study of the 1992 Presidential Election." *Economics and Politics* 11:51–82.

Hibbing, J. R., and E. Theiss-Morse. 1995. *Congress as Public Enemy: Public Attitudes toward American Political Institutions*. Cambridge: Cambridge University Press.

Hibbs, D. A., Jr. 1977. "Political Parties and Macroeconomic Policy." *American Political Science Review* 71:1467–87.

Hillman, A. L. 1989. *The Political Economy of Protection*. Switzerland: Harwood, Chur.

———. "Protection, Politics, and Market Structure," in *International Trade and Trade Policy*, edited by E. Helpman and A. Razin. Cambridge: MIT Press.

Hillman. A. L., and H. Ursprung. 1988. "Domestic Politics, Foreign Interests, and National Trade Policy." *American Economic Review* 78:729–45.

Hine, R. C. 1985. *The Political Economy of European Trade: An Introduction to the Trade Policies of the EEC*. Brighton and New York: Wheatsheaf.

Hirano, S. 2002. "Changing Electoral Systems and Changing Influence of the Personal Vote in Japanese Politics." Ph.D. dissertation, Harvard University.

Hiscox, M. 2001. *International Trade and Political Conflict: Commerce, Coalitions, and Mobility*. Princeton: Princeton University Press.

HMSO. 1979, 1983. "Analysis of UK Manufacturing Industry by Employment Size." *Business Monitor* PR 1003. Various years.

Huber, J. 1996. "The Vote of Confidence in Parliamentary Democracies." *American Political Science Review* 90:269–82.

Huber, J., and G. B. Powell, Jr. 1994."Congruence between Citizens and Policymakers in Two Visions of Liberal Democracy." *World Politics* 46:291–326.

Hudson, R., and D. Sadler. 1989. *The International Steel Industry: Restructuring, State Policies, and localities*: London: Routledge.

Hudson, R., D. Sadler, and A. Townsend. 1992. "Employment Change in UK Steel Closure Areas during the 1980s: Policy Implications and Lessons for Scotland." *Regional Studies* 26:633–46.

ILO. Iron and Steel Committee11th Session. 1986. "Productivity Improvement and its Effects on the Level of Employment and Working Conditions in the Iron and Steel Industry." Geneva: ILO.

Indridason, I. H. 2001. "To Dissent or Not to Dissent? Informative Dissent in Parliamentary Governance." Paper presented at Midwest Political Science Association Annual Meeting.

Johnman, L., and H. Murphy. 2002. *British Shipbuilding and the State since 1918: A Political Economy of Decline*. UK: Regatta Press.

Johnston, Richard. 1986. *Public Opinion and Public Policy in Canada*. Toronto: University of Toronto Press.

Jones, K. 1986. *World Industry Studies, 4: Politics versus Economics in World Steel Trade*. London: Allen and Unwin.

Jones, R. W. 1971. "A Three-Factor Model in Trade, Theory, and History." In *Trade, Balance of Payments and Growth*, edited by Bhagwati et al. Amsterdam: North Holland.

Kaempfer, W. H., S. Marks, and T. D. Willett. 1988. "Why Do Large Countries Prefer Quantitative Trade Restrictions?" *Kyklos* 41:625–46.

Kalandrakis, A. 2000. "General Equilibrium Parliamentary Government." PhD. Dissertation in Political Science, University of California, Los Angeles.

Krueger, A. O. 1998. "Why Trade Liberalization Is Good for Growth." *Economic Journal* 108:1513–22.

Krugman, Paul. 1991. *Geography and Trade*. Cambridge: MIT Press.

Laird, S., and A. Yeats. 1990. *Quantitative Methods for Trade Barrier Analysis*. New York: New York University Press.

Laver, M. 1997. "In Search of the 'Big' Model of Political Competition." *European Journal of Political Research* 31:179–92.

Laver, M., and I. Budge. 1992. *Party Policy and Coalition Government*. London: Macmillan.

Laver, M., and N. Schofield. 1990. *Multiparty Government: The Politics of Coalition in Europe*. Oxford: Oxford University Press.

Laver, M., and K. Shepsle, eds. 1994. *Cabinet Ministers and Parliamentary Government*. New York: Cambridge University Press.

Lavergne, R. P. 1981. *The Political Economy of Tariffs: An Empirical Analysis*. Ph.d. thesis. University of Toronto.

Lavergne, R. P. 1983. *The Political Economy of Tariffs: An Empirical Analysis*. Ontario: Academic Press Canada.

Lawson, N. 1993. *A View from N.11*. London: Random House.

Lenway, S., K. Rehbein, and L. Starks. 1986. The Impact of Protectionism on Firm Wealth: The Experience of the Steel Industry. *Southern Economic Journal* 56:1079–93.

Levin, J., and B. Nalebuff. 1995. "An Introduction to Vote-Counting Schemes." *Journal of Economic Perspectives* 9:3–26.

Levine, M. K. 1985. *Inside International Trade Policy Formulation: A History of the 1982 US-EC Steel Arrangments*. New York: Praeger.

Levy, P., I. 1997. "A Political-Economic Analysis of Free Trade Agreements." *American Economic Review* 87: 506–19.

Lijphart, A. 1984. *Democracies*. New Haven: Yale University Press.

———. 1990. "The Political Consequences of Electoral Laws, 1945–1985." *American Political Science Review* 84:873–90.

———. 1994. *Electoral Systems and Party Systems: A Study of Twenty-Seven Democracies, 1949–1990*. Oxford: Oxford University Press.

Lilien, D. 1982. "Sectoral Shifts and Cyclical Unemployment." *Journal of Political Economy* 90:777–93.

Lindbeck, A., and J. Weibull. 1987. "Balanced-Budget Redistribution as the Outcome of Political Competition." *Public Choice* 52:273–97.

———. 1993. "A Model of Political Equilibrium in a Representative Democracy." *Journal of Public Economics* 51:195–209.

Lizzeri, A., and N. Persico. 2001. "The Provision of Public Goods under Alternative Electoral Incentives." *American Economic Review* 91:225–45.

Lohman, S., and S. O'Halloran. 1994. "Divided Government and U.S. Trade Policy: Theory and Evidence." *International Organization* 48:225–48.

Loungani, P., M., Rush, and W. Tave. 1990. "Stock Market Dispersion and Unemployment." *Journal of Monetary Economics* 25:367–88.

Mackie, T. T., and R. Rose. 1983. *The International Almanac of Electoral History*. Washington, D.C.: Congressional Quarterly.

Magee, S. 1973. *International Trade Distortions in Factor Markets*. New York: Marcel Dekker.

———. 1980. "Three Simple Tests of the Stolper-Samuelson theorem." In *Issues in International Economics*, edited by Peter Oppenheimer. London: Oriel Press.

Magee, S., W. Brock, and L. Young. 1989. *Black Hole Tariffs and Endogenous Policy Theory*. Cambridge: Cambridge University Press.

Mahdavi, M., and A. Bhagwati. 1994. "Stock Market Data and Trade Policy: Dumping and the Semiconductor Industry." *International Trade Journal* 8:207–21.

Mainwaring, S. 1999. *Rethinking Party Systems in the Third Wave of Democratization: The Case of Brazil*. Stanford, Calif.: Stanford University Press.

Mansfield, E. D., and M. Busch. 1995. "The Political Economy of Non-tariff Barriers: A Cross-National Analysis." *International Organization* 49:723–49.

Mansfield, E. D., H. Milner, and B. P. Rosendorff. 2000. "Free to Trade: Democracies, Autocracies, and International Trade." *American Political Science Review* 94:305–22.

Marklew, V. 1995. *Cash, Crisis, and Corporate Governance*. Ann Arbor: University of Michigan Press.

Marks, S. V., and J. McArthur. 1990. "Empirical Analyses of the Determinants of Protection: A Survey and Some New Results." In *International Trade Policies: Gains from Exchange between Economics and Political Science*, edited by J. S. Odell and T. D. Willett. Ann Arbor: University of Michigan Press.

Martin, L., and B. Simmons 2001. *International Institutions*. Cambridge: MIT Press.

Marvel, H. P., and E. J. Ray. 1983. "The Kennedy Round: Evidence on the Regulation of International Trade in the USA." *American Economic Review* 73:190–97.

Mayer, W. 1984. "Endogenous Tariff Formation." *American Economic Review* 74:970–85.

Mayer, W., and R. Riezman. 1987. "Endogenous Choice of Trade Policy Instruments." *Journal of International Economics* 23:377–81.

Mayhew, D. 1974. *Congress: The Electoral Connection*. New Haven: Yale University Press.

McGillivray, F. 1995. "The Comparative Properties of Political Institutions." Ph.d. Dissertation. University of Rochester, Rochester, New York.

———. 1997. "Party Discipline as a Determinant of the Endogenous Formation of Tariffs." *American Journal of Political Science* 41:584–607.

———. 2003. "Redistribution and Stock Price Dispersion." *British Journal of Political Science* 33:367–95.

McGillivray, F., and A. Smith. 1997. "Institutional Determinants of Trade Policy." *International Interactions* 23:119–43.

McGillivray, F., and W. Schiller. 1998. "The Political Geography of Lobbying: Forming Coalitions to Maximize Influence in Trade Policy." Unpublished ms.

McGillivray, F., I. McLean, R. Pahre, and C. Schonhardt-Bailey. 2001. *International Trade and Political Institutions*. London: Edward Elgar.

McKelvey, R. D., and N. Schofield. 1987. "Generalized Symmetry Conditions at a Core Point." *Econometrica* 55:923–33.

Meny, Y., and V. Wright. 1986. "State and Steel in Western Europe." In *The Politics of Steel: Western Europe and the Steel Industry*, edited by Y. Meny and V. Wright. Berlin: Walter de Gruyter.

———. 1987. *The Politics of Steel: Western Europe and the Steel Industry in the Crisis Years (1974–1984)*. Berlin: Walter de Gruyter.

Mershon, C. 2002. *The Costs of Coalition*. Stanford, Calif.: Stanford University Press.

Milesi-Ferretti, G. M., R. Perotti, and M. Rostagno. 2001. "Electoral Systems and Public Spending." International Monetary Fund Working Paper WP/01/02.

Milner, H. V. 1983. "Maintaining International Commitments in Trade Policy." In *Do Institutions Matter?* edited by K. Weaver and B. Rockman. Washington, D.C.: Brookings.

———. 1988. *Resisting Protectionism: Global Industries and the Politics of International Trade*. Princeton: Princeton University Press.

Mitchell, P. 1999. "Coalition Discipline, Enforcement Mechanisms, and Intraparty Politics. In *Party Discipline and Parliamentary Government*. Edited by Bowler, D. Farrell, and R. Katz. Columbus: Ohio State University Press.

Monroe, B. L. 1995. "Fully Proportional Representation." *American Political Science Review* 89:925–40.

Morgan, K. 1983 "Restructuring Steel: The Crises of Labour and Locality in Britain." *International Journal of Urban and Regional Research* 7:175–201.

Muller, W. C., and K. Strom. 1999. *Policy, Office, or Votes? How Political Parties in Western Europe Make Hard Decisions*. New York: Cambridge University Press.

Murphy, K., A. Schleifer, R. Vishny. 1993. "Why Is Rent-Seeking So Costly to Growth?" *American Economic Review* 83: 409–14.

Mussa, M. 1982. "Imperfect Factor Mobility and the Distribution of Income." *Journal of International Economics* 12:125–41.

Myerson, R. B. 1993. "Incentives to Cultivate Favored Minorities under Alternative Electoral Systems." *American Political Science Review* 87:856–69.

Nelson, D. 1988. "Endogenous Tariff Theory: A Critical Survey." *American Journal of Political Science* 21:285–300.

Nicita, A., and M. Olarrenga. 2001. *Trade and Production, 1976–1999*. Companion paper to The World Bank Trade and Production Database, 1976–1999.

Nogues, J. J., A. Olechowski, and L. A. Winters. 1986. "The Extent of Non-tariff Barriers to Imports of Industrial Countries." World Bank Staff Working Paper, no 789. Washington D.C.

Nordhaus, W. 1975. "The Political Business Cycle." *Review of Economic Studies* 42:169–90.

Norton, P. 1978. *Conservative Dissidents: Dissent within the Parliamentary Conservative Party, 1970–1974*. London: Temple Smith.

OECD. Various years. *Main Economic Indicators: Historical Statistics: 1955–1971*. Paris: OECD.

OECD. Various years. *Macro Indicators, 1962–91*. Paris: OECD.

Olson, M., Jr. 1965. *The Logic of Collective Action: Public Goods and the Theory of Goods*. Cambridge, Mass.: Phillips.

ONS (Office of National Statistics). 2001. *Size Analysis of UK Business: 2001 Business Monitor PA1003* (Various Years). London: Office for National Statistics.

Ordeshook, P., and O. Shvetsova. 1994. "Ethnic Heterogeneity, District Magnitude, and the Number of Parties." *American Journal of Political Science* 38:100–123.

Osborne, Martin J. 1995. "Spatial Models of Political Competition under Plurality Rule: A Survey of Some Explanations of the Number of Candidates and the Positions They Take." *Canadian Journal of Economics* 28: 261–301.

Pahre, R. 2001. "Most-Favored-Nation Clauses and Clustered Negotiations," *International Organization* 55:859–90.

———. 2002. *Agreeable Customs: The Politics of Trade Cooperation, 1815–1913*. Ann Arbor: University of Michigan Press.

Pearce J., and J. Sutton, with R. Batchelor. 1985. *Protection and Industrial Policy in Europe*. London: Routledge and Kegan Paul.

Pecorino, P. 1996. Is There a Free-Rider Problem in Lobbying? Endogenous Tariffs, Trigger Strategies, and the Number of Firms. *University of Alabama*. Dept. of Economics, Finance and Legal Studies.

Persson, T., and G. Tabellini. 1999. "The Size and Scope of Government: Comparative Politics and Rational Politicians." *European Economic Review* 43:699–735.

Pincus, J. J. 1975. "Pressure Groups and the Pattern of Tariffs." *Journal of Political Economy* 53:757–78.

Powell, G. B. 1982. *Contemporary Democracies: Participation, Stability, and Violence*. Cambridge: Harvard University Press.

———. 2000. *Elections as Instruments of Democracy: Majoritarian and Proportional Visions*. New Haven: Yale University Press.

Powell, G. B., and G. D. Whitten. 1993. "A Cross-National Analysis of Economic Voting: Taking Account of the Political Context." *American Journal of Political Science* 37:391–414.

Pressman S. 1984. "Pressure Mounts on Protectionist Trade Bills." *Congressional Quarterly Weekly Report*, August 4/84.

Quinn, D. P., and R. Jacobson. 1989. "Industrial Policy through the Restriction of Capital Flows: A Test of Several Claims Made about Industrial Policy." *American Journal of Political Science* 33:700–736.

Rae, D. 1971. *The Political Consequences of Electoral Laws*. New Haven: Yale University Press.

———. 1995. "Using District Magnitude to Regulate Political Party Competition." *Journal of Economic Perspectives* 9:65–75.

Reidel, J. 1977. "Tariff Concessions in the Kennedy Round and the Structure of Protection in West Germany." *Journal of International Economics* 7:133–43.

Richardson, J. J. 1988. "British Steel and Government: Governance Success and Failure and Problematic Learning as a Policy Style." Essex Papers in Politics and Government. No. 135.

Richardson, J. J., and G. F. Dudley. 1986. "Steel Policy in the UK: The Politics of Industrial Decline." In *The Politics of Steel: Western Europe and the Steel Industry*, ediated by Y. Meny and V. Wright. Berlin: Walter de Gruyter.

Riezman, R., and J. D. Wilson. 1992. "Politics and Trade Policy." Paper presented at the Inaugural Conference of the Wallis Institute of Political Economy, University of Rochester, New York.

Riker, W. H. 1962. *The Theory of Political Coalitions*. New Haven: Yale University Press.

Roberts, Brian. 1990. "Political Institutions, Policy Expectations, and the 1980 Election: A Financial Market Perspective." *American Journal of Political Science* 34:289–310.

Robertson, D. 1976. *A Theory of Party Competition*. New York: Wiley.

Rodriguez, F. and D Rodrik. 2000. "Trade Policy and Economic Growth: A Skeptic's Guide to the Cross-National Evidence." Center for Economic Research Discussion Paper 2143.

Rodrik, D. 1986. "Tariffs, Subsidies, and Welfare with Endogenous Policy," *Journal of International Economics* 21:285–99.

———. 1995. "Political Economy of Trade Policy." In *Handbook of International Economics*, vol. 3, edited by G. Grossman and K. Rogoff. Amsterdam: North-Holland.

Roemer, J. E. 2001. *Political Competition*. Cambridge: Harvard University Press.

Rogowski, R. 1987. "Trade and the Variety of Democratic Institutions." *International Organization* 41:203–24.

———. 1989. *Commerce and Coalitions: How Trade Affects Domestic Political Alignments*. Princeton: Princeton University Press.

Rogowski, R. 1996. "Trade, Economic Concentration, and U.S. Political Institutions." Unpublished Ms.

——. 1997. "Pork, Patronage, and Protection in Democracies: How Differences in Electoral Systems Govern the Extraction of Rents." Manuscript.

——. 1998. "Electoral Systems and Vote-Buying: Why PR Works Best When Voters Are Loyal, Majoritarian Systems When Voters Are Fickle." Mimeo, UCLA.

Rogowski, R., and M. Kayser. 2000. "Effects of European Economic Integration on the Timing, Mode, and Distortionary Effects of Domestic Elections." Paper presented at the American Political Science Association, 2000.

——. 2002. "Majoritarian Electoral Systems and Consumer Power: Price-Level Evidence from the OECD Countries." *American Journal of Political Science* 46:526–39.

Rogowski, R. M. Kayser, and D. Kotin. 1999. "How Geographical Concentration Affects Industrial Influence: Evidence from U.S. Data." Paper presented at the annual meeting of the American Political Science Association.

Rohde, D. W. 1991. *Parties and Leaders in the Post Reform House*. Chicago: University of Chicago Press.

Roubini, N., and J. D. Sachs. 1989. "Political and Economic Determinants of Budget Deficits." *European Economic Review* 33:903–38.

Rustow, D. A. 1950. "Some Observations on Proportional Representation." *Journal of Politics* 12:107–27.

Sabel, C. 1989. "Flexible Specialization and the Reemergence of Regional Economies. In *Reversing Industrial Decline?* edited by P. Hirst and J. Zeitlin. Oxford: St. Martin's Press.

Sadler, D. 1984 "Works Closure at British Steel and the Nature of the State." *Political Geography Quarterly* 3:297–311.

Sartori, G. 1986. *Parties and Party Systems*. Cambridge: Cambridge University Press.

Schattschneider, E. E. 1935. *Politics, Pressure, and the Tariff*. Englewood Cliffs, N.J.: Prentice-Hall.

Scheuerman, W. 1986. *The Steel Crisis: The Economics and Politics of a Declining Industry*. New York: Praeger.

Scheve, K., and M. J. Slaughter. 2001. "What Determines Individual Trade-Policy Preferences?" *Journal of International Economics* 54:267–92.

Schiller, W. 1999. "Trade Politics in the American Congress: A Study of the Interaction of Political Geography and Interest Group Behavior." *Political Geography* 18: 769–89.

——. 2000. "Has Free Trade Won the War in Congress, or is the Battle Still Raging?" *NAFTA Law and Business Review of the Americas* 6: 363–87.

Schnietz, K. E. and J. Oxley. 1999. "Globalization Derailed? Multinational Investors' Response to the 1997 Demise of Fast-Track Trade Authority." *Journal of International Business Studies* 32: 479–96.

Schofield, N. 1993. "Political Competition and Multiparty Coalition Government." *European Journal for Political Research* 23:1–33.

——. 1996. "MultiParty Electoral Politics." In *Perspectives on Public Choice*. Edited by D. Mueller. Cambridge: Cambridge University Press.

——. 1997. "Political Competition." *European Journal for Political Research* 31:179–92.

———. 1998. "Contributions of Rational Choice Theory to Comparative Politics." *Political Economy Seminar Series*. Yale 1997/98.

———. 2003. "Power, Prosperity, and Social Choice: A Review." *Social Choice and Welfare* 20:85–118.

Schofield, N., and M. Laver. 1985. "Bargaining Theory and Portfolio Payoffs in European Coalition Governments, 1945–1983." *British Journal of Political Science* 15:143–64.

Schonhardt-Bailey, C. 1991. "Lessons in Lobbying for Free Trade in 19th-Century Britain: To Concentrate or Not." *American Political Science Review* 85:37–59.

Scott, A. J. 1988. *Metropolis: From the Division of Labor to Urban Form*. Berkeley: University of California Press.

Shepherd, G., F. Duchene, and C. Saunders. 1983. *Europe's Industries*. London: Frances Pinter.

Smith, A. 1996. "Endogenous Election Timing in Majoritarian Parliamentary Systems."*Economics and Politics* 8:85–110.

———. 2004. *Election Timing in Majoritarian Parliaments*. Cambridge: Cambridge University Press.

Smith, S. 1988. "An Essay on Sequence, Position, Goals, and Committee Power." *American Political Science Review* 81:85–104.

Snyder, J. 1989. "Political Geography and Interest Group Power." *Social Choice and Welfare* 6:102–25.

———. 1990. "Resource Allocation in Multiparty Elections." *American Journal of Political Science* 34:59–73.

Sobel, A. 1999. *State Institutions, Private Incentives, Global Capital*. Ann Arbor: University of Michigan Press.

Staiger, R. W., and G. Tabellini. 1987. "Discretionary Trade Policy and Excessive Protection." *American Economic Review*, 77:23–837.

Stein, R., and K. N. Bickers. 1995. *Perpetuating the Pork Barrel: Policy Subsystems and American Democracy*. Cambridge: Cambridge University Press.

Stigler, G. J. 1974. "Free Riders and Collective Action: An Appendix to Theories of Economic Regulation." *Bell Journal of Economics* 5: 359–65.

Strater, F. 2003. "The Structural Change: Chances and Risks for the Future of Solingen." *http://212.19.45.244/e_deu/b110/buch011/page/7inhalt.htm*. May.

Stratmann, T., and M. Baur (2002). "Plurality Rule, Proportional Representation, and the German Bundestag: How Incentives to Pork-Barrel Differ across Electoral Systems." *American Journal of Political Science* 46:506–14.

Strom, K. 1990a. "A Behavioral Theory of Competitive Political Parties." *American Journal of Political Science* 34:565–98.

———. 1990b. *Minority Government and Majority Rule*. Cambridge: Cambridge University Press.

Sugden, R. 1984. "Free Association and the Theory of Proportional Representation." *American Political Science Review* 78:31–43.

Taagepera, R., and M. Shugart. 1989. *Seats and Votes: The Effects and Determinants of Electoral Systems*. New Haven: Yale University Press.

Tharakan, P.K.M. 1980. "The Political Economy of Protection in Belgium." World Bank Staff Working Paper no. 431. Washington, D.C.

Trefler, D. 1993. "Trade Liberalization and the Theory of Endogenous Protection: An Econometric Study of U.S. Import Policy." *Journal of Political Economy* 101:138–60.

Tsebelis, G. 1990. *Nested Games: Rational Choice in Comparative Politics*. Berkeley: University of California Press.

———. 1995. "Decision Making in Political Systems: Veto Players in Presidentialism, Parliamentarism, Multicameralism, and Multipartyism." *British Journal of Political Science* 25:291–325.

———. 1999. "Veto Players and Law Production in Parliamentary Democracies: An Empirical Analysis." *American Political Science Review* 93:591–608.

———. 2002. *Veto Players: How Political Institutions Work*. New York: Russell Sage Foundation; and Princeton: Princeton University Press.

Tsoukalis L., and R. Strauss. 1986. "Community Policies on Steel, 1974–1982: A Case of Collective Management." In *The Politics of Steel: Western Europe and the Steel Industry*, edited by Y. Meny and V. Wright. Berlin: Walter de Gruyter.

Tweedale, G. 1995. *Steel City: Entrepreneurship, Strategy, and Technology in Sheffield, 1743–1993*. Oxford: Clarendon Press.

Underhill, G. 1998. *Industrial Crisis and the Open Economy: Politics, Global Trade, and the Textile Industry in the Advanced Economies*. New York: St. Martin's Press.

USITC. 1978. "Certain Stainless Steel Flatware: Report to the President on Investigation TA-201-30 under Section 201 of the Trade Act of 1974." Washington, D.C.: U.S. International Trade Commission.

USITC. 1985. "Summary of Trade and Tariff Information: Handtools, Cutlery, and Related Products: TSUS items 648.51–651–75." Washington, D.C.: U.S. International Trade Commission.

U.S. Cenus Bureau. Various Years. *U.S. Census of Manufacturers*. Washington, D.C.: U.S. Department of Commerce.

Warwick, P. V., and J. N. Druckman. 2001. "Portfolio Salience and the Proportionality of Payoffs in Coalition Government." *British Journal of Political Science* 31:627–49.

Weiss, F. D. 1983. "The Structure of International Competitiveness in the Federal Republic of Germany: An Appraisal." World Bank Staff Working Paper no 571. Washington, D.C.

White, A. 1997. " 'We Never Knew What Price We Were Going to Have Till We Got to the Warehouse': Nineteenth-Century Sheffield and the Industrial District Debate." *Social History* 22:307–17.

Wilkinson, B. W., and K. Norrie. 1975. *Effective Protection and the Return to Capital*. Ottawa: Information Canada.

Wilks, S., and M. Wright, eds. 1987. *Comparative Government—Industry Relations*. Oxford: Clarendon Press.

Zagorsky, J. L. 1994. "Stock Market Data, Vacancies, and Sectoral Dispersion." *Journal of Macroeconomics* 19:509–22.

Zardkoohi, A. 1988. "Market Structure and Campaign Contributions: Does Concentration Matter? A Reply." *Public Choice* 58:187–91.

Index